Sri Lanka
a travel survival kit

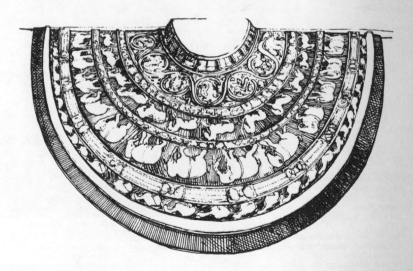

Front cover: Palm Paradise, Tangalla
Back cover: Tami-Ul-Alfar mosque, Pettah, Colombo

Sri Lanka – a travel survival kit

Published by
Lonely Planet Publications
PO Box 88, South Yarra, Victoria 3141, Australia
Also at: PO Box 2001A, Berkeley, CA 94702, USA

Printed by
Colorcraft, Hong Kong

Photographs by
Paul Steel – 177ABC
Tony Wheeler – all others

Illustrations by
Peter Campbell

Design by
Graham Imeson

Typeset by
Anne Logan

First Published
February 1980

This Edition
September 1984

National Library of Australia
Cataloguing-in-publication entry

Wheeler, Tony
Sri Lanka, a travel survival kit.

3rd ed., rev. and updated.
Previous ed.: South Yarra, Vic.: Lonely Planet, 1982.
Includes index.
ISBN 0 908086 62 8

1. Sri Lanka – Description and travel – Guide-books.
I. Tittle.

915.49'3043

Tony Wheeler was born in England but spent most of his younger years overseas due to his father's occupation with British Airways. Those years included a lengthy spell in Pakistan, a shorter period in the West Indies and all his high school years in the US. He returned to England to do a university degree in engineering, worked for a short time as an automotive design engineer, returned to university again and did an MBA, then dropped out on the Asian overland trail with his wife Maureen.

They've been travelling, writing and publishing guidebooks ever since, having set up Lonely Planet Publications in the mid-70s. Tony has written or co-written a number of the Lonely Planet series as well as contributing to other guidebooks. Travelling for Tony and Maureen is now considerably enlivened by their three-year old daughter Tashi and one-year old son Kieran, both of whom have visited and enjoyed Sri Lanka. In 1984 the Wheelers are living in Berkeley, California, setting up Lonely Planet's US office.

THIS EDITION

To research this third edition of *Sri Lanka – a travel survival kit* I returned to the island for the third time. On our first trip Maureen and I made a fairly lengthy trip around – we covered Sri Lanka from Dondra at the extreme south to Jaffna in the extreme north, from the coral gardens underwater at Hikkaduwa to sunrise at dawn on top of Adam's Peak. That was in the days when bus travel in Sri Lanka was somewhat of a nightmare experience and by the end of our travels we never wanted to see another CTB bus!

For the second edition I returned to Sri Lanka alone and made a whirlwind trip around the main centres followed by a week catching up on lost sleep. This third trip fell between the two. On this occasion we hired a car and drove around. We revisited almost every place of interest, an activity somewhat complicated by what felt like continuous rain on the east coast. Researching this edition was also complicated by another factor – the violent upheavals of 1983. Although I do not think any foreign visitors were in any way personally involved in the riots and violence the number of visitors to Sri Lanka fell dramatically for the rest of the year. Conditions in the tourist business are now returning to normal but I had some difficulty in finding if prices were 'normal condition' ones or 'we've still not got enough visitors and therefore we're cutting the price' ones!

Additionally some Tamil-run hotels and restaurants were destroyed in the riots and in some places I've had to guess if they would be rebuilt or not. Damage was most severe in the Tamil areas of Colombo and in the southern hill country towns – damage in Kandy was relatively minor but Nuwara Eliya, Bandarawela, Badulla and Haputale were all badly hit.

OTHER PEOPLE

In Sri Lanka I must thank Mrs Jayanti Savanadasa of the Sri Lankan Tourist Board, Mrs Claudette Pathmanathan of Mack Transport, Mr Thomson Rodrigo of the Ratnapura Rest House and the many other people all around the country who made my trip so pleasant. And thanks to all the hard workers at Lonely Planet who have aided my research, typeset, drawn maps, designed the book and so on.

As important as my own research were, once again, the many letters we received from travellers in Sri Lanka. A surprising number of you sat down to write to us during the '83 riots – the curfew kept some of you locked in your hotels where you thoughtfully decided to put pen to paper and tell us about Sri Lanka! Grateful thanks to you intrepid travellers:

Linda Ackerman (USA), Bill Allen, Ian Anderson (UK), Kim Atkinson (UK), Ruby Aver (USA), Karin Back (Sw), Nick Baker, Bonnie Baskin (USA), John Beasley (UK), Christian Belaud, Mathias Bev (UK), Margaret Blake, Annie Border (UK), Anne Britton, Martyn Brown (UK), Tim Brown (UK), Jan & Jill Burnes (UK), Michelle Burrow, Sue Bush, R D C Clarke (USA) Ade Colley, Mark Connelley, Joe Corrigan, Ian Courtis (UK), Sue Cox, Rod Cunningham (Aus), Alan Drayton (Aus), Peter J M Ducrot (Aus), Christina Durst, Lee Epstein (UK), G C Evans (Aus), John Fitzpatrick (UK), Rosyln Garavaglia, Mr & Mrs Gilden, Kay Gladstone (Aus), Harry Golding (USA), Bent Graungaard (Dk), Robert Dale Hajek (USA), Ian Hamilton (Aus), Bryan Hanson (UK), Louise Hardy, Joe Hatz, Greg Hay, Roger Hee, Mark Holtom (UK), Angela Huisman (Nl), Henry Irving (USA), Mark Irving, Brian Isbell, Ella & Banke Jeninga (Nl), Sue Joiner (UK), Jonathan, Gareth Jones, Steve & Mandy Jones (Aus), Maya Kar, Dr N Katz (USA), Rob Kay (NZ), Philip Keating (UK), Tinken Keteks, Judith Klenninan (UK), Gerhard Kotschenseuther, Jack Krieger, Shu Kuin, Mike Ledwith, Debbie Lodd, Keith Lott (Aus), Mrs E McCarthy, Nicky McCreanor, Mick McGowan, Robyn MacKenzie (Aus), Sharon McKenzie (Aus), Ian McMaster, Mike & Gerry McMaster, Ellyn Martin (Aus),

Charlotte Meldgaard & Ivar Moltke (Dk), Benita & Bill Mikulas (USA), Nancy Mitchell (USA), Hilary Moore, Graham Morgan (Aus), Margrit & Beat Muller (CH), Caroline Nixon (UK), A Philipps, Joachim Pietzsch (J), Mark & Desi Pigott, Peter Pimm (UK), P H Piyasena, John A Plampoin, Robert Porter, Deva Punit (USA), Alison Randall (UK), Jean Rannie, Mary Reckham, Manon Richard (Nl), Jacky & Roy Richards, Huw Robson, John Rogers (UK), Judith Roper (NZ), Lisa Ropfogel (USA), Anna Sabastearski (UK), Bob Sanders (UK), Brenda Silver (C), John Slade (UK), Susanne Smit (Nl), Linus Smith (Aus), Chris Spencer (Aus), Michael Spinks (Aus), Serban Stanciulescu, Jos Stevens (Nl), Morris Stewart (UK), Glenn Strachan (USA), John Stubbs (NZ), Paul Suhler (USA), Brian H Taylor, Sybe Terwee (Nl), Ian Thom (UK), Joan Underwood, Gahi Vamross?? (C), Carla Vandersloot (Nl), Martin & Kath Van Der Voorn, Loretta Ventuosoui (Aus), Charles Waheley (UK), Geoff Wallis, John Weaver (NZ), Joe Weiss, Elliot Wheelwright, P Gary White (Nep), Rick Wicks (USA), Robert Widin, Susan Williams, D W Winkworth (UK), Leon Winsky (UK), Mr & Mrs W A Withers (UK), George Wood (Sw), Phil Woods, Chris Zinn, Rolf Zuhlsdorf.

Aus – Australia, C – Canada, CH – Switzerland, D – Germany, Dk – Denmark, Nep – Nepal, Nl – Netherlands, NZ – New Zealand, Sw – Sweden, UK, USA

And the Next Edition

Things change – prices go up, good places go bad, bad places go bankrupt and nothing stays the same. So if you find things better, worse, cheaper, more expensive, recently opened or long ago closed, please don't blame me but please do write and tell me. The letters we get from 'our' travellers, out there on the road, are one of the real pleasures of Lonely Planet. As usual the best letters win a free copy of the next edition – or another LP guide if you prefer.

Contents

Introduction

It's easy to think of Sri Lanka as just an offshoot of India – a miniature, tropical-island India where the people are Buddhist, not Hindu, and there aren't so many of them. It's a complete misconception for Sri Lanka is nothing like India. It's a totally different place and enormously appealing. In fact it's hard to disagree with Marco Polo's impression that this is the finest island in the world – for no matter what you want Sri Lanka is likely to have it. Beaches? – the coastal stretch south of Colombo has beach after beach as beautiful as anywhere in the world. Culture? – try the Kandyan dances or the demon mask dances for size. Ruins? – if you like ruins you'll find your fill in the ancient cities of Anuradhapura and Polonnaruwa. Scenery? – head for the hill country where the heat of the plains and the coast soon fade away. Wildlife? – they say you can see leopards in the national parks, I did! All this comes with friendly people, good food, pleasant places to stay, reasonably low costs and in a handy, compact package. Sri Lanka? – I love it.

On leaving the Island of Andoman and sailing a thousand miles, a little south of west, the traveller reaches Ceylon, which is undoubtedly the finest Island of its size in all the world.

Marco Polo

CEYLON OR SRI LANKA?

Changing the country's name from Ceylon to Sri Lanka caused considerable confusion

Robert Knox's 1681 map of Ceylon

7

but in actual fact it has always been known to the Sinhalese (the people of Sri Lanka) as Lanka or to the Tamils as Ilankai. Indeed the two thousand year old Hindu epic, the *Ramayana*, tells of Rama's beautiful wife being carried away by the evil king of Lanka. Later the Romans knew it as Taprobane and Moslem traders talked of the island of Serendib, from which was derived the word serendipity – the faculty of making happy and unexpected discoveries by accident. The Portuguese called it Ceilao, a corruption of the native name Sinhala-dvipa. In turn the Dutch altered this name to Ceylan and the British to Ceylon. In 1972 the name was officially altered to the original Lanka with the addition of Sri which means 'auspicious' or 'resplendent'.

CHANGES

This is the third edition of this guidebook and my third trip to Sri Lanka. I wrote in the second edition that the changes had been enormous and the pace of tourism development was simply astonishing. The rate of escalation of prices at that time was also somewhat mind-boggling! In 15 years the annual flow of visitors has increased from just 16,000 to a third of a million so it's hardly surprising that there have been great changes.

The changes have not been nearly so great between that second trip and this third one. Of course there have been more hotels and guest houses opening but little clusters of guest houses have not suddenly turned into whole resorts! Nor have prices risen so steeply, in part due to the upheavals of 1983 which scared away many visitors and has forced the tourist business in Sri Lanka to become very competitive.

The pace of tourist development in the country is worrying because in many places it wipes out what people most like about Sri Lanka. The quiet and unhurried pace of coastal villages can hardly be found when they have become tourist ghettoes besieged by a constant barrage of noisy and smelly traffic. Unhappily not all visitors do their part to preserve the tranquility either – a little politeness and consideration goes a long way in Asia. greater effort is now required to escape to the unspoilt and relaxed Sri Lanka, the real and beautiful Sri Lanka. With effort you still can find it and it's an effort that is amply repaid.

Facts about the Country

HISTORY

Sri Lanka is definitely one of those places where history can be said to fade into the mists of legend. Is not Adam's Peak said to be the very place where Adam set foot on earth, having been cast out of heaven? Isn't that his footprint squarely on top of the mountain to prove it? Or is it Buddha's, visiting an island half way to paradise? And isn't Adam's bridge (the chain of islands linking Sri Lanka to India) the very series of stepping stones which Rama, aided by his faithful ally the monkey god Hanuman, skipped across in his mission to rescue Sita from the clutches of the evil demon Rawana, king of Lanka, in the epic Ramayana?

It is probable that the story of the Ramayana actually does have some frail basis in reality for Sri Lanka's history recounts many invasions from the south of India. Perhaps some early, punitive invasion provided the background for the story of Rama and his beautiful wife, a story which is recounted over and over again all around Asia. Whatever the legends the reality points towards the Sinhalese people first arriving in Sri Lanka around the 5th or 6th century BC and gradually replacing the original inhabitants, the Veddahs, who still linger on in remote parts of the island.

The Rise & Fall of Anuradhapura

In the centuries that followed, more settlers came in from India and the kingdom of Anuradhapura developed in the dry, northern plain region of the country. Later other kingdoms rose up in the south and west coast regions but Anuradhapura remained the strongest. At this time, around the 3rd century BC, the great Buddhist-Emperor Ashoka reigned in India and his son, Mahinda, came to the island with a retinue of monks to spread the Buddha's teachings. He soon converted the king and his followers to Buddhism and his sister planted a sapling of the sacred bo-tree under which the Buddha attained enlightenment in Bodh Gaya in northern India. It can still be seen flourishing in Anuradhapura today. Buddhism went through a rejuvenation in Sri Lanka and it was here that the Theravada, Hinayana or 'small vehicle' school of Buddhism developed and later spread to other Buddhist countries. Even today the Buddhists of Burma, Thailand and other Theravada-school countries look to Sri Lanka for spiritual leadership.

Buddhism gave the Sinhalese people a sense of national purpose and identity and also inspired the development of their culture and literature – factors which were to be important in the tumultuous centuries that followed. Although Anuradhapura was the centre of Sinhalese kingdoms for over a thousand years, from around the 4th century BC to the 10th century AD, it suffered repeated invasions by the Pandyan and later Chola kingdoms of south India. Each time some Sinhalese leader arose to repel the invaders; one of the most famous being Dutugemunu (around the 1st century BC) and later Vijayabahu (1055-1110 AD). The repeated invasions took their toll and Vijayabahu decided to abandon Anuradhapura and move his capital south to Polonnaruwa. Today the majestic ruins of his earlier capital are not the only reminders of this period of Sri Lankan history. Scattered throughout the country are enormous 'tanks', artificial lakes developed for irrigation purposes in the dry regions of Sri Lanka. Even today they would be amazing engineering feats.

The Rise & Fall of Polonnaruwa

Polonnaruwa survived as a Sinhalese capital for three more centuries after the fall of Anuradhapura and provided two other great kings, apart from Vijayabahu. His nephew Parakramabahu (1157-1186 AD), not content with Vijayabahu's expulsion of the Cholas, carried the war to south India and later followed this military feat with a daring raid on Burma. Internally he indulged in an orgy of building at his capital and constructed many new tanks around the country. But his warring and architectural extravagances wore the country out and probably shortened Polonnaruwa's lifespan. His successor, Nissankamalla (1187-1196) was the last great Polonnaruwa king. He was followed by a series of weak rulers and once more Sri Lanka was subject to invasions from south India. Another Tamil (south Indian) kingdom rose in the north of the island, tanks were neglected or destroyed, malaria started to spread due to the decay of the irrigation system and finally, like Anuradhapura before it, Polonnaruwa was abandoned.

The Portuguese Period
The centre of Sinhalese power now shifted to the south-west of the island and between 1253 and 1400 AD there were five Sinhalese capital cities. During this period Sri Lanka also suffered from attacks by Chinese and Malaysians as well as the periodic incursions from the south of India. Finally the most powerful invaders of all, the colonial European powers, arrived on the scene in 1505.

At this time Sri Lanka had three main kingdoms – Jaffna in the north, Kandy in the central highlands and Kotte, the most powerful, in the south-west. In 1505 Lorenco de Almeida arrived in Colombo, established friendly relations with the King of Kotte and gained for Portugal a monopoly on the spice and cinnamon trade, which would soon become of enormous importance in Europe. Attempts by the kingdom of Kotte to utilise the strength and protection of the Portuguese only resulted in Portugal taking over and ruling not only their regions but all the rest of the island, apart from the central

highlands around Kandy. Remote and inaccessible the kings of Kandy were always able to defeat attempts by the Portuguese to annex them and on a number of occasions drove them right back down to the coast.

The Dutch Period
Portuguese rule was characterised by European greed, cruelty and intolerance at its worst but attempts by the kingdom of Kandy to enlist Dutch help in expelling the Portuguese only resulted in the substitution of one European power for another. In 1656, just 151 years after the first Portuguese contact, the Dutch took control over the coastal areas of the island. In many ways the 140 years of Dutch rule were a carbon copy of the Portuguese period for the Dutch too were involved in constant, and unsuccessful, attempts to bring the highland power of Kandy under their control. The Dutch were much more interested in trade and profits than the Portuguese, who also had a strong interest in spreading their religion and extending their physical control. They also indulged their national penchant for canal building and you can still find many canals in Sri Lanka today, particularly around Negombo.

The British Period
The French revolution resulted in a major shake-up amongst the European powers and in 1796 the Dutch were easily supplanted by the British, who also managed to subdue the kingdom of Kandy and became the first European power to control the whole island. Until 1802 the British administered Sri Lanka from Madras in India but in that year it became a Crown Colony and in 1818, three years after the incorporation of Kandy, a unified administration for the entire island was set up.

In 1832 sweeping changes in property laws opened the doors to British settlers – at the expense of the Sinhalese who did not have clear title to their land, in British

An Execution by an Eliphant.

One of many fascinating illustrations from Robert Knox's 1681 book *An Historical Record of Ceylon.*

when it was replaced by Sinhala, nevertheless English is still widely spoken today.

Coffee was the main cash crop and the backbone of Sri Lanka's economy but a disastrous leaf blight virtually wiped out the coffee business in the 1870s and the plantations quickly switched over to growing tea or rubber. Today Sri Lanka is the world's largest tea exporter but tea production is subject to considerable price fluctuations on the international market and the taking over of privately owned British tea-plantations has often resulted in drastically lowered yields.

Rubber is grown as an intermediate crop – between the high country tea plantations and the low country coconut belt. The arrival of rubber in Sri Lanka has a distinct flavour of Victorian industrial espionage. Little more than 100 years ago rubber was a Brazilian monopoly but in 1876 Sir Henry Wickham quietly departed from the Amazon with 700,000 rubber tree seeds. They were whisked across the Atlantic and taken to Kew Gardens in London, where all the flowers had been removed from the greenhouses in readiness for this illicit crop.

From these seedlings a rubber tree nursery of 2000 plants was set up 30 km from Colombo in the Heneratgoda Botanical Gardens and all the rubber trees in Sri Lanka, and later Malaysia, came from this first planting. You can still see the very first rubber tree planted in Asia and there was another grove of these original trees at the Royal Botanical Gardens at Peradeniya, near Kandy. Today Sri Lanka and Malaysia produce 70% of the world's natural rubber.

The development of the plantations had a secondary, yet equally important, effect upon the country. The British were unable to persuade the Sinhalese to work cheaply and willingly so they imported large numbers of Tamil labourers from south India. The natural enmity between the Sri Lankans and the south Indians was exacerbated by this additional Tamil influx and it remains a serious problem to this very day. Attempts by the Sinhalese to repatriate the 'plantation Tamils' are

eyes. Soon the country was dotted with coffee, cinnamon and coconut plantations and a network of roads and railways were constructed to handle this new economic activity. English became the official language and remained so until 1956 considerably confused by the fact that there are many other Tamils who are descendants of the Tamil invaders of a thousand or more years ago.

Independence

Between the first and second world war political stirrings started to push Sri Lanka towards eventual independence from Britain – but in a considerably more peaceful and low-key manner than in India. At the close of WW II it was evident that independence would come very soon, in the shadow of Sri Lanka's larger neighbour. In February 1948 Sri Lanka, or Ceylon as it was still known at that time, became an independent member of the British Commonwealth. The country had emerged in remarkably good shape from WW II and the Sinhalese politicians were confident that the path ahead would be a smooth one, now that the 'colonial yoke' had been cast aside.

The first independent government was formed by D S Senanayake and his UNP (United National Party). His main opponents were a mixed bag of Communists, Marxists and Bolsheviks and the Tamil parties, either from the north of the country or the tea plantations. Sri Lanka's transition to independence went through very smoothly and at first everything else went smoothly too. The economy remained strong; tea prices, already running at a high level from WW II, were further bolstered by the Korean conflict. The government concentrated their energies on improving social services and keeping the opposition as weak as possible. Disenfranchising the plantation Tamils certainly helped the latter programme.

In 1952 D S Senanayake was killed in an accident and was followed by his son Dudley Senanayake. His first, of four, periods as Prime Minister was very short. One of the first moves following independence was to institute a policy of providing a free ration of rice to every Sri Lankan and also to heavily subsidise imports of this important staple. World-wide the price of rice had started to escalate and since minimal progress had been made in improving rice production the balance of payments started to run the wrong way. An attempt in 1953 to increase the price of rice resulted in mass riots, a large number of deaths and the declaration of a state of emergency. Dudley Senanayake resigned – he was not to be the last Sri Lankan leader to be brought down by the 'rice issue'.

Sir John Kotelawala took his place; since he just happened to be Dudley Senanayake's uncle the degree of nepotism in the UNP had by now resulted in the nickname of the 'Uncle Nephew Party'. Kotelawala was forceful but often careless and made many enemies both within Sri Lanka and abroad; not least being Nehru, leader of India. In 1956 he went to the polls and to his surprise was stunningly defeated, retaining only eight seats in the 101 member Parliament. The new leader was Solomon Bandaranaike, until his resignation from the UNP in 1951 he had been one of the few members of the UNP cabinet who was not related to Senanayake!

Bandaranaike's MEP (Mahajana Eksath Peramuna) coalition defeated the UNP primarily on nationalistic issues. Nearly 10 years after independence English remained the national language and the country continued to be ruled by an English speaking elite. The MEP's first moves included elevation of Sinhala to the role of national language and recognition of Buddhism as the national religion. The Tamils were caught in the middle of this English-Sinhala and Christian-Buddhist disagreement. The Tamils now put their weight behind the Federal Party, pressed for a degree of autonomy in the heavily Tamil areas in the north and east and bitterly opposed the position of Sinhala as the national language. Substituting a Sinhala letter for a Roman letter on car licence plates was just one government decision which led to considerable violence. When Bandaranaike tried to ease back on the Sinhala language decision and assure the Tamils that they would still have 'reasonable use' of their own language the 'Sinhala only' lobby turned on him, backed up by the opportunistic UNP which had been so strongly opposed to the substitution of Sinhala for English in the first place.

Inevitably this inter-communal bickering, fanned on by the opportunism of the political parties, led to violence, deaths and another state of emergency. Sri Lanka's major Sinhala-Tamil difficulties really date from this time although they had clearly been simmering long before.

Undeterred by these difficulties Bandaranaike set out on a huge programme of nationalisation and the setting up of state monopolies. The most visible of these was the Ceylon Transport Board (CTB) which took over every private bus line in the country and managed to make bus travel an uncomfortable and thoroughly chaotic experience absolutely everywhere. Fortunately free enterprise has been re-introduced to bus travel and there is now a flourishing minibus network which has also taken the load off the CTB.

Bandaranaike soon came into outright conflict with the still privately run press which proved to be just as opportunistic as the opposition parties. In 1958 Phillip Gunawardhene, his right-hand man, left the MEP to join the opposition SLFP (Sri Lanka Freedom Party) but before he could accomplish very much there Bandaranaike was assassinated by a Buddhist monk in late 1959. To this day Bandaranaike is looked upon as a national hero who brought the government of Sri Lanka back to the common people. It was this creation of a national sentiment which was his main accomplishment.

The MEP soon ran into trouble without Bandaranaike and in the 1960 elections, only a few months after his death, Dudley Senanayake came back to power. The SLFP ran a narrow second to the UNP but in the Tamil dominated north the Federal Party held a majority. The UNP did not, however, hold a clear majority and a

second election in mid-1960 swept the SLFP, now led by Mrs Sirimavo Bandaranaike, widow of the late Prime Minister, into power. She was the first woman Prime Minister in the world.

Strong arm tactics on the Tamils, and a continuing state of emergency in the north, kept the racial pot from boiling over and she pressed on with her husband's nationalisation policies and at least temporarily soured relations with the US by taking over the oil companies. Sri Lanka had earlier decided to follow an even-handed foreign relations policy and had enjoyed friendly relations with China, which purchased a large part of the country's rubber output. Meanwhile the economy was running from bad to worse and an attempt by the Finance Minister (yet another Bandaranaike, the UNP was not the only party to play the nepotism game) to abolish the rationed rice policy led to massive opposition and his resignation. In 1962 a plot was uncovered to overthrow the government by force.

In late 1964 the SLFP was defeated in Parliament and in the following election in 1965 Dudley Senanayake scraped back into power with the support of the Federal Party. As was by now becoming usual in Sri Lankan politics his policies turned out to have more bark than bite and his reluctance to turn back the clock on the SLFP's nationalisation programme soon lost him much of his support. Nevertheless he managed to survive his full five year term and led the UNP to a massive defeat in 1970. Major issues were unemployment, the cost of living, the poor state of the economy, the bungled development of the Mahaweli irrigation project and, once again, the rice issue.

Mrs Bandaranaike was again in power but in turn squandered her huge majority by failing to come to grips with the disastrous economic conditions and in 1971 an outright insurrection broke out, led by students and young people under the banner of the JVP (People's Liberation Army). The JVP had supported Mrs

Bandaranaike's election but were bitterly disappointed by her reluctance to confront the country's problems. Poorly organised, they were quickly defeated by the army, but at enormous cost both in property and lives. North Korea was accused of aiding the revolt and their diplomats were booted out of the country.

The revolt did hand the government a mandate to make sweeping changes including a strengthened armed forces, a new constitution, abolition of the upper house (the Senate) and the changing of the country's name from Ceylon to Sri Lanka. Nevertheless the economy continued to deteriorate and attempts to continue the free importation of rice at all costs led to drastic shortages of almost everything else. Long queues became commonplace at shops all over the country and in the 1977 elections the SLFP (in its new guise of the ULF – the United Left Front) went down to a stunning defeat at the hands of the UNP. Politics in Sri Lanka seems to be a continued succession of either shaky victories or stunning defeats!

The Present Government

J R Jayawardene (universally referred to in Sri Lanka as JR) was the new leader of the UNP and he was determined to follow a more pragmatic path than his predecessors. This involved back-pedalling on the socialisation and nationalisation programmes and an all out effort to lure back some of the foreign investment which was so comprehensively chased away by Mrs Bandaranaike. It's still early days to pass judgement on his efforts but the institution of a free trade zone has attracted many foreign companies to take advantage of Sri Lanka's high educational standards and low wage levels. In late 1981 Queen Elizabeth II visited Sri Lanka to finally open part of the long delayed Mahaweli irrigation project. Major efforts to improve rice production have also been undertaken and Sri Lanka is also taking maximum advantage of its tourist boom.

Jayawardene has also taken some controversial steps to stabilise the country's volatile political chemistry. These changes, which included a change from a British style parliamentary system to a presidential system, have also strengthened his own powers and made it much easier for him to stay in control.

Unhappily the Tamil question continues to bedevil the government and in mid-1981 another round of racial violence broke out with bloodshed on both sides. Emergency law was proclaimed to bring the situation under control but this was just a subdued preview of what was to happen in 1983. The events of '83 followed an increasingly familiar pattern but with a final explosion that dwarfed previous outbreaks of violence. The spark that lit the explosion was an ambush and massacre by Tamil 'Tiger' extremists of an army patrol in the northern Jaffna region. The government, aware of the effect of similar events in the past, tried to suppress the news but, inevitably, it leaked out with horrifying results. For days on end mobs rampaged through towns all over the island looting and burning Tamil shops and businesses and slaughtering any Tamils they could lay their hands on.

The government, police and armed forces were unable to control the extremists and areas with a large Tamil population – such as the Pettah district of Colombo or the business districts of some of the hill country towns – were virtually levelled. Even prisons were not safe as Tamil prisoners were murdered in Colombo's jails. Thousands of Tamils fled from the south to the relatively safer Tamil dominated Jaffna region or left the country completely.

Although the loss of life and property was high the violence also had great costs for Sri Lanka's improving yet still fragile economy. Many businesses were destroyed and obviously many Tamils, who provide a disproportionate part of the country's investment and enterprise, will be reluctant to reinvest in the country. The tourist trade fell flat on its face with the major European package tour operators cancelling en masse. By early '84 tourism was picking up again, rebuilding was underway and loud promises were being made that such events would never happen again, but an answer to the inter-communal friction will remain high on the problem list for any Sri Lankan government. As of yet it's hard to say if any real steps have been taken to prevent yet another recurrence of what seems to have almost become a biennial event in Sri Lanka.

PEOPLE

Sri Lanka today has a population of around 14 million, the resulting population density of around 200 people per square km is one of the highest in Asia. Like many other Asian countries Sri Lanka has suffered from explosive population growth over the past few decades. Approximately 70% of the population live in the rural areas and another 10% or so work on the great plantations.

The Sinhalese people, originally settlers from India, constitute about 70% of the population. They speak Sinhala, are predominantly Buddhist and have a reputation as an easy-going, warm-hearted people. Like the Hindus of India the Sri Lankans have a developed caste system although it is of nowhere near the same overall importance.

The Tamils are the second largest group, constituting about 20% of the population. Tamils will often claim that the actual percentage is rather higher and that there is a Sinhalese plot to underestimate their numbers in order to maintain Sinhalese superiority and control. Many Tamils have been living in Sri Lanka since the series of Tamil-Sinhalese wars and invasions of a thousand or more years ago but there are also a great number of 'plantation' Tamils who were brought over by the British to work on the tea plantations. Attempts by the Sinhalese to disenfranchise or repatriate these Tamils has caused considerable bitterness. The Sri Lanka Tamil population is concentrated in the east and north, particularly around Jaffna. They are predominantly Hindu, speak Tamil and caste distinctions are more important than amongst the Sinhalese although nowhere near as important as in the north of India.

The remaining 10% (actually a bit less) of the population is composed of a number of elements. The Burghers are Eurasians, primarily descendants of the Portuguese and Dutch, more frequently the former than the latter. For a time, even after independence, the Burghers had a disproportionate influence over the political and business life of Sri Lanka but growing Sinhalese and Tamil nationalism has reduced their advantage and many Burghers have moved abroad. Nevertheless, names like Fernando, de Silva or Perera are still very common.

There is also a small Moslem community described as either Ceylon Moors, Indian Moors or Malays. The Ceylon Moors date from Portuguese times and were probably the descendants of Arab or Indian Moslem traders. The Malays generally came with the Dutch from Java while the Indian Moors are more recent arrivals from India or Pakistan. There are also smaller Chinese and European communities and a small, down-trodden group of low-caste south Indians brought in to perform the most menial tasks. In the more remote parts of the country there are still a few groups of Veddahs; the aboriginal people who inhabited Sri Lanka long before the Sinhalese came on the scene.

Westerners interested in assuming more permanent residence in Sri Lanka may be interested in the government's policy – if you can prove you have a regular external income the government will allow you to settle in Sri Lanka. The longest resident westerner under this programme is science fiction author Arthur C Clarke.

The Tamil Question

You're not going to be able to spend long in Sri Lanka without seeing, reading or hearing something about the 'Tamil Question' since it's far and away the country's greatest problem. As an outsider it's impossible to really understand but any understanding is better than none. Basically it comes down to animosity between the easy-going Sinhalese and the dourer, hard working Tamils. The spark that seems to periodically light the fuse is 'Eelam', a Tamil cry for independence for the Tamil region of Jaffna in the north.

Most Tamils recognise that cutting off a slice from this already small island nation is simply not on, but all it seems to take is some random act of violence by an extremist group to send the whole country up in flames. And once the mobs start marching it's the Tamil minority who suffer the consequences.

The whole evil brew that goes to make up this on-going problem is difficult if not impossible to analyse but clearly there are a number of factors you can easily pinpoint and feed into the equation. First any analysis of the Tamils has to take account of the 'Sri Lankan Tamils' and the 'stateless' or 'Indian Tamils'. The latter are the Tamils who came in under the British and have neither managed to gain Sri Lankan citizenship nor been repatriated to India during the campaign to export the Tamil problem. They're predominantly found in the hill country tea plantations and although they have the least they probably lost the most from the '83 violence. They're stateless so they have no say in the country's government, they're generally not economically well off and it was the hill country that bore the brunt of the violence.

Secondly the Tamils are unquestionably good businesspeople and in many areas control the economic strings. They're the small shopkeepers, the local industrialists. They're not, however, by any means excluded from the government – there are important Tamil ministers in the government, Tamils are high officers in the police force, they hold powerful positions in the civil service. Furthermore, although efforts have been made to increase the percentage of Sinhalese in higher education, Tamils still win a disproportionate number of college and university places.

It's interesting to compare Sri Lanka and its problems with two other countries. In Malaysia friction between an introduced race, the Chinese, and the indigenous people, the Malays, has led to similar violence although not now for a number of years. In Malaysia, however, the Chinese form a much larger percentage of the population than the Tamils in Sri Lanka; their economic control is much greater and much more evident; and the Malay-dominated government's efforts to raise the Malay position has been much greater.

The other interesting comparison is to another small island; one where the minority population has achieved their 'eelam' and carved out their own little northern state. And where that division has not solved any problems at all. For Jaffna and the Tamils read Belfast and the Northern Irish.

You'll undoubtedly get plenty of opportunity to discuss the problem in Sri Lanka. Visitors from abroad are a neutral party so both sides of the question will discuss it more openly than they would with another Sri Lankan. Foreign residents in Sri Lanka will probably give you yet another view of the whole situation. Despite some horror stories in the more colourful western press visitors to Sri Lanka have not really been involved in the problem – it's strictly Sri Lankan versus Sri Lankan. Although European package tour groups deserted the country in the latter half of '83 the west coast, where these groups generally head, was probably least affected of the whole island. I don't think I saw any damage along the east coast whereas towns in the hill country and parts of Colombo looked as if they'd been blitzed.

Although it's difficult to see any simple solution to the 'Tamil Question' several results are very clear. One is that each outbreak of violence does the country's fragile economy great harm – businesses are ruined, investment is scared away and tourism plummets. Secondly communal violence creates the very situation which the Sinhalese least want – more and more Tamils move north to the relative safety of the Jaffna region and in turn more and more Sinhalese leave that area. In effect a separate Tamil state is being created in the north by the very opposition to it. Finally a major fear lurks on the horizon – just how far can a situation similar to 1983 develop before India, with its huge population and disciplined armed forces, decides to step in to 'keep the peace'?

ECONOMY

Prior to independence it was a constant source of complaint that the British had forced upon Sri Lanka a typical colonial economy. All effort was concentrated upon a limited number of commodities whose production was probably more beneficial to the coloniser than the colonised. It's a sad reflection on the government bungling that Sri Lanka has been subject to that – 30 years after independence – tea, rubber and coconuts are still overwhelmingly the mainstays of the economy.

Tea remains the single largest export by a very large margin. Despite Sri Lanka's abundant fertility it is still unable to produce sufficient rice and other staples to feed its population and a large part of the import bill is devoted to food. In 1984, however, were it not for unseasonal rains the country would have been self-sufficient in rice. It is hoped that with the completion of major new irrigation projects the rice production shortfall will be dramatically reduced. Similarly the island has a long coastline and is surrounded by waters teeming with fish, yet is unable to provide sufficient fish;

large quantities are imported either fresh or canned. This despite large sums of money spent on a national Fisheries Corporation.

Sri Lanka's fame as a gem centre no doubt brings in large amounts of foreign exchange although much of this comes in via the black market and illegal exports. And of course there is tourism, which has been storming ahead as people realise what a delightful little paradise Sri Lanka is. It's perhaps just as well since, gems apart, Sri Lanka is virtually devoid of natural resources apart from its stunning attractiveness.

Since the election of Jayawardene's government in 1977 great efforts have been made to attract foreign investment through a free trade zone and promises of low levels of government intervention. Gradually it is hoped to build a manufacturing industry to complement the current agricultural bias. The hydro electric power that Sri Lanka desperately needs for these developments will come, in large part, from the huge Mahaweli project. Although the events of '83 were a major setback to the government's hopes there was clear evidence that the new economic policies were starting to bear fruit and Sri Lanka was making important steps forward in new industries.

GEOGRAPHY

Sri Lanka is a relatively small island shaped like a teardrop falling from the southern end of India. From north to south it is just 353 km (220 miles) long and only 183 km (114 miles) at its widest. Its area of 66,000 square km (25,000 square miles) is about the same as Ireland or the Australian state of Tasmania.

The central hill country rises a little south of the centre of the island and is surrounded by a low-lying coastal plain. The flat north-central and northern plain extends from the hill country all the way to the northern tip of the island and this region is much drier than the rest of the island. The best beaches are on the south-

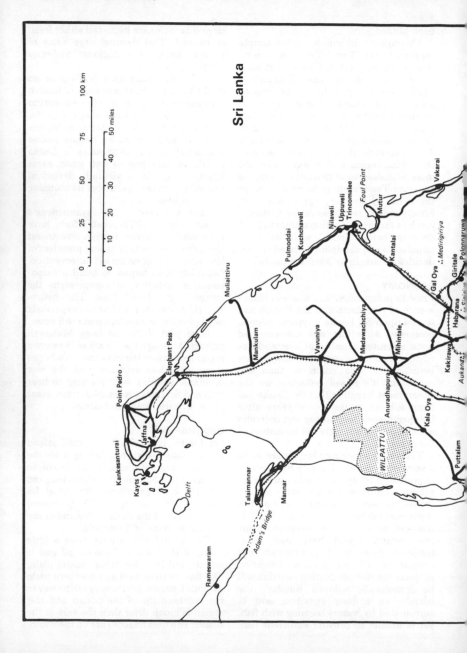

Sri Lanka

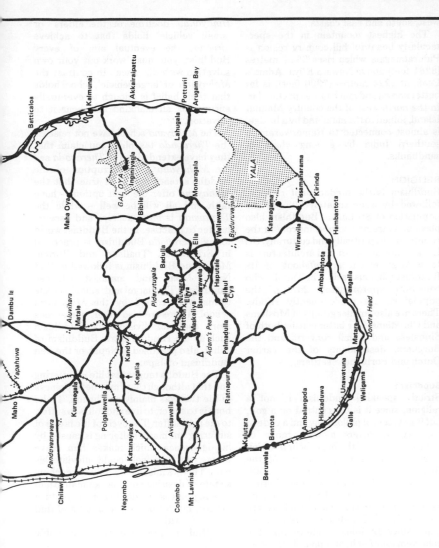

west, south and east coasts.

The highest mountain in the spectacularly beautiful hill country region is Piduratalagala which rises 2524 metres (8281 feet) above Nuwara Eliya. Adam's Peak, at 2224 metres (7300 feet), is far better known and much more spectacular. In the north-west of the country Mannar Island, joined to the mainland by a bridge, is almost connected to Rameswaram in southern India by a long chain of sandbanks.

RELIGION

Buddhism is the predominant religion, followed by approximately 70% of the population of Sri Lanka. Buddhism also plays an extremely important role in the country both spiritually and culturally. Sri Lanka's literature, art and architecture is to a large extent an offshoot of its Buddhist religious basis. The Tamils, who constitute approximately 20% of the population, are predominantly Hindu. There are also smaller groups of Moslems and Christians. The latter consist both of Sinhalese and Tamil converts and the Burghers, descendants of the earlier Dutch and Portuguese settlers.

Buddhism

Strictly speaking Buddhism is not a religion, since it is not centred on a god, but is a system of philosophy and a code of morality. It covers a wide range of interpretations of the basic beliefs which started with the enlightenment of the Buddha in northern India around 2500 years ago. Siddhartha Gautama, born a prince, was not the first Buddha nor is he expected to be the last. Gautama is said to be the fourth Buddha or 'enlightened one'. Since Buddhists believe that the achievement of enlightenment is the goal of every being, eventually we will all reach Buddhahood.

The Buddha never wrote his *Dhamma* (teachings down and a schism later developed so that today there are two major schools of Buddhism. The *Theravada,*

Hinayana, 'doctrine of the elders' or 'small vehicle' holds that to achieve *nirvana,* the eventual aim of every Buddhist, you must 'work out your own salvation with diligence'. In contrast the *Mahayana,* or 'large vehicle', school holds that their belief is enough to eventually encompass all mankind and bear it to salvation.

The *Mahayana* school have not rejected the *Theravada* teachings but claim that they have extended it; the *Theravada* see the *Mahayana* as a corruption of the Buddha's teachings. It is true that the *Mahayana* offer the 'soft option' – have faith and all will be well – while the *Theravada* is more austere and ascetic; harder to practise. In the Buddhist world today *Theravada* Buddhism is practised in Sri Lanka, Thailand and Burma. *Mahayana* Buddhism is followed in Viet Nam, Japan and amongst Chinese Buddhists. The 'large' and 'small' vehicle terms were coined by the *Mahayana* school. There are also other, sometimes more esoteric, divisions of Buddhism such as the Hindu-Tantric Buddhism of Tibet, also practised in Nepal, or the Zen Buddhism of Japan.

The Buddha taught that life is suffering and that although there may be happiness in life this was mainly an illusion. To be born is to suffer, to live and toil is to suffer, to die is to suffer. The cycle of life is one of suffering but man's suffering is caused by his ignorance which makes him crave things which he feels could alleviate his pain. This is a mistake for only by reaching a state of desiring nothing can man attain true happiness. To do this one must turn inward, master one's own mind and find the peace within.

Buddha preached the four noble truths:

1. all life is suffering
2. this suffering comes from selfish desire
3. when one forsakes selfish desire suffering will be extinguished

4. the 'middle path' is the way to eliminate desire

The middle path to the elimination of desire and the extinction of suffering is also known as the 'eight-fold path' which is divided into three stages: *Sila* – the precept, *Samadhi* – equanimity of mind, *Panna* – wisdom and insight. The eight 'right' actions are:

1. right speech
2. right action
3. right thought
4. right exertion
5. right attentiveness
6. right concentration
7. right aspiration
8. right understanding

This, is an evolutionary process through many states of spiritual development until the ultimate goal is reached – death, no further rebirths, entry to *nirvana*. To the western mind this often seems a little strange – for us death is the end, not something to be looked forward to, but something to be feared.

Buddha taught that all things are part of the whole, that there is no part of man which is called the soul: 'In the beginning is the One and only the One is. All things are one and have no life apart from it; the One is all things and incomplete without the least of them. Yet the parts are parts within the whole, not merged in it.'

Supreme enlightenment is the only reality in a world of unreality, the teachings continue. All else is illusion and there is no unchanging soul which is reborn after life, but a consciousness which develops and evolves spiritually until it reaches the goal of *nirvana* or oneness with the all. *Karma* is central to the doctrine of rebirth, but this is not 'fate' as it is sometimes described. *Karma* is the law of causation, each rebirth results from the actions one has committed in the previous life, thus in Buddhism each

person alone is responsible for their life. The Buddha did not claim that his way was the only way, since in the end all beings will find a path because the goal is the same for all.

Ashoka, the great Indian emperor who was a devout Buddhist, sent missions to all the known world and his son Mahinda brought Buddhism to Sri Lanka. It took a strong hold on the country almost immediately and Sri Lanka has been looked upon as a centre for Buddhist culture and teaching ever since. It was in Sri Lanka that the *Theravada* school of Buddhism first developed and was later passed on to other countries.

Buddhism emphasises love, compassion, gentleness and tolerance and this tolerant outlook on other religions has often resulted in Buddhism being absorbed into other religions, as eventually happened with Hinduism, or absorbing already extant beliefs. The personal experience one has of Buddhism remains the same from country to country despite local adaptations, changes, amalgamations and inclusions – it's an overriding impression of warmth and gentleness; a religion practised by friendly people who are always eager to explain their beliefs.

Books

If you'd like to read more about Buddhism a good book to start with is Christmas Humphrey's *Buddhism* (Pelican paperback London, 1949). There are many books on Buddhism available in Sri Lanka, a particularly good place to look is the Buddhist Publication Society, which is located by the lakeside in Kandy. There is also a Buddhist Information Centre at 50 Ananda Cumaraswamy Mawatha, Colombo 5; the Buddhist Book Shop at Green Path, Colombo 7 and a Museum of Buddhism at the Gangaramaya Bhikku Training Centre, 61 Sri Jinaratana Rd, Colombo 2.

FESTIVALS & HOLIDAYS

Sri Lanka has a wide variety of festivals and holidays related to the Buddhist,

Hindu, Christian and Moslem religions. Many of the holidays are based on the lunar calendar so they vary in date from year-to-year by our Gregorian calendar. Moslem holidays, such as the festival of Id-ul-Fitr, move forward 10 days each year.

In addition every full moon day is a holiday, whether it coincides with some other holiday or not. The tourist office has a colourful brochure describing the many festivals.

January On the full moon day in January the Duruthu Perahera is held at the Kelaniya temple in Colombo. Second in importance only to the huge Kandy Perahera, this festival celebrates a visit by the Buddha to Sri Lanka. On January 14th the Thai Pongal harvest festival is held by Hindus in honour of the Sun God.

February Independence Day, celebrating independence from Britain, features parades, dances, processions and national games all over the country on February 4th. In late February or early March the Hindu festival of Mahasivarathri commemorates Parvati, the consort of Lord Shiva, in her winning of the god. At the February full moon Navam Poya a big perahera is held in Colombo near the lake. About a hundred elephants take part and this is now bigger and more impressive than the Kelaniya perahera.

The usually uninhabited islands of Kachchaitivu and Palativu, off the Jaffna Peninsula, are the scene for Roman Catholic festivals at churches consecrated to St Anthony.

March An Easter passion play is performed on the island of Duwa off Negombo.

April A month of festivals and holidays with both the Sinhala and Tamil new years falling in April. This is an occasion for hospitality and it also coincides with the end of the harvest season. The new year also marks the start of the south-west monsoon and the end of the pilgrimage season to climb Adam's Peak. During the Sinhala new year period it can be very difficult to find transport or even a meal. Even the restaurants in some hotels may be shut down.

May Workers' Day falls on May 1st as in other parts of the world and May 22nd is celebrated as Republic Day but Wesak is the important holiday in this month. This two-day holiday over the full moon day in May celebrates the birth, enlightenment and death of Lord Buddha. Villages are decorated with huge panels showing scenes from the Buddha's life; puppet shows and open-air theatre performances take place. The temples are crowded with devotees bringing flowers and offerings. High point of the Wesak festivities are the lighting of countless paper lanterns and oil lamps which turn the whole island into a fairyland.

June The full moon day in June celebrates the festival of Poson when Mahinda, the son of Ashoka, brought Buddhism to Sri Lanka. Anuradhapura and Mihintale, where Mahinda met and converted the Sinhalese king, are the main sites for this celebration. Thousands of white-clad pilgrims climb the staircase to the summit of Mihintale.

July In late July or early August fire-walking ceremonies take place at Udappu and Mundel. The annual pilgrimage from Batticaloa to Kataragama also starts at this time. The important Kandy Esala Perahera and the Vel festival take place in late July or early August. A host of Hindu festivals are held in the Jaffna area in July-August. They include events at Maviddapuram and Nallur where ritual acts like those at Kataragama take place, but much less as a show for tourists.

The Catholic festival of Madhu on July 2nd commemorates the meeting in the jungle of two parties of Portuguese and Sinhalese Catholics fleeing from Dutch oppression to the safety of the Kingdom of Kandy.

August At the full moon in the Sinhalese month of Esala the huge Kandy Esala Perahera, the most important and spectacular festival in Sri Lanka, takes place. This great Perahera or procession honours the Sacred Tooth Relic of Kandy. The festival continues for 10 days and nights with peraheras from the four principal devales or shrines. Thousands of dancers, drummers and temple chieftans take part in the parade which also features 50 or more magnificently decorated elephants including the most splendid of them all, the mighty Maligawa Tusker which carries the golden relic casket. Smaller peraheras are held at other locations around the island.

August At the full moon in the Sinhalese month of Esala the huge Kandy Esala Perahera, the most important and spectacular festival in Sri Lanka, takes place. This great Perahera or procession honours the Sacred Tooth Relic of Kandy. The festival continues for 10 days and nights with peraheras from the four principal devales or shrines. Thousands of dancers, drummers and temple chieftans take part in the parade which also features 50 or more magnificently decorated elephants including the most splendid of them all, the mighty Maligawa Tusker which carries the golden relic casket. Smaller peraheras are held at other locations around the island.

The Hindu festival of Vel is held in Colombo at the same time. The gilded chariot of Skanda, the God of War, complete with his ayudha (weapon) the vel (trident) is ceremonially hauled from the Hindu temple in Sea St, Pettah to the kovil at Bambalapitiya. Other important Hindu festivals are held in and around Jaffna and at Kataragama where Hindu devotees put themselves through the whole gamut of ritual masochism. Skewers are thrust through their tongues and cheeks, others tow heavy carts or suspend weights from hooks piercing their skin. The grand finale is the fire-walking ceremonies as the devotees prance barefoot across beds of red-hot embers.

September Bandaranaike Commemoration Day takes place on September 26th.

October The Hindu festival of Deepavali, the festival of lights, takes place in late October or early November. Thousands of flickering oil lamps celebrate the triumph of good over evil, the return of Rama after his period of exile and welcome Lakshmi, the Goddess of Wealth.

December The pilgrimage season to climb Adam's Peak starts during this month. The full moon day commemorates Sangamitta, Ashoka's daughter who accompanied Mahinda to Sri Lanka and brought a sapling from the sacred Bo-tree. The tree grown from that original sapling still stands in Anuradhapura over two thousand years later.

Poya Warning
On the monthly full-moon poya holidays no alcohol may be sold in hotels, restaurants, bars or stores. If you feel you're likely to be thirsty it's wise to stock up in advance! Some hotels may provide their needy guests with a bottle of beer 'under the table', so long as it isn't too obvious.

LANGUAGE
It's very easy to get by in Sri Lanka with English. Although Sinhala is now the official national language English is still widely spoken and in all the major centres you'll have no problem finding somebody who can understand you. If you get off the beaten track you'll quickly find that knowledge of English fades away so it's nice to know at least a few words of Sinhala – it's pleasant to be able to greet people in their own language anyway.

Remember that Sinhala is not the only local language, a substantial minority also speak Tamil.

The Sinhalese alphabet has about 50 letters in it so you're unlikely to find yourself able to read signposts in a short stay in Sri Lanka! One considerable achievement of the post-independence Sri Lankan governments has been excellent progress in the educational field – today Sri Lanka has a very high, by Asian standards, literacy rate.

Sinhalese is somewhat simplified by the use of many 'eka words'. *Eka* is used more or less similarly to the English definite article 'the', *ekak* is used like 'a' or 'any'. English words for which there is no Sinhalese equivalent have often been incorporated straight into Sinhalese with the simple addition of *eka* or *ekak*. Thus if yu're in search of a telephone it's simply *telifoon ekak* but if it's a specific telephone then you want *telifoon eka*. Similarly specifically English definitions of people have been included in Sinhala simply by adding *kenek* – if you hire a car the driver is the *draiwar kenek*.

A simple Sinhalese phrasebook is a cheap item to pick up in Colombo. Look for *Say it in Sinhala* by J B Disanayaka (Lake House, Colombo, 1974). If you're going to be staying any length of time in the north it's worth picking up a Tamil-English phrasebook in a Jaffna bookshop.

Greetings & Civilities

In common with may other Asian countries our multitude of greetings – hello, good morning, how are you, goodbye – simply don't exist. Saying *aaibowan* more or less covers them all. Similarly there isn't really a Sinhalese word for 'thank you'. You could try *bohoma stutiy* but it's a rather awkward thing to say – better to smile. Appreciation of a meal could be covered by *bohoma rahay* which serves as appreciation and a compliment – sort of 'that was good'. *Hari shook* covers our expressions like 'wonderful, terrific' or even 'fine'. Remember that,

as in India, the head gesture for 'yes' is a side to side wiggle of the head, more akin to our 'no' and initially very confusing.

Personal Terms

Again, as in some other Asian countries, the word 'you' is studded with pitfalls – in Sinhalese there are over 20 different ways to say 'you' depending on the person's age, social status, sex, position and even (as in French and German) how well you know him. It's best to simply avoid saying you! The word for Mr is *mahatteya* and Mr Jayawardene is Jayawardene mahatteya since the word comes after the name, not before. Similar Mrs is *noona*. Any non-eastern foreigner is defined as white so a male foreigner is a *suda mahatteya*.

Useful Words & Phrases

yes	ou
no	naa
OK	hari honday
room	kaamare
bed	anda
food	kaama
tea	tea
eggs	bittara
vegetables	eloolu
fish	maalu
hoppers (local snacks)	aappa
bank	bankuwa
post office	tapal kantooruwa
certainly, of course	nattan
really?	habaata?
wait a minute	poddak inna
so so?	itin itin?
this/that	mee/oya
what/where	mokadda/koheda
how much?	kiiyada?
my name is........	ma-ge nama........
what is this?	meeka mokadda?
when is the bus?	bas-eka kiiyata da?
where is the hotel?	hootale koheda?
how much is this?	meeka kiiya da?

Two useful little Sinhalese words are *da* and *ge*. *Da* turns a statement into a question – thus if *noona* means a lady then *noona-da* means 'this lady?' or 'is this the lady?'. *Ge* is the Sinhalese equivalent of apostrophe s; thus 'Tony's book' in Sinhala would be *Tony-ge pota*. *Ta* is like the English preposition to – if you want to go 'to the beach' it's *walla-ta*.

1	eka
2	deka
3	tuna
4	hatara
5	paha
6	haya
7	hata
8	ata
9	namaya
10	dahaya
100	siiya
1000	daaha

Place names

Sri Lanka's often fearsome looking place names become much simpler with a little analysis. *Pura* or *puram* simply means town – as in Ratnapura (town of gems) or Anuradhapura. Similarly *nuwara* means city and *gama* means village. Other common words that are incorporated in place names include *gala* or *giri* (rock or hill), *kanda* (mountain), *ganga* (river), *oya* (large stream), *ela* (stream), *tara* or *tota* (ford or a port), *pitiya* (park), *watte* (garden), *deniya* (rice field), *gaha* (tree), *arama* (a park or monastery) and *duwa* (an island).

Not surprisingly many towns are named after the great tanks – *tale*, *wewa* or *kulam*. The same word can appear in Sinhala, Sanskrit, Pali and Tamil! Finally *maha* means great. Put it all together and even a name like Tissamaharama makes sense – it's simply '(King) Tissa's great park'.

FLORA & FAUNA

The following description of Sri Lanka's flora and fauna and its national parks and wildlife sanctuaries was contributed by Constance S Leap Bruce and Murray D Bruce. See also the Wildlife Parks chapter (page 194) for further information.

The recent development of a National Parks and Reserves system is but the latest episode in a long history of a coordinated conservation practice in Sri Lanka. The early edicts of the country's Buddhist leaders and the Sinhalese culture itself have allowed much of the island's natural richness to remain undisturbed for centuries. Sir Lanka can boast of the world's first wildlife sanctuary dating back to the 3rd century BC, created by King Devanampiyatissa in whose reign Buddhism was introduced. Succeeding monarchs continued this tradition as recorded on rock inscriptions throughout the island, perhaps the most famous being the proclamation written in Polonnaruwa by King Nessankamella (1187-1196 AD) which called for a ban on killing all animals within seven 'gaw' (39 km) of the city. These rulers were also aware of the importance of undisturbed forests and set aside large tracts of land called 'Thahanankalle' (Forbidden Forests) as wilderness areas and watersheds. Some of these ancient reserves in existence today are the Sinharaja Rain Forest Reserve and Udawattekelle Wildlife Sanctuary (in Kandy).

Today's system of reserves is mostly a synthesis of traditionally protected areas and those established by the British, who were also responsible for clearing large tracts of forest for their coffee, tea and rubber plantations and the slaughter of 'big game'. There are close to 100 protected areas now acknowledged by the Government, including an extensive system of bird sanctuaries, jungle corridors, 'man and biosphere reserves', and five national parks – Wilpattu, Yala (Ruhuna), Gal Oya, Uda Walawe and Lahugala.

Inside the national parks visitors' movements are restricted and you must be accompanied by a guide. This policy has been established to ensure minimal disturbance by visitors and maximum protection to the area. Guided tours by minibus are arranged at park headquarters and it is not generally recommended to hire the private 'safari' vehicles which flourish at the park's perimeters. Reservation of accommodation available within the parks should be made at the Department of Wildlife Conservation, Zoological Gardens, Dehiwela (tel 714146). However, around the parks you will also find a good selection of accommodation in all price ranges.

The most important of the reserves are Horton Plains, Knuckles Hill Range (of hills) and the Peak Wilderness Sanctuary (Adam's

Peak). Entry is not restricted here and visitors can move about freely. Of the 'man and biosphere' reserves, the most important is the Sinharaja Rain Forest Reserve, the last remaining patch of virgin rainforest and the richest in endemic flora and fauna. Entry here is only via permits issued by the Forest Department, PO Box 509, Colombo 1.

The varied climate and topography of Sri Lanka allows for a large diversity of plant and animal life. The south-western Wet Zone is tropical rainforest with characteristic dense undergrowth and a tall canopy of hardwood trees, including ebony, teak and silkwood. Here also are some of the most spectacular orchids and many of the plants used in Ayurvedic (traditional) medicine. The central Hill Zone, such as at Horton Plains, is typical of the cold, damp highland areas with hardy grasslands, *Rhododendron* and Elfin (stunted) Forests, with trees often draped in *Sphagnum* moss. The remainder forms the arid Dry Zone, with a sparser cover of trees with shrubs and grasslands, which may erupt into bloom with the first rains.

The animals of Sri Lanka are some of the most unusual and varied found anywhere. The 86 species of mammals include the famous elephant, seen in all National Parks (notably Gal Oya and Lahugala) and leopard (Wilpattu and Yala). Many species of deer, including spotted deer, hog deer, sambhar and mouse deer are in all the national parks. Monkeys, especially the long-tailed grey langur and the toque macaque, are common throughout the island. Other interesting mammals include the sloth bear, porcupine, wild boar, dugong, and flying foxes (roosting in huge treetop colonies during the day, such as at Peradeniya Botanical Gardens, near Kandy).

The birdlife is a major attraction of Sri Lanka, with about 450 species recorded, including around 250 species found here throughout the year (21 are only found in Sri Lanka). As there is no land south of Sri Lanka except Antarctica, it is a very important winter home for the bird migrants coming from as far as western Europe and Siberia. From August to April the migratory birds can be seen in their hundreds and thousands at tanks, lagoons and other wetland areas. The best time for birds, and hence wildlife in general, is January to April, when visibility and field conditions are good everywhere.

The network of bird sanctuaries in Sri Lanka

not only play host to the thousands of visitors, but are important breeding grounds for many other species. Perhaps the showiest bird is the flamingo, arriving in large numbers, but also to be seen are ducks, storks, herons, egrets and other waterbirds. Some 54 species of fish are also found in these waterways and marshlands, including many highly prized aquarium varieties such as the red scissortail barb and the ornate paradise fish. The British also introduced several kinds, including trout, which are still common around the Horton Plains. Also found in these areas are 40 species of frogs and toads, and amongst the large variety of reptiles are two species of crocodile and five species of turtles. Most reptiles, however, are land dwellers, including the beautiful star tortoise and the infamous cobra. Of the 83 species of snakes recorded, only five are poisonous (cobra, Russell's viper, Indian & Sri Lankan krait and the saw-scaled viper), but they are relatively common.

Only 25 to 35% of the island is still under forest cover and a large amount of this is threatened by the massive Mahaweli Development Project in the east. Fortunately, the improvement of the system of protected areas is considered to be an important priority. New areas are under proposal as national parks and reserves, while the upgrading of existing places continues. The five current national parks are listed here. These are all in the Dry Zone, where the elephant and other large animals are confined. Also listed are several other areas of interest in all zones. As some of these places, notably Wilpattu and Yala, are mentioned also in the Wildlife Parks chapter, they are only briefly covered in this section.

Wilpattu National Park The 'Land of Lakes' is 176 km north of Colombo, and most famous for its leopards, bears and birdlife. A single morning's visit is unlikely to be enough to appreciate the diversity of the park. If you decide to spend two or three nights in the park, try booking into the park bungalows at Kali Villu or Manikepola Uttu, both towards the northern end of the park, and also handy to the larger lakes near Portugal Bay and the north-west coast.

Yala (Ruhana) National Park Yala is at the opposite end of the island, 305 km south-east from Colombo, and much more convenient from the west coach beaches where day trips can even be arranged. It also offers open, undulating country, studded with rocky formations and lagoons, and is famous for its elephants. About 12 herds occur here, but solitary males may provide your first glimpses of elephant (a far cry from a century ago when professional hunters and 'sportsmen' were very active, with one man claiming to have shot 1400).

As at Wilpattu you may want to stay inside the park at a bungalow, try Buttawa or Mahsilawa, both on the coast. In the eastern part of Yala, and cut off from the main section by a strict nature reserve, is the Kumana Bird Sanctuary, the most popular in Sri Lanka, with a large variety of waterbirds in spectacular numbers. Access is by a jeep road from Pottuvil, via Panama (about 50 km).

Gal Oya National Park North of Yala and 312 km from Colombo, this smaller park in the foothills of Uva Province near Inginiyagala surrounds a large man-made lake (tank) called Senanayaka Samudra and protects another important area for elephants. Its isolation has provided sanctuary for a large variety of wildlife. If you prefer to avoid a jolting ride in a jeep, try a peaceful exploration of the waterways by boat (check on permits before making arrangements).

Uda Walawe National Park This is about the same size as Gal Oya and also featuring a tank (but this one is less than half the size). It is about 200 km south-east from Colombo and close to the southern end of the highlands. It can be reached from Ratnapura or Embilipitiya. There are two good campsites at Ranagala and Mauara.

Lahugala National Park A recently-declared, small park also located near Pottuvil. It protects the twin tanks of Mahawewa and Kitulana, which attract good numbers of elephants. Also very good for birdlife.

Sinharaja Rainforest Reserve The most important reserve in the south-west, offering spectacular rainforest scenery and its associated wildlife (the highest concentration of animals unique to Sri Lanka can be found here). If you want to visit, check with the Forest Department not only about permits, but if anyone from there is planning as visit, you may be able to accompany them.

Horton Plains Nature Reserve If you go to World's end you also visit this reserve. The forests at this altitude (over 2000 metres) offer unusual plant and animal life adapted to its harsher climate. It is worth a few days to explore the area, as well as enjoy a cool change from the lowlands.

Peak Wilderness Man & Biosphere Reserve The forest around Adam's Peak offer a spectacular variety of birds, butterflies, and other wildlife. If you visit during the pilgrimage season, it's also the best time for wildlife.

Udawattekelle Wildlife Sanctuary This ancient reserve now surrounded by Kandy offers pleasant walking as well as opportunities to see birds and other wildlife. You may not have to go far to see the monkeys here (toque macaques) as they usually come to you first – we had them stealing fruit from out hotel room.

Chundikula & Kokkilai Lagoon Bird Sanctuaries Located on the north-east coast, these two sanctuaries are on the eastern migration route and can offer spectacular numbers of birds on the spring and autumn days when the birds are flying through. If you miss these events, there are still large numbers of birds and other wildlife to be seen.

Warawila-Tissa Bird Sanctuary If you stay at Tissamaharama during a visit to and from Yala, you cannot miss the extensive network of lagoons filled with birds which represent this sanctuary. It is centred on a large tank, where cattle can wade far out when the water is low, and many parts are carpeted in lily or lotus flowers. It's just such places as this that can start people off on the bird-watching trail.

Pallemalala & Bundala Bird Sanctuaries On the south coast between Hambantota and Tissamaharama are these two sanctuaries. For migratory birds this is the end of the line and the concentrations which can build up make them one of the best places to bird-watch, with flamingos one of the star attractions.

– Constance S Leap Bruce
& Murray D Bruce

Facts for the Visitor

VISAS

If you are from Britain, Australia, New Zealand, Canada, the USA or from most west European nations no visa is needed to enter Sri Lanka. Initial entry is for one month which can be extended beyond that time.

Recent visitors report, however, that visa extensions are now much more difficult to obtain and you may only get a single two week extension after the first month. Others say that extensions are much easier if you have a ticket out and even better a confirmed ticket out. Bags of money, it appears, do not count for as much as airline tickets although a figure of $15 per day seems to have been established as the 'survival level' permitting you to extend your visa. In other words if you've been there 30 days already then you should have changed 30 x $14 $450. You have to produce bank receipts to show you have changed that amount of money (so save them). If you have not changed enough you'll just have to zip round to the bank and change more. You're quite free to change it back again afterwards.

A possible way round this problem, if you intend to stay for a longer period of time, is to apply for a longer visa before going to Sri Lanka – even if you don't need a visa for a short visit. It appears that going and getting a three month visa before you depart is much simpler than simply obtaining a one month stay permit on arrival and then trying to extend it. You may have to say you plan to spend lots of money, though! In places where there is no Sri Lankan diplomatic representation the British embassy will issue visas – US$10 for a three month visa for Europeans. When you arrive, however, you may find that this means 'up to three months' and you'll just get one month like everybody else.

Extensions of stay are granted by the Department of Immigration & Emigration (tel 29851, 21509), Galle Buck Rd, Colombo l. Follow the sign for 'Registration for Indian Nationals (People of Indian Origin)'! You usually have to leave your passport and application form here and come back in a couple of hours but the procedure is generally quite straightforward. There is a nominal charge for the extension and if you're wondering what all those kids are doing hanging around the windows outside, they've got the postage stamps with which you have to pay for the extension! You have a choice of a long walk back to the post office or paying their small mark up.

Extensions of stay beyond three months are very difficult if not impossible. You'll probably have to go back to India and re-enter and you may have to stay out of the country for some period of time. Beyond six months there is a Rs 500 residence tax.

Non-Commonwealth citizens have another hurdle to leap before getting an extension beyond 30 days. They have to register at the Aliens Bureau, 4th floor, New Secretariat Building, Colombo 1. Whatever your nationality you must either have an onward ticket or 'sufficient' foreign exchange before being allowed to enter Sri Lanka. On the ferry from Rameswaram this problem was handled with typical Indian panache – if you didn't have 'sufficient' funds they simply insisted that you buy a return ticket on the ferry.

Some relevant Sri Lanka consular offices abroad include:

Australia	High Commission of the Republic of Sri Lanka, 35 Empire Circuit, Forrest, Canberra ACT 2603
Canada	High Commission of the Republic of Sri Lanka, Suites

	102-104, 85 Range Rd, Ottawa, Ontario KLM 8J6
Germany (West)	Embassy of the Republic of Sri Lanka, Rolandstrasse 52, 5300 Bonn 2, Bad Godesberg
India	High Commission of the Republic of Sri Lanka, 27 Kautilya Marg, Chanakyapuri, New Delhi 110021 (also in Madras & Bombay)
Indonesia	Embassy of the Republic of Sri Lanka, 70 Jalan Diponegoro, Jakarta
Singapore	High Commission of the Republic of Sri Lanka, 1207-1212 Goldhill Plaza, Singapore 11
Thailand	Embassy of the Republic of Sri Lanka, Mailart Building, 87 Sukhumvit Rd, Bangkok 11
UK	High Commission of the Republic of Sri Lanka, 13 Hyde Park Gardens, London W2 2LU
USA	Embassy of the Republic of Sri Lanka, 2148 Wyoming Avenue NW, Washington DC 20008

MONEY

A$1	= SL Rs 22.10
US$1	= SL Rs 24.25
£1	= SL Rs 33.50
IRs 1	= SL Rs 2.20
NZ$1	= SL Rs 15.75
C$1	= SL Rs 18.70
DM1	= SL Rs 8.75
S$1	= SL Rs 11.60

The Sri Lankan unit of currency is the rupee (Rs) divided into 100 cents (c). There are coins of 1, 2, 5, 10, 25 and 50c and of 1, 2 and 5 rupees. Notes come in Rs 2, 5, 10, 20, 50, 100, 500 and 1000 rupee denominations. The usual Asian rules apply to Sri Lanka's currency:

First break down larger notes when you change money – this is not as big a problem as in the past, due to Sri Lanka's rocketing inflation rate, but it can still be a problem to change a large note. Sri Lanka's small-change shortage has also been cured, perhaps partly by the inflation rate. The second rule is never to accept very dirty or torn notes as they are often difficult to dispose of, except to a bank. Again this is not as big a problem as in some other Asian countries.

Travellers' cheques get a better rate of exchange than cash in Sri Lanka and the rate may vary slightly from bank to bank. For some reason the variance seems to be rather more on pounds sterling or Deutsche marks than for other currencies. Commission charges for changing travellers' cheques also vary from bank to bank. Daily rates for major currencies are shown in the *Ceylon Daily News*. Banking hours are 9 am to 1 pm on Mondays, to 1.30 pm on other weekdays. In Colombo there is a special exchange counter at the Bank of Ceylon on York St, Fort, which is open from 8 am to 8 pm every day of the week, including on holidays. The Hotel Taprobane, also on York St, also has an exchange counter which is open extended hours. You can change rupees back to foreign currency at the airport on departure but you must have proof that you changed money into rupees in the first place.

Recently there have been a number of operators hanging round the Fort area offering black market exchange rates. Just how real their offers are is open to question but what is absolutely certain is that many of them are superb sleight of hand tricksters who will perform folded money or cash in the envelope tricks quicker than you can shout 'rip off'.

Sri Lanka is no better than any other country in Asia for getting money sent to – well perhaps not that bad but getting on that way. If you have to get money sent to you ask your home bank to send it by telegraphic transfer and specify one of the commercial banks such as Grindlays. With a Visa Card you can get instant cash from the Bank of America on the Galle Rd. British account holders can cash UK cheques if backed with a Visa Card/Barclay Card at the travel department of the main branch of the Bank of Ceylon.

American Express have their office on York St in Fort, opposite the Taprobane Hotel. American Express and Diners Club cards are widely accepted in Sri Lanka.

COSTS

Sri Lanka is still a pleasantly economical country to travel around. The upheavals of 1983, which scared away so much of the country's tourist trade, has kept accommodation and other travel-related prices fairly static. Hotel prices, which zoomed upwards between the 1st and 2nd edition of this book, have virtually stood still between the 2nd and this 3rd edition. Transportation and other costs have still increased but overall the costs to a visitor have not changed greatly over the past few years.

Almost anywhere in the country pleasant shoestring doubles can be found for Rs 100 to 150 (say US$5 to 7.50) and in many places for much less. If you really want to economise you can get a single or at least a dormitory bed for Rs20 to 30. In many places quite good doubles are available for Rs 30 to 50. You'd be hard pressed to spend more than Rs 25 on a day's bus travel. At the other end of the scale Rs 250 is the usual price for Sri Lanka's delightful rest houses now, although many are still cheaper. There are also many 'international' hotels which start at Rs 500 to 1000 a night.

Some places, even low-price guest houses, are loading on service charges these days. This is not a local custom so be aware of it or you may find accommodation, food and so on is all costing you 10% more than you expected.

Two Level Costs

There is, however, one part of the cost picture in Sri Lanka which many visitors find very irritating – the two level cost structure. In many places there is one price for local residents and another, much higher one, for visitors. At places like the Colombo Zoo, the ancient cities of Polonnaruwa and Anuradhapura, even the Peradeniya Botanical Gardens in Kandy, the admission charge for overseas visitors is 15 times as much as for local residents!

Worse than this, many visitors have felt that in its headlong chase after tourist dollars parts of Sri Lanka are being turned into a sort of tropical Costa del Sol, tourists are tending to be looked upon as prime candidates for any rip-off going and by instituting such two-tier pricing policies the government is seeming to sanction such an attitude. The alternative view is that the prices aren't that bad and tourists, who are well off compared to the average Sri Lankan, might as well do some subsidising ....

Ancient Sites

You can obtain an all-in ticket to the ancient sites at the Cultural Triangle Centre, 212 Bauddholaka Mawatha for Rs 225. It covers Polonnaruwa, Anuradhapura, Sigiriya and Dambulla.

CLIMATE

Sri Lanka is a typically tropical country in that there are distinctly dry and wet seasons but the picture is somewhat complicated by the fact that it is subject to two monsoons. From May to August the south-west monsoon brings rain to the southern and western coastal regions and the central hill country. From October to January it's the north-east monsoon that blows – bringing rain to the north and east of the island. This peculiar monsoon pattern does have the distinct advantage that it is always the 'right' season somewhere on the island. If it is raining on one coast you simply have to shift across to the other. Don't count on the weather following the rules though – it often seems to be raining where it should be sunny; sunny where it should be raining.

In the low-lying coastal regions the temperature is uniformly high year round – Colombo averages 27°C. The temperatures rapidly fall with altitude so if you don't feel like cooling off in the sea you have simply to go up into the hill country. At Kandy (altitude 305 metres) the average temperature is 20°C and at Nuwara Eliya (at 1890 metres) you're down to 16°C. The climate is generally a sort of eternal spring up in the hills but you should come prepared for chilly evenings.

The highest temperatures usually come in March to June but the mercury rarely climbs above 35°C. November to January is usually the coolest time of the year. The sea can be counted upon to remain at around 27°C year round although it is much less suitable for swimming during the monsoon period when it can be choppy and murky.

There is also an inter-monsoon period in October and November when rain and thunderstorms can occur in many parts of the island. The south, south-west and central highlands are much wetter than the dry central and north-central regions

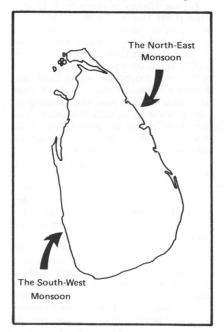

The North-East Monsoon

The South-West Monsoon

In the latter area annual rainfall averages only 100 cm (40 inches) and the many 'tanks', built over a thousand years ago to provide irrigation water, indicate that this is by no means a new problem. In the wetter part of the country the annual rainfall reaches 400 cm (150 inches) or more per year.

BOOKS & BOOKSHOPS

Sri Lanka is well endowed with bookshops, particularly in Colombo. Probably the widest selection of books will be found at the Lake House Book Shop at 100 Sir Chittampalam Gardiner Mawatha in Colombo 2. Other good Colombo bookshops include K V G de Silva (Kandy) in the YMBA Building on Sir Baron Jayatilaka Mawatha in Fort; M D Gunasena on Olcott Mawatha in the Pettah area of Colombo 11; K V G de Silva (Colombo) at 415 Galle Rd in Colombo 4 and the various hotel bookshops, in particular the branches of Charles Subasinghe at the Taprobane Hotel and the Inter-Continental. M D Gunasena has a particularly wide selection of Sinhalese books as well as many books in English. Cargill's and H W Cave, both on Sir Baron Jayatilaka Mawatha in Fort, also have books.

Some of the most interesting finds are likely to turn up in second-hand bookshops like Ashoka Trading at 183 Galle Rd, Colombo 4 which has a marvellous collection of tatty old books where you're quite likely to find something interesting. In Kandy there is another branch of K V G de Silva (Kandy) at 86 D S Senanayake Veediya.

History

Dr K M de Silva's monumental *A History of Sri Lanka* (Oxford University Press, 1981) at last brings Sri Lankan history up to the present time. Until it's publication there had been something of a gap for a book covering the country's recent political upheavals. it was easy to find out about the pre-European history of the island or the fortunes of the various European powers, not so simple to decipher recent events.

The Story of Ceylon by E F C Ludowyk (Faber, London 1962) and *The Modern History of Ceylon* by the same author (Praeger, New York, 1966) provide a good introduction to Ceylonese history. *Sri Lanka in Transition* by W M K Wijetunga (Lake House Bookshop, Colombo, 1974) is a cheap and concise paperback that provides a readable description of the country economically and culturally and covers the turbulent post-WW II history almost up to the present day. It may be out of print.

Guidebooks

Every time I go to Sri Lanka I find another locally produced guidebook but rarely do I find the same one available on the next trip. They all seem to be one time efforts. Probably the best one I found on my first trip. Now out of print the *Handbook for the Ceylon Traveller* (Studio Times Publications, Colombo, 1974) covered almost every place of historic or cultural interest in Sri Lanka in considerable (and poetic!) detail.

The Thorana Guide to Sri Lanka (Lever Brothers Cultural Conservation Trust, Colombo, 1979) has some interesting material on temples and buildings not found elsewhere. *Guide to Ceylon (Sri Lanka)* by H A I Hulugalle (Lake House, Colombo, 1969) is another locally produced guidebook.

There are a series of useful booklets produced by the Ministry of Cultural Affairs including *A Guide to Polonnaruwa, A Guide to Anuradhapura* and one titled simply *Kandy*. For those in search of unusual guides there's even *A Guide to the Waterfalls of Sri Lanka* by Eberhard Kautzsch (Tisara Prakasakayo, Dehiwala, 1983).

The *Insight Guide Sri Lanka* (Apa Productions, Singapore, 1983) is a beautiful coffee table paperback on the country. One to read before you go and to

remind yourself of the country after your return. If you're continuing on to the Maldives then *Maldives via Sri Lanka* (Other People, Padstow, Australia, 1982) has more information about those beautiful islands than anything else available.

General

Now back in print again, *An Historical Relation of Ceylon* by Robert Knox (Tisara Prakasakayo, Colombo), is a fascinating book to read. Robert Knox was an Englishman, captured near Trincomalee and held captive by the King of Kandy for nearly 20 years. His captivity was relatively loose and he had considerable freedom to wander around the kingdom and observe its operation. When he eventually escaped and returned to England his description of the kingdom of Kandy became an instant bestseller. It's equally readable today and far and away the best book on pre-European Ceylon.

Ceylon, History in Stone by R Raven-Hart (Lake House, Colombo, 1973), is a much more modern description of a lengthy visit to Sri Lanka. *Seeing Ceylon* by R L Brohier (Lake House, Colombo, 1965) is a surveyor's account of his wanderings around the island. Tea is still the country's major money earner but the plantation workers, most of them impoverished 'stateless' Tamil labourers, lead hard lives in poor living conditions. Read *Born to Labour* by C V Vellupillai (Gunasena, 1970) to find out more.

Sri Lanka by Akira Uchiyama (Kodansha International, Tokyo, 1973) is another of the Japanese 'This Beautiful World' series with plenty of pretty photographs. There are a number of glossy coffee table books on Sri Lanka – it's a photogenic place.

'A must for anyone who goes to the Kataragama fire-walking festival', suggested one visitor, is *Medusa's Hair* by Gannanath Obeyesekere. 'It explains a lot about Sinhalese society which is not readily apparent to the passing visitor'. First published in 1913 and now available in a modern paperback (Oxford University Press, 1981) Leonard Woolf's *The Village in the Jungle* is a readable, but depressing, story set in a small and backward Sinhalese village around the turn of the century. Leonard Woolf later went on to found the Hogarth Press and become a leader of the literary Bloomsbury set between the wars.

Sri Lanka's best known writer is, of course, Arthur C Clarke and his science fiction novel *The Fountains of Paradise* (Pan paperback, 1980) is set on an imaginary island called Taprobane and features places remarkably like Adam's Peak and Sigiriya. A good book to read while you're on the spot! You'll find Arthur C Clarke books widely available and prominently displayed in Sri Lanka.

Maps

A variety of quite adequate locally produced maps of Sri Lanka are available. Lake House have recently produced two which cover everything you need to know − *Pictorial Tourist Map of Sri Lanka* and *Pictorial Tourist Map of Colombo*. If you need to know more Apa Productions of Singapore have also recently published a Sri Lanka map which looks to be of higher quality than previous maps of the country as a whole.

Sri Lanka has a surprisingly good collection of reasonably priced survey maps available. If you really want to study the island closely then pay a visit to the Highway Department Building on York St in Fort or to the Map Sales Branch (tel 85111) on Kirula Rd, Narahenpitiya.

The Serendib Gallery at 100 Galle Rd, Colombo 4 often has some interesting old maps of Ceylon.

NEWSPAPERS & MEDIA

Sri Lanka has a number of daily and Sunday English language papers. The main English daily is the *Ceylon Daily News* which is 'worth reading for the style alone'. It gives a good coverage of local and international news. Others include the tabloid *Ceylon Observer*, the *Sun*, *The Island* and the *Mirror*. *The Island* is Sri Lanka's only real opposition paper, recommended for not following the 'government line' as closely as the others. *Time* and *Newsweek* are readily available and their newsstand price is rather less than in neighbouring India.

The Sri Lanka Broadcasting Corporation has news and other programmes both with and without commercials and in English as well as in Sinhalese and Tamil. There's also a new English language service with FM stereo, known as Studio SLX. You can also hear English programmes on the new regional radio station in Kandy. TV has recently arrived in Sri Lanka, programmes are broadcast from 6 to 11 pm nightly in colour. The transmitter is atop Pidurutalagala, the highest mountain in Sri Lanka, just outside Nuwara Eliya. There are two networks, both government controlled and although there are also some locally produced programmes much of it comes from the west.

Tamil and Sinhalese films make an entertaining insight into the peoples' culture and they're easily comprehensible. Outside Colombo 'first class seats' are Rs 5 or less. Western films tend to be rather scratched and old by the time they appear in Sri Lanka.

FILM & PHOTOGRAPHY

Film is more readily available and more reasonably priced than it was a couple of years ago but it is still wise to bring film with you rather than count on buying it there. Supply is erratic, quality uncertain and prices a bit higher than in the west. A very good place to try is Millers on the corner of Mudalige Mawatha and York St in Fort, they usually have a good supply at reasonable prices. Kodachrome 64, 36 exposure slide film is Rs 335 but you can get much better prices if you shop around the camera shops in Fort and buy 10 or 15 rolls at a time. For camera repairs try Photo Technica, 264 Galle Rd, Colombo 3.

The usual Asian and tropical rules apply to photography in Sri Lanka – ask peoples' permission before taking pictures and better results are obtained earlier in the morning or later in the afternoon, before the sun gets too high and everything looks washed out.

HEALTH

Vaccination certificates for smallpox, yellow fever or cholera are only required if you arrive from or have recently visited an 'infected area'. Smallpox has now been eradicated worldwide and yellow fever basically applies to South America only but I think cholera protection is a wise precaution for any Asian traveller. Outbreaks of cholera are not unknown in almost any Asian country. For Rs 20 vaccinations are available from the Vaccination Clinic in the Anti-Tuberculosis Clinic, General Hospital, Regent St, Colombo 2 opposite Hayley's Building. Or from the Assistant Port Health Office (tel 597422), 385 Deens Rd, Colombo 10.

Visitors to Sri Lanka should also take precautions against malaria – a weekly or daily anti-malarial tablet, prescribed by your doctor, is the usual answer. There is certainly malaria present in parts of the country. Tap water is not drinkable in Sri Lanka and a little care with food quality is a good idea – but overall Sri Lanka is a remarkably healthy country and if you're only slightly careful you should suffer no stomach problems.

If, however, you do come down with a stomach upset it's wise to have some sort of medication available as a back up. Lomotil is the usual travellers' standby but, as with any medicine, don't turn to it immediately. You'll be better equipped to withstand a further attack if your body has been able to build up a little immunity. You've got something worse than ordinary diarrhoea if you're also running a temperature or passing blood in your movements.

Pharmacies in Sri Lanka usually stock a fairly wide range of proprietary drugs but you have to be aware of possible brand name changes from those used in the west. Generic names are not used so widely as in the west. Medical attention in Sri Lanka is not what you're used to in the west, if you need hospitalisation it's probably best to hightail it for Colombo. One traveller wrote of the unwanted 'adventure' of being hospitalised in Haputale – you have to do a fair amount of the work yourself and it's very useful to have someone handy to make sure you get food, drugs and other ordinary medical attention!

POST

The GPO in Colombo is on Janadhipathi Mawatha in Fort, just down from the lighthouse. It has an efficiently run poste restante service and there is often a tourist-only counter where you can avoid the usual crush for getting stamps. Aerograms cost Rs 3.50, postcards Rs 4 to 5. Stamp collectors should head for the Sri Lanka Philatelic Bureau, 4th floor, Ceylinco House on Janadhipathi Mawatha, Fort, where they will find a wide selection of first day covers and stamp packs.

TELEPHONE

Although phone calls in Sri Lanka are cheap the lines are often out of order so don't rely on being able to book accommodation ahead by phone. Many towns are now linked by direct dialing and calls generally go through without difficulty. Apart from Colombo numbers the phone numbers in this book are generally shown with their long distance codes. This initial code is dropped when you are dialing locally. International calls, at least from Colombo, are also fairly straightforward.

ELECTRICITY

230-240 volt, 50 cycles, alternating current.

BUSINESS HOURS

The working day is usually 8.30 am to 4.30 pm.

TIME

Sri Lankan time is 5 hours 30 minutes ahead of Greenwich Mean Time. When it is 12 noon in Sri Lanka the time is 6.30 am in London, 1.30 am in New York, 10.30 pm the previous day in San Francisco and 4.30 pm in Sydney. Make allowances for summer time changes in the west. There is some discussion about advancing the time in Sri Lanka by half an hour, which would make the time six hours ahead of GMT.

INFORMATION

The Ceylon Tourist Board has offices at the airport and at the Travel Information Centre, 41 Glen Aber Place, Colombo 4 (tel 89585-6). This is a temporary address following the demolition of the old Samudra Hotel on Galle Face. It is not a very convenient location and it is probable that at some time in the future the information centre will move to a more central site although they have been in their present home for a couple of years now. There are also smaller offices in Colombo Fort and by the lakeside in Kandy.

The tourist office is friendly and reasonably informative. Amongst the various brochures and maps they put out the most useful is the *Sri Lanka Tourist Information* booklet. This has a great deal of useful information including all the main train schedules. Pick up a copy at the airport on arrival. They also put out a separate *Accommodation Guide*. Although this is rather haphazardly organised it is very useful for its long listings of rooms available in private homes. Pick up a copy at the airport on arrival.

In Sri Lanka there is only one other tourist office – at the handicraft centre by the lake in Kandy. Overseas offices of the Ceylon (Sri Lanka) Tourist Board include:

Australia	241 Abercrombie St, Chippendale NSW 2008 (tel 02 698 5226) 439 Albany Highway, Victoria Park WA 6100 (tel 09 362 4579)
Canada	2 Carlton St £1519, Toronto, Ontario M5B 1K2
Denmark	Sollerodgardsvej 38, DK 2840 Holte
Germany (West)	6000 Frankfurt Main, Kaiserstrasse 13 (tel 280010, 283750)
Japan	AMO, 2/1 Atago 1-chome, Minato-ku, Tokyo (tel 433 6377-8)
Thailand	1/18 Soi 10, Sukhumvit Rd, Bangkok
UK	52 High Holborn, London WC1V 6RI (tel 01 405 1194)
USA	4405 Riverside Drive £204-205, Burbank CA 91505 (tel (213) 846 4002) 35 East Wacker Driver £1212, Chicago IL 60601 (tel (312) 372 5268) 3300 West Mockingbird Lane £534, Dallas TX 75235 (tel (214) 350 1592) 62 Princess St, Sausalito CA 94965 (tel (415) 331 5348) 1111 Fourth Avenue Bldg £630, Seattle WA 98101 609 Fifth Avenue £308, New York, NY 10017 (tel (212) 935 0369)

ACCOMMODATION

There is quite a selection of places in Sri Lanka which I will arbitrarily divide into several categories. The tourist office's *Accommodation Guide* lists accommodation in all the various brackets all around the country – but does not cover every establishment, particularly at the bottom end of the market and in the more out-of-the-way locations. Many places will also have rooms at lower prices than those quoted in the booklet – it's always worth asking if there are any cheaper rooms available. The Travellers' Halt network of low price hostels also puts out a useful little booklet listing their locations.

Note that Sri Lanka is very seasonal, particularly along the beach strips. Prices quoted in this guide are generally the high season rates but you can often find spectacular bargains in the off-season. A number of travellers have written to say that the weather is often fine in the off-season or that reefs may protect a beach area and make swimming quite feasible at places like Hikkaduwa. Additionally the season officially starts on a certain date irrespective of weather conditions. It's certainly not unknown for the monsoon to have ended well before the season starts. Big hotels often charge as little as 20% of their high season rates during the off-season. It's a great chance for shoestring travellers to enjoy some real luxury.

Sri Lanka is besieged by hotel touts in some areas. These characters meet tourists at the bus or railway stations (or even on the buses or trains, or even before they depart) and steer them towards places where they know they can get a healthy commission. In many cases this is as high as 50 to 100% of your first-night accommodation cost. Not surprisingly this tends to drive the accommodation prices upwards and equally unsurprisingly you will often be told that place A (where you wanted to go) is 'full', 'closed down' or has 'gone downhill' simply because the tout gets a better rake-off in place B. My advice is to avoid them if at all possible. If you know where you want to go, then go there no matter what you are told. You'll make yourself much more popular with hotel proprietors if you turn up without a tout in tow.

Guest Houses These are often the best deals in Sri Lankan accommodation. They're more-or-less rooms with local families, sometimes just a couple of rooms in the house are rented out like English bed-and-breakfast places. Other times they're like small hotels. You'll find some very cheap places to stay in this category plus some in the medium price bracket and even the occasional more expensive place. It's a good idea to pin down exactly what you're getting or be prepared, in some places, for an unpleasant surprise when you find out how many cups of tea you've had and how much each of them has cost!

In the family-style guest houses you'll also often find very good food – better Sri Lankan food, in fact, than almost any of the restaurants and better than a lot of the more expensive hotel restaurants. The Sri Lankans are proud of their cuisine and asking for seconds is the best compliment you can give. They will usually be only too happy to show you round the kitchen and explain how dishes are prepared. Apart from low cost the 'meeting people' aspect is the big plus of guest house accommodation.

Rest Houses Originally established for the use of travelling government officials they're now mainly used by foreign visitors – or at least the rest houses in the tourist centres are. Small town rest houses are still principally for government people. There are rest houses all over the country, many being the only regular accommodation in smaller or out-of-the-way centres.

Although they vary widely in standards and prices (some are even privately run these days) many of them are the most pleasant accommodation in town – attractively old fashioned, well kept and usually very well situated. This last virtue particularly applies in the ancient cities where the rest houses were the first on the scene and usually the only places actually within the precincts of the ruins. Later regulations have required that modern buildings be put up in adjacent 'new town' areas. Wherever you go you'll find the rest houses enjoy the view from the highest hill, along the best stretch of beach or in some other way have grabbed the best position around. Prices in the rest houses vary from the medium price range to the bottom end of the upper price range. A room only double generally costs around Rs 250.

Other Government Accommodation A step down from the rest houses are the archaeological bungalows, circuit bungalows and the like. They're intended very much for government officials but may be open to visitors if there is space. Facilities and standards are much simpler and you'll usually have to provide your own bed sheets or even food. Prices are also lower— as little as Rs 10 for a double. Don't count on them though – apart from some of the archaeological bungalows or the wildlife park cottages accommodation is often only available if you have written and applied far in advance.

Travellers' Halts All over the country you'll find the travellers' halts, a loosely organised network of places for the shoestring travellers. If you're back-packing around Asia they're a good place to start looking. Their actual connection is no more than one recommends another and they all appear in a jointly produced booklet listing their locations.

Hotels Prices of hotels have zoomed up in the past couple of years but more so in Colombo and along the coastal strips than elsewhere. Finding a double room under Rs 100 is no longer so easy although even in Colombo it can still be done and in the country you can still often find places at less than Rs 50. Medium price hotels generally cost from around Rs 150 to 300 – this price category will include the more expensive guest houses. Finally in the 'international standard' hotels RS 500 is probably the median price although in Colombo there are plenty of places at Rs 1000 and over per night. Colombo will soon, no doubt, have its US$100 a night rooms.

FOOD & DRINK
Sri Lanka does not have one of the great Asian cuisines but it's certainly quite enjoyable and the food quality is generally quite high. If you insist on eating just like back at home the Sri Lankans also manage to make a very reasonable stab at cooking 'English style', unlike some nationalities who are most definitely best left to their own cuisines. A Sri Lankan taste treat not

to be missed though, is fruit. Sri Lanka rates right up there with the best places in south-east Asia when it comes to finding the knock-out best of tropical fruits.

Food
Like many other aspects of Sri Lankan life the food is closely related to that of India – but rice and curry Sri Lankan style still has many subtle variations from the Indian norm. Curries in Sri Lanka can often be very hot indeed but adjustments will often be made to suit sensitive western palates! If you find you have taken a mouthful of something that is simply too hot, relief does not come from a gulp of cold water. That's like throwing fuel on a fire. Far better is a fork of rice or better still some cooling curd (yoghurt) or even cucumber. That's what those side dishes are for. Of course if it's not hot enough the solution to that is there too – simply add some *pol sambol*, a red-hot, grated coconut, chilli and spice side dish. *Sambol* is the general name for any spicy-hot dish.

Sri Lankan rice and curry usually consists of a variety of small curry dishes – vegetable, meat or fish. Surprisingly, for the amount of rice eaten in Sri Lanka, the rice is not always so special. Sri Lankan rice often seems to me, to have a very musty, 'old' taste to it. Certainly not of the same standard as Thai rice. The spices used to bring out the subtle flavours of Sri Lankan curry, and remember that 'curry powder' is purely a western invention, are all from Sri Lanka. It was spices, particularly cinnamon, that first brought Europeans to the island and even today a selection of Sri Lankan spices is a popular item to take home when you leave.

The usual Indian curry varieties are also available of course; south Indian vegetarian *thali* or the delicate north Indian *biriyani*. From the northern Jaffna region comes *kool* a boiled, fried and then dried in the sun, vegetable combination.

Naturally Sri Lanka has a wide variety of seafood – they do excellent fish and chips in many coastal towns, Negombo is famous for its prawns and in Hikkaduwa, Unawatuna and Trincomalee (to name but a few places) you can find delicious and very economical steamed crab. In the south of the island a very popular fish dish is *ambul thiyal* which is usually made from tuna and translates literally as 'sour fish curry'. Negombo is renowned for its seerfish – a small and tasty flat-fish.

Moving through the day there are a number of Sri Lankan specialities starting with hoppers which are usually a breakfast or evening snack. A string hopper is a tangled little circle of steamed noodles, use them as a curry dip. Or try a regular hopper which is rather like a small pancake; with an egg fried into the middle of it you have an egg hopper. Another rice substitute is *pittu* – a mixture of flour and grated coconut which is steamed in a bamboo mould so that it comes out as a cylinder. *Lamprai* is a popular Sinhalese dish of rice boiled in meat stock then added to vegetables and meat and slowly baked in a banana leaf wrapping.

At lunchtime my favourite Sri Lankan meal is a plate of 'short eats'. A selection of assorted goodies, spring rolls, vegetable patties, meatballs and other snacks is placed in the middle of the table. You eat as many as you feel like and the bill is added up from how many are still left. At the Pagoda Tea Room in Colombo Fort, a favourite place for short eats, they even follow it up with what I suppose you could call 'short desserts'.

Desserts & Snacks

The Sri Lankans also have lots of ideas for desserts, such as *watalappam* a Malay originated egg pudding. Curd and treacle, which often seems to get mis-spelt to 'curd and tricle' is the not-to-be-missed dessert – nice at any time of the day. Curd is like yoghurt but made from buffalo milk – it's rich and tasty but certainly does not come in a handy plastic container. A street stall curd container is a shallow clay pot, complete with a handy carrying rope and

so attractive you'll hate to throw it away. The treacle (*kitul*) is really palm syrup, another stage on from toddy! If it's dried into hardened blocks you have *jaggery*, an all-purpose Sri Lankan candy or sweetener.

Like the Indians the Sri Lankans waste no opportunity to indulge their sweet tooth – sweets are known as *rasa-kavili*. You could try *kavun*, spiced flour and treacle batter-cake fried in coconut oil. Or *aluva* – rice flour, treacle and cashew nut fudge. Coconut milk, jaggery and cashew nuts give you dark and delicious *kalu dodol*.

Fruit

I'll always carry one taste from my first foray around south-east Asia – after you've tried rambutans, mangosteens, jackfruit and durians how could anybody live with boring old apples and oranges again? Well, if you're already addicted, Sri Lanka is a great place to indulge. If you've not yet developed a taste for tropical fruits then it's a great place to get into it. Just a few favourites:

Rambutan The name, it's a Malay word, means spiny and that's just what they are, large walnut or small tangerine size and covered in soft red spines. You peel the spiny skin off to reveal a very close cousin to the lychee. The cool and mouth watering flesh is, unfortunately, often rigidly attached to the central stone.

Pineapple In season Sri Lanka seems to be afloat in pineapples. They're generally quite small and very thirst quenching. In Colombo there seems to be a stall virtually every 50 metres where you can get a whole quarter of a (small) pineapple for a rupee.

Mangosteen One of the finest tropical fruits, the mangosteen is about the size of a tangerine or small apple. The dark purple outer skin breaks open to reveal pure-white segments shaped like orange segments – but with a sweet-sour flavour which has been compared to a combination of strawberries and grapes. Queen Victoria, so the story goes, offered a considerable prize to anybody able to bring a mangosteen back intact from the east for her to try.

Mango The Sri Lankans claim that it is the mango which grows best on their island. It comes in a large variety of shapes and tastes although generally in the green-skinned, peach-textured variety like that found around Jaffna – Sri-Lanka's mango-capital.

Custard Apple The custard apple that grows in Australia is not the real thing (to my Asian-inclined tastes) whereas the Sri Lankan variety definitely is. Actually there are a number of custard apple types with a variety of flavours. It's the refreshing, slightly lemon/tart flavour which I love. Outwardly custard apples are quite large (say the size of a grapefruit but more pear shaped). The thin skin is light green and dotted with little warts but a custard apple isn't ready for eating until it has gone soft and squishy and the skin is starting to go grey-black in patches.

Jackfruit This enormous fruit (water-melon size but it hangs from trees) breaks up into hundreds of bright orange/yellow segments with a slightly rubbery texture. It's also widely used as a vegetable, cooked with rice or curries. While ripening on the tree jackfruits are often shrouded in sacking – to keep birds away?

Coconut The all-purpose coconut palm provides far more food value than the obvious coconut itself would suggest. For a refreshing drink, though, you can't go far wrong with a *thambili*, the golden king-coconut. All over Sri Lanka there will be some lad sitting with a huge pile of coconuts, machete at the ready to provide you with a thirst-quenching drink.

Other There is a wide variety of bananas which are often referred to as plantains. Or papayas (pawpaw), that best known of tropical fruits with the golden orange, melon-like flesh – a delicious way to start the day with a dash of lemon. Or woodapples, a hard wooden-shelled fruit which is used to make a delicious drink, a creamy dessert topping or a uniquely Sri Lankan jam. Or melons, passion fruit, avocados, guavas (particularly the little pink variety, like crispy pears) and many others I've still got to discover. Not to mention the famous durian – a big, green hand-grenade of a fruit which breaks open to reveal a smell like a disgustingly blocked up sewer! But what a taste!

Drinks
As in most Asian countries you're advised not to drink water unless you're certain that it has been carefully boiled. Of course you've got no way of telling if that really has been done, should a restaurant tell you so. Plus you get awful thirsty at times so you may just have to take the risk.

Safe substitutes? Well there's Sri Lanka's famous tea although, unfortunately, it's another place which is famous for the quality tea it produces but is generally unable to make a decent cup of it! A cup of Sri Lankan tea may not be as bad as the horrible 'mixed' tea (tea, milk and too much sugar all brewed up together) the Indians specialise in, but it is still too often an over-strong, over-stewed concoction.

The other side of the drinks menu will usually be labelled 'cool drinks', which doesn't necessarily mean they're cool at all. It simply means they're the sort of drinks which could (if there was a fridge, if it worked, if they cared to use it) possibly be served cool! There'll be excellent lime juice, made from the questionable water, and a range of soft drinks. Coca Cola is widely available in Sri Lanka but is usually rather more expensive than the local brands. Most widespread of the Sri Lankan soft drinks is Elephant House – a wide variety of flavours (including a not very good cola), generally quite palatable, big 400 ml bottles and reasonably cheap at Rs 3 to 5 depending on where you buy it and whether it's cold or not. Beware of special tourist rip-off prices – the legal maximum price is printed on the label.

Alcoholically there are a couple of Sri Lankan beer brands (Lion and Three Coins). Cost per 'big' bottle starts from around Rs 18 and goes up to Rs 25, 30 even 35 depending on where you buy it. Once again there is a legal maximum price. Sri Lankan beer is quite OK but will certainly win no prizes from any beer fancier. Note that alcohol cannot be sold on the monthly full moon 'poya' holiday.

Sri Lanka also has two extremely popular local varieties of intoxicating beverage. Toddy is a natural drink, a bit like cider, produced from one or other of the palm trees. Getting the tree to produce toddy is a specialised operation performed by people known as 'toddy tappers'. Your typical toddy tapper will have as many as 100 trees in his territory and his daily routine involves tightroping from the top of one tree to another on shaky ropeways to remove full buckets of toddy, lower them to the ground and replace them with empty buckets. Toddy tapping is not a particularly safe occupation although fewer toddy tappers manage to fall out of the trees than you'd expect.

Fermented and refined toddy becomes arrack. It's produced in a variety of grades and qualities – some of which are real firewater. Proceed with caution! The town of Kalutara, 40 km south of Colombo on the way to Bentota and Beruwela, is the toddy and arrack capital of Sri Lanka. Annually Sri Lanka produces five million gallons of toddy and 7½ million bottles of arrack. With a soft drink mixer arrack is very pleasant.

THINGS TO BUY
Sri Lanka has a wide variety of very attractive handicrafts on sale, most of which you can find in shops and street stalls in Colombo although you will,

naturally, find greater variety 'at source'. Whatever you do, don't miss the government run Laksala in Colombo. Here you will find a very representative collection of items from all over the country – generally of reasonably good quality and at reasonable prices. The Laksala doesn't, however, seem to get the really excellent pieces. Even if you do intend to look for some particular item elsewhere in the country the Laksala will give you a good idea of what to look for and how much to pay.

Masks Sri Lankan masks are a very popular collectors' item for visitors. They're carved at a number of places, principally along the south-west coast, but the town of Ambalangoda, slightly north of Hikkaduwa, is the mask carving centre. There are a number of mask specialists here but, surprisingly, I thought some of the 'pupils' had better masks than the 'masters'.

The Laksala in Colombo is a good place to get an initial impression of styles, qualities and prices but there is not the variety here that you will find in Ambalangoda. If you'd like to know a lot more about masks there are some expensive coffee-table quality books and a rather haphazard booklet: *The Masks of Sri Lanka* by M H Goonatilleka (Department of Cultural Affairs, 1976) – it's very scathing on the 'tourist' masks which are all you really see in Sri Lanka today, outside of museums.

There are two basic types of masks. One is the *kolam* mask, the name literally means a mask or form of disguise and these masks are used in rural dance-dramas where all the characters wear masks. The other type is the devil dancing-mask where the dancers wear masks in order to impersonate disease causing demons and thus exorcise these demons. *Kolam* masks generally illustrate a set cast of characters but although these masks are still made for dance performances, and even some new characters have been introduced, they are not produced for tourist consumption.

The masks you see on sale are all of two devil styles. One is the cobra king where the demonic face, complete with pro- truding eyeballs, lolling tongue and pointed teeth is topped with a 'coiffure' of writhing cobras. The other masks you will see on sale, but much less frequently, are the '18 disease' mask. A demon figure,

18 disease masks

clutching one or more victims and often with another clenched in his teeth, is flanked by 18 faces representing the whole gamut of diseases which the dance can exorcise. The whole ensemble is bordered by two cobras and others sprout from the demon's head.

Touristic or not the masks are remarkably well made, low in cost and look very nice on the wall back home. I've got one. They're available from key ring size for a few cents up to high quality (and large) masks at prices over Rs 2000.

Batiks The Indonesian art of batik making is a relatively new development in Sri Lanka but one they have taken to with alacrity. You'll see batiks made and sold in many places around the island but the best, in my opinion, were the batik pictures from Fresco Batiks on the Peradeniya road outside Kandy. Other good places are Buddhi Batiks, north of Colombo, with a tremendous selection, and Artlanka. ' . . . . ..Kandy batiks were very poor compared with the superb ones at the batik village of Mahawewa beyond Negombo', wrote a visitor. 'The ones at Buddhi were breathtaking'. Batik pictures start from Rs 50 or less and go up to over Rs 1000. Batik is also used for a variety of clothing items.

Leather You can also find some very low-priced and quite reasonable quality leatherwork – particularly shoulder bags. Look in the Laksala in Colombo Fort or in other leatherwork shops and shoe shops around Fort. The stalls on York St are much cheaper than the Laksala for similar quality goods. There is a Ceylon Leather Products Corporation with sales outlets in the YMBA building in Fort and on the Galle Rd at Kollupitiya.

Gems Sri Lanka's famous gemstones remain one of the most important (and interesting!) cornerstones of the economy. Initially gems were found mainly around Ratnapura and this remains one of the most important areas for gemming, but they are now also found in many other localities.

In Colombo you can inspect and purchase gems at the State Gem Corporation's showroom at 24 York St, Fort or at their branch offices in the Lanka Oberoi Hotel, the Hotel Inter-Continental, at the Katunayake airport or at the Bentota resort. The People's Bank also has a Co-operative Gem Society with showrooms at their bank offices in Ceylinco House, Fort and in Ratnapura. Plus, of course, there are countless private gem dealers and showrooms. In Ratnapura everybody and his brother is a spare-time gem dealer! All gems purchased from the State Gem Corporation are guaranteed and they will also test, free of charge, any gem you care to bring in to them.

For more information on gems see the section under Ratnapura in the Hill Country. High quality though Sri Lanka's gemstones may be the jewellery settings are often abysmal – stones often simply fall out.

Several letters since the first edition have had something to say on the subject of gem stones. One said that a government guarantee was nothing to write home about – 'what does it guarantee?' the writer asked. Another said that Chatham St in Colombo was the best place to buy gems, in his experience. He said that a reputable dealer would accompany you to the State Gem Corporation for free testing of a selected gem. 'If and when they are proved to be what they are supposed to be, you can then pay for them.' The writer found that The Jewel Shop at 117-119 Chatham St was fairly priced and reputable, in his opinion, and stated that he later made a good profit on selling the loose stones overseas. I still think the only people who make money on that sort of deal are people who really know what they are about.

Other There are countless other purchases waiting to tempt your travellers' cheques out of your moneybelt. The ubiquitous coconut shell is carved into all manner of souvenirs and useful items. Like the Thais and Burmese the Sinhalese also make lacquerware items like bowls and ash trays – layers of lacquer are built up on a light framework, usually of bamboo strips. There is much interesting antique jewellery but modern jewellery is often not terribly exciting. Brassware is popular, particularly in Kandy. Try a hefty brass elephant-head door knocker for size.

Modern reproductions of antique Dutch furniture are very popular. Coir, a rope fibre made from coconut husks, is made into baskets, bags, mats, and many other useful items. All the usual travellers' - style clothes are available, particularly in Hikkaduwa; although the quality is often low the prices are even lower. Tortoise-shell and ivory are best left on the backs of turtles or in the tusks of elephants.

Cargill's Department Store in Fort, Colombo, will pack items in cardboard or wooden boxes – they do a good job at reasonable prices. The CPO has a side door leading to an office especially set up for foreign parcels. Sailing dates are posted on a blackboard there.

WHAT TO BRING
Not too much! Apart from up in the hill country, where the temperatures can sink surprisingly low at night, Sri Lanka is definitely a place for high-summer gear only. In the hill country, and Nuwara Eliya in particular, you'll need a sweater or light coat for the evenings. If you intend to make the pre-dawn ascent of Adam's Peak you'll need all the warm gear you can muster – wearing a T-shirt, shirt, sweater and ski-jacket I still found it bitterly cold until the sun rose, when the temperature became comfortable almost immediately. At times in the hill country it can also get very wet.

The usual Asian rules of decorum apply – one should be decently dressed if you do not wish to risk offending the locals. Shorts, particularly on women, are really

only for the beach. Of course on the beach almost anything goes although at the more crowded beaches like Hikkaduwa there has been a campaign to reinvent the bikini top. If you're a snorkelling fan then bring your mask and snorkel along with you. It's easy enough to rent them in Hikkaduwa but not so simple in other beach centres.

You'll find all the usual Asian ethnic gear on sale in Sri Lanka, particularly at Hikkaduwa, so if you want a new blouse, shirt, T-shirt, lightweight trousers or whatever you'll have no problem.

Sri Lanka is not as staunch as Burma in insisting that visitors barefoot-it in Buddhist temples but you should be prepared to discard your footwear so it makes more sense to wear sandals or thongs than shoes when you're out sightseeing. Some sort of head cover is also a wise precaution when you're exploring the ruins in the dry, hot, ancient cities area of Sri Lanka.

Soap, toothpaste (some terrible local brands but also most western brands) and other general toiletries are fairly readily available but, like India, toilet paper can sometimes be hard to find. When you do locate it the cost/quantity ratio is much better than in India but I suggest that you stuff a number of rolls into your baggage – if you're staying at the cheaper hotels where toilet paper is a luxury not regularly provided. That is a very useful way of ensuring that you have enough room in your baggage to put all the items you'll inevitably end up buying – toilet paper is very light but kind of bulky!

Other useful items include insect repellent and anti-histamine cream to treat mosquito bites with. A sink plug can also be useful as can a padlock, often useful for securely locking cheap hotel rooms. Buy some mosquito coils, you never known when you're going to find the mosquito-infested hotel room.

Getting There

You can fly to Sri Lanka from almost anywhere in the world with a number of scheduled or charter carriers. Bear in mind the steady increase in air fares when you read the fare details that follow. From most regions to Sri Lanka it's fairly easy to get tickets at prices that considerably undercut the regular fares. From Asian neighbours there are direct flights from Singapore, Kuala Lumpur, Bangkok, Kathmandu, Karachi and several cities in India.

These days there are no regular scheduled shipping services to Sri Lanka, although it is still a fairly regular stop for cruise ships. There is a ferry service between Rameswaram at the southern end of India and Talaimannar; it operates three times a week except at the height of the monsoon season.

FROM EUROPE

Discounted tickets are readily available from London travel agents for around £200 one-way or £350-400 return. These will usually be with Air Lanka or Garuda, but you can also find tickets with Pakistan International, KLM, Gulf Air and other airlines. Air Lanka's service is very good with free booze and movies; their aircraft appear to be much better kept than other things-mechanical in Sri Lanka!

It's also quite easy to find tickets from London to Australia via Sri Lanka. One-way fares will be around £350 to 450 depending on the airline and stop-overs. Typical connections would be with Air Lanka to Colombo then Singapore, Thai International from there to Sydney or Melbourne.

To find agents for cheap tickets check the travel ads in *Time Out*, *Australasian Express* or other London information sources. Trail Finders on Earls Court Rd or STA Travel on Old Brompton Rd are two reputable and reliable travel agents for cheap tickets.

Even cheaper tickets may be available with Aeroflot or eastern European airlines. There are a wide variety of charter flights from Germany and other countries in western Europe. Regular economy fares to Sri Lanka are over twice as expensive as the discounted tickets.

There are numerous charter flights from Germany to Sri Lanka. Although you can get good prices on flights from Athens in Greece to Sri Lanka and other places in Asia obtaining visas there, if you need them, is very difficult as there is little Asian consular representation. Athens-Moscow-Colombo with Aeroflot is about the cheapest way to Sri Lanka.

FROM AUSTRALIA

You can find one-way tickets to Sri Lanka from the Australian east coast for A$500 to 600. Or one-way tickets to Singapore or Bangkok are available for A$360 to 400 and you can then fly on from there. Apex fares to Singapore and Bangkok are somewhat higher. As of yet there are no Apex fares to Sri Lanka direct although there are Apex fares to India – they vary from A$600 to 710 one-way or A$875 to 1050 return. The regular economy one-way fare to Sri Lanka is A$873. There is a 10 day minimum stay, 270 day maximum stay return excursion fare of A$1268.

Only KLM operate regular flights between Australia and Europe via Sri Lanka. Otherwise you will have to change airlines en route, usually at Singapore from where you continue with Air Lanka or Singapore Airlines. Until the flag carriers – Air Lanka and Qantas – start services between the two countries it is unlikely that there will be any particularly interesting official fares. Cheap fares to Europe via Sri Lanka are easy to find, however.

FROM THE USA

Interesting discounted airline tickets to Asia are now much more readily available from the US than a few years ago – particularly on the west coast. Cities like San Francisco or Los Angeles now have specialist agents dealing in discounted tickets just like the 'bucket shops' of London. Interestingly many of them are Asian operations – originally set up as a pipeline for excess discounted tickets which Asian airlines were happy enough to pass on to the 'ethnic' market, but not so keen on seeing anybody getting their hands on. These days all you have to do is scan the travel section of a Sunday paper to find adverts for these agents.

From the west coast, fares to Sri Lanka are pretty similar whether you travel east or west. Fares are available from around US$1300 to US$1450 return either via London (from where you would normally fly Air Lanka) or via Bangkok. On the other hand you can get return tickets to Hong Kong for approximately US$650 to 750 and try your luck from there, but it would probably work out at much the same fare as a ticket straight through from the west coast. From the east coast you would definitely be better flying to London and on from there.

Since fares to Sri Lanka are so similar travelling east or west an interesting alternative would be to get a round-the-world ticket, available from around US$1500. Then you could stop in Europe on one leg, in other parts of Asia on the other.

FROM ASIA

Apart from connections to India there are also regular flights to a number of Sri Lanka's Asian neighbours – in particular Nepal, Thailand, Malaysia and Singapore.

Air fares from Singapore and Bangkok usually don't bear too close a relation to what 'the book' says. Count on around US$200 for Singapore-Colombo or similar prices from Bangkok. Royal Nepal Airlines flies Colombo-Kathmandu with fares around US$160. If you're going to Nepal the Nepalese Consulate General in Colombo is not much more than a table in a sports good shop at 92 Chatham St, opposite the Pagoda Tea Rooms. A four-week visa costs Rs 105 plus an additional charge for same day service. Visas can be applied for from Monday to Friday between 10 am and 12 noon.

With Air Lanka it's Rs 1557 from Colombo to Male in the Maldives. The regular fare to Singapore is Rs 4597. Typical fares to Bangkok are Rs 4500 or to Karachi Rs 4350. One-way fare to Hong Kong is around Rs 7750 or Rs 10,800 return, Rs 11,500 with a Bangkok stopover. Coming from Hong Kong you can get tickets via Sri Lanka to London (or other European cities) for HK$2700. Try Student Travel in Star House, Kowloon.

FROM INDIA

As you might expect there are more connections to Sri Lanka from India than from any other country. There are flights from several Indian cities and also for much of the year there is a regular ferry service.

If you're intending to fly one direction and ferry the other between the two countries there are several schools of thought on which way to do it. From Sri Lanka you can book the ferry in Colombo while from India it can only be booked at the port of departure, Rameswaram. If you don't want the uncertainty of getting to the port without knowing if you're going to get on the boat or not, then Sri Lanka-India is the better direction to go by ferry. On the other hand airline tickets Sri Lanka-India tend to be available somewhat cheaper than the same tickets India-Sri Lanka. So if saving money is important then it's preferable to fly from Sri Lanka.

Special Note

Transportation between India and Sri Lanka has often been rather chaotic. For a time in the late '70s Sri Lanka was without an airline and since Indian Airlines was drastically under-equipped and over-booked at that time, getting a seat was often very difficult. When Air Lanka commenced operations and Indian Airlines expanded their fleet this problem was temporarily resolved only to develop once again as Sri Lanka liberalised its trade policies.

Sri Lanka's new economic open door policy flooded the country with consumer products – everything from pocket calculators to air-conditioners, Japanese minibuses to stereo equipment. Indian consumers had been equally starved of these goodies and Sri Lanka quickly became a convenient back door for a flood of consumer products on to the Indian market. Getting to Sri Lanka was simple and cheap and individual visitors could import items purchased there with much greater ease than from, say, Singapore or Europe. To take maximum advantage of this handy loophole Indian entrepreneurs would round up contingents of 'visitors' to pop over to Sri Lanka on the ferry, buy up products unobtainable in India and head straight back. The end result was that despite all the extra flights getting a seat once again became difficult and the ferry – the cheapest way of travelling between the two countries – was a near impossibility.

The violence of mid-83 and the ensuing frosty relations between India and Sri Lanka has dramatically diminished this freelance importing business but it's wise to bear the vagaries of India-Sri Lanka traffic in mind and book well in advance.

By Air
Flights are operated between India and Sri Lanka by Indian Airlines and by Air Lanka. Both airlines use Boeing 737s on roughly parallel routings and frequencies. It's much easier to do things with Air Lanka (computerised) than with Indian Airlines (quadruplicate forms, carbon paper, running up and down the stairs, join the queue and wait all morning) although the long awaited Indian Airlines

booking computer is said to be nearly ready.

One-way fares from Colombo are Rs 936 to Trivandrum, Rs 983 to Trichy, Rs 1392 to Madras, Rs 2987 to Bombay.

By Ferry
Rameswaram is the final south Indian town from where Adam's Bridge points the way across to Sri Lanka. On Mondays, Wednesdays and Fridays a ferry operates the short, 3½ hour crossing from here to Talaimannar in Sri Lanka. The return trip is made on Tuesdays, Thursdays and Saturdays. The service is suspended during the worst of the monsoon, usually November and December. At that time the only way to travel between India and Sri Lanka is to fly.

To get to Rameswaram means rail – it's actually an island connected to the mainland by a rail-only causeway. A road bridge is a future possibility, meanwhile cars intended for shipment to Sri Lanka have to be loaded on to the train at Mandapam where the road ends. You can rail to Rameswaram direct from Madras or pick the train up further along the route. The trip from Madurai is agonisingly slow and although the ferry is not scheduled to depart until 2 pm – and is often very late – it is wise to get to Rameswaram as early as possible. Accommodation can be a bit difficult at Rameswaram so don't count on arriving there the night before and finding a place to stay too easily.

From the railway station to the ferry terminal is only a few minutes walk – say Rs 3 by a horse cart. You can get tickets for the ferry at the harbour booking office starting at 7 am – at present it appears there is no advance booking. The boat is often overbooked and if you don't get on board the only answer is to sit back and wait a few days for the next departure. Westerners have one advantage in that they are let through the gates to buy tickets first. The ferry costs:

	from Talaimannar	from Rameswaram
upper deck	SL Rs 220	I Rs 89
lower deck	SL Rs 165	I Rs 65

It is still possible to get through tickets from Madras Egmore to Colombo for I Rs 162. The terminal gates are swung back at 7 am and the usual mad stampede takes place as everybody rushes to do battle with Indian bureaucracy. It's strictly first in, first served and once the boat is full the boom is lowered and nobody else gets on. Buying your ferry ticket is the first operation once you get inside. After that the long, slow process goes something like this:

1. Fill in a form for the Shipping Corporation of India stating that should the Sri Lankan immigration authorities not want you – due to your lack of finance, lack of airline tickets to far-away-places, 'hippy' characteristics, or whatever, you'll quietly turn around and come back to Rameswaram.
2. Show that you have US$500 or an airline ticket from Sri Lanka to your home country or purchase a return ticket to Rameswaram.
3. Pay any 'port charges' – these seem to come and go.
4. Have your name checked in a huge ledgerbook listing, one suspects, all the possible foreign undesirables wishing toescape from India. This takes a long time since there is only one big book to check everybody from and you're searched for under both Christian name and surname.
5. Wait – you can change back Indian Rs to dollars while you wait.
6. Go through customs, after first queueing up to have your number of bags entered on a form. The number one question from the customs officials is 'do you have any opium or contraband?'
7. Another lengthy queue to have your passport stamped out.

If you were at the ferry terminal entry gate at 7 am it could well be after 11 am by the time you've finished all this. There is no suitable dock facility at Rameswaram so to get out to the ferry you have to transfer in creaky, old, wooden lighters which are towed out two or three at a time. Cars for shipping to Sri Lanka are brought out precariously balanced on two lighters lashed together side-by-side. It's great entertainment, but not for the car owners. Instead go to the office of

The *Ramanujam* is an elderly ship (built in 1929) but in reasonably good shape. Even the toilets are fairly clean! The upper deck is definitely a little more comfortable and commodious than the lower deck, but it isn't just comfort that makes it worth laying out the extra money for the top deck. At the other end the uppers are let off the ferry (to do battle with Sri Lanka's bureaucracy) first and this can be very important.

Finally, if things have gone pretty smoothly and everybody has got through the paperwork OK, you sail at 2 pm. Or later. There's quite a good canteen on the ship where you can get a pleasant banana-leaf wrapped biriyani or a thali – but they often run out of food and of drinks so be early. The trip across is straightforward although perhaps a bit uncomfortable if it's close to the monsoon season. If the departure has been delayed at all, which is quite likely since simply loading all the passengers on by lighter takes a long time, you may not arrive in Talaimannar until after dark.

After docking at Talaimannar the Sri Lankan immigration officials come aboard and start the lengthy process of checking the passengers through. Upper deck gets cleared first – this is the main reason for opting for the more expensive tickets. Once off the ship you have a long stroll down the pier to the customs hall and railway terminal. You can change Indian rupees into Sri Lankan rupees at Rameswaram before departure but one traveller wrote that you get a better rate at banks in Sri Lanka. Since Talaimannar port charges are now paid in India before departure it is no longer absolutely necessary to have some Sri Lankan rupees with you on arrival.

Having cleared the ship you're then whisked through customs and you're in Ceylon. If you want your first Sri Lankan journey to be a comfortable one you've now got to be very fast. Don't change money, don't join the queue for railway tickets. Instead go to the office behind the ticket counter and ask for a sleeping berth booking. There are only a dozen or so berths, half the people on the boat would like one (if they knew about them), so getting on is a matter of getting quickly off the boat, quickly through customs and wasting no time changing money. If you are lucky and can get one you'll find a berth the best Rs 30 (2nd class) investment you make in Sri Lanka. Booking note in hand you can now change money at leisure, buy your train ticket (at the counter) and pay for the berth charges.

The train for Colombo should leave around 10.30 pm but it usually departs only when the last passenger has been cleared. It has been known to leave right on time, stranding half the passengers from a late ferry arrival so don't be too confident that it will leave late. If you've got a berth you'll have a comfortable little room all to yourself (with two or four berths), padded fold-down bunks and all the comfort you could ask for. In first class you even get sheets! If you've not got a berth (and most people don't) you'll have a crowded, fairly sleepless night and you're advised to keep a close eye on your gear on this particular train journey; tired travellers are easy picking for thieves who work the trains. Recently the night train service from Talaimannar has not always been operating. If it isn't you'll probably have to face an uncomfortable night on the station platform.

If you can't face the long trip to Colombo – arrival is usually around 9.30 to 10.30 am the next morning – there are a couple of outs. One is not to take the train at all but to stay in Talaimannar or nearby Mannar. See the Jaffna & the North section for more details. Next morning you could then take the less crowded day train onwards and be able to see the countryside.

The ferry between Sri Lanka and India can be somewhat chaotic, as this newspaper clipping indicates! Getting to the ferry terminal at Talaimannar involves a long (usually overnight, crowded and sleepless) train journey and once there you will find virtually nothing apart from the railway platform and ferry pier – certainly nothing much by the way of accommodation. So if the ferry is full all you can do is sit and wait for a couple of days until it returns from India. Wouldn't you storm it? Bookings are particularly heavy around March when many travellers start heading back through India to the north before the height of the hot season makes things unbearable in the south. Additionally 'Indian repatriates will have preference on the ferry' at any time. It's hardly surprising that Colombo Airport figures indicate that while 406,940 people flew into Sri Lanka in 1980, 434,675 flew out. The difference is probably '28,000 disillusioned Rameswaram-Talaimannar boat travellers. Like every single traveller we met who went to Sri Lanka by the ferry – we flew out', reported a traveller.

Hippies storm Indo-Ceylon ferry

About 100 foreigners, described by the Police as hippies, stormed the Indo - Ceylon ferry at Talaimannar yesterday after they had been told there was no room for them.

Police said last night that 250 persons bound for India were shut out for want of space. The hippies who had boarded the ferry, were later ordered ashore by the Police.

Another alternative to going straight to Colombo from Talaimannar is to detrain at Anuradhapura around 1 or 2 am and start your Sri-Lankan travels there rather than in Colombo. Or you can push straight through – you'll find Sri Lankan train travel curiously quiet and hassle free after the all-singing-and-dancing Indian variety. No hordes at every station, no raucous cries of 'chai, chai' to periodically rouse you. And if you're lucky enough to grab a berth you'll have a very comfortable night.

Fares from Talaimannar to Colombo are Rs 168.50 in 1st class, Rs 107.90 in 2nd, Rs 43.90 in 3rd. 1st class is only available with sleeping berths (Rs 50 extra), 2nd class as seats or berths (Rs 30 extra), 3rd class as seats or sleeperettes (Rs 10 extra).

Coming from Colombo the pre-ferry departures are at 6.50 pm arriving in Talaimannar at 4.45 am for the 10 am (supposedly) departure for India. On other days the Talaimannar train departs Colombo at 7.25 pm and arrives at 5.15 am plus there is a daily departure at 6.42 am arriving at 5.45 pm after a train change at Anuradhapura. Tickets for the ferry and for Indian railways are available between 7.30 am and 2 pm from counter 4 at Colombo Fort station. These times may not be correct if there are still no overnight services from Talaimannar to Colombo.

It also appears that at present it may not be possible for foreigners to book lower deck tickets on the ferry. The whole ferry story seems a little confused at present. Travellers have written that reservations could only be made up to five days in advance although it appears that having a good reason why that would be inconvenient for you could circumvent that problem. Also the booking process in Colombo Fort Station appears to be very slow although

one traveller wrote that judicious baksheesh turned up a clerk with a 'relative' in each department which made things go much faster. Or try the Station Superintendent's office.

FLYING OUT OF SRI LANKA

Colombo is not like Bangkok or Singapore for hunting out cheap flights but there are quite a few travel agents around Colombo Fort and a little scouting around will always turn up some interesting fares. Approximate costs in Rs and US dollars include:

Europe	Rs 8,000	US$350
Singapore	Rs 4,200	US$185
Bangkok	Rs 4,200	US$185
Kathmandu	Rs 4,500	US$195
Australia (east coast)	Rs 13,200	US$575
USA (west coast)	Rs 12,500	US$545

I'm not approving of it but one traveller wrote how he got a student discount on a flight to India by having a student card and a letter purportedly from Madras University saying he was studying English there, signed by 'Professor Baksheesh'!

Booking & Reconfirming

At the height of the summer season flights out of Sri Lanka can be very heavily booked and if you do not have a reservation you could find yourself waiting weeks for a seat. Equally important, if you do have a firm reservation, make sure you reconfirm at least 72 hours ahead. Otherwise your seat confirmation will be cancelled and you may end up joining in the general melee trying to find a flight out.

Airport Tax

There is a Rs 100 airport tax on departure.

Getting Around

RAIL

Train travel in Sri Lanka can be pretty good. It's generally nowhere near as crowded as in India and the simple act of buying a ticket or making a reservation involves none of the Indian-style bureaucratic hassles. Plus, although the trains are quite slow, the distances are short so there are few overnight or all day ordeals to contend with. As in India, station masters often have considerable local discretionary powers. When the seats are all 'booked out' a polite request will often find a seat for a foreign visitor. Timetables are available in Kandy and Colombo although there are often last minute changes.

On many services there is only a choice of 2nd or 3rd class and we felt that 2nd was a much better bet than 3rd – even though it is about 50% more expensive. Not because it was more comfortable, there was very little difference in that department, but because 2nd class was generally much less crowded than 3rd. However, several travellers have since written to say that does not always apply. One wrote that it was impossible to get a seat Colombo-Kandy in 2nd class while 3rd class was virtually empty and the 3rd class carriages were new and comfortable.

When 1st is available the cost is about 3½ times the 3rd class level and seats can always be booked. Actually it will be more expensive still since 1st class always means either an observation saloon, air-conditioned coach or a sleeper berth – any of which involves extra charges.

At night there are additional possibilities thrown in. There may be 2nd or 3rd class sleeperettes, which in 2nd class are very comfortable individual reclining seats. Or there may be sleeping berths which are individual twin-bunked rooms and are the absolute last word in Asian train comfort – if you've just come from India anyway.

They're only available in 1st or 2nd class versions – main difference is the 1st class berths have a sink and sheets on the bunk.

The timetables in the Ceylon Tourist Board booklet and the information in this guide refers only to express trains. There are also some slower local trains which stop everywhere and take a long, long time. Recently new Inter-City Express services have been introduced on the Colombo-Galle, Colombo-Kandy and Colombo-Anuradhapura-Jaffna routes. These trains make only limited stops, are all one-class and charge fares slightly higher than the regular 2nd class fare. You can buy return tickets with a 50% discount on the return half so long as you make the round trip within 10 days. Seats on the Inter-City services must be booked at least a day in advance.

Supplementary costs over the standard fares are Rs 25 for the 1st class observation saloon (on the hill country services) or Rs 50 for the air-conditioned coach in 1st class. Sleeping berths cost an additional Rs 50 in 1st, Rs 30 in 2nd. In 2nd class at night you have a choice of berth or sleeperette (if you can get them). The sleeperettes (reclining seats) are Rs 15 extra. The only night possibility on 3rd class is a sleeperette at Rs 10 extra. Note that on any rail journey over 50 miles you can break the trip for up to 24 hours without any extra ticketing. Thus if you were going by rail from Colombo to Polonnaruwa, for example, you could hop off the train at Aukana, go to see the huge Buddha image, then catch another later train.

Life does not revolve around the railway stations in Sri Lanka to anything like the same extent it does in India. Railway station restaurants are generally terrible in Sri Lanka whereas they're little havens of safe, reasonable-quality food in India.

But there are railway retiring rooms at certain stations and they're worth remembering when all else fails. There are rooms at Anuradhapura, Galle, Jaffna, Polgahawela, Trincomalee, Kandy and Talaimannar Pier.

Be a little cautious on the trains, particularly at night. The Talaimannar-Colombo service is particularly notorious for thieves relieving sleepy travellers of their belongings. One traveller wrote of a far more frightening incident on board a train. He was sitting in an open doorway as a train approached Colombo one night when somebody simply pushed him out. Luckily he landed from the slow-moving train with nothing more than cuts and bruises but, of course, all his possessions were gone.

BUSES & MINIBUSES

At one time, not so many years ago, the CTB – Ceylon Transport Board – had turned bus travel in Sri Lanka into a nightmare. This huge, unwieldy and inefficient monster had a monopoly on every bus service in the country and provided a totally miserable service. There weren't enough operating buses, they were unreliable and they rarely ran to schedule. Because there were too few buses actually in running order (there always seemed to be plenty broken down at the depots) the overcrowding was horrendous. Bus travel in Sri Lanka was a start to finish horror story. It was just as bad in towns as out in the country, only the trips were mercifully shorter.

Fortunately all that has changed. Private bus operators are once again in operation and there is a whole string of private bus services operating in parallel with the CTB or even on their own unique routes. They operate in the country and on local town services. They use Japanese minibuses, usually charge a little more than the CTB for equivalent trips and get you there in much greater comfort and at much greater speed. Sometimes at too great speed – 'a good alternative for those

whom reckless speed doesn't faze', wrote one traveller. The introduction of the minibuses has, however, had a secondary benefit. Because of the intense competition between minibus operators their fares on some busy routes (Colombo-Negombo, Colombo-Kandy) may actually be lower than the CTB fare!

By taking the pressure off the CTB they have made those buses much more feasible to travel on – CTB buses now tend to be far less crowded than before and hence also rather faster. In fact many travellers find the CTB buses preferable to the minibuses – less cramped, more room for baggage, less chance of being overcharged and less crazy driving.

To ensure you're not overcharged on a private bus check the price before you get on and make sure you get a ticket. The minibus fares are usually only marginally higher than CTB fares so ascertaining the CTB price will give you a pretty good idea of what you should be paying. For what it's worth it is said that the bus's insurance will not cover you if you do not have a ticket.

So all in all bus travel is now a much easier operation than it was a few years ago. Of course the CTB still has a monopoly on many quieter routes where the business isn't sufficient to attract private operators. And, of course, this is still a third world country and you can't expect western standards of comfort, convenience and safety. Local CTB buses have white signs, the long distance buses have yellow signs.

On buses and trains there are certain seats reserved for ladies. Like the 'smoking prohibited' signs this injunction is completely ignored; it's first-come first-served. On the other hand the first two seats are always reserved for 'clergy' (ie Buddhist monks) and this is never ignored – a pregnant woman would probably have to stand if a strapping teenage monk hopped on!

CARS

By Asian standards car rental is reasonably expensive in Sri Lanka. The rental companies still, to some extent, discourage self-drive rental but this seems to be changing. Nevertheless, costs are generally somewhat lower for chauffeur-driven rentals than for self-drive; excess mileage charges are about the same but the chauffeur-driven cars, although they have both types available. Some of their self there is an insurance charge for self-drive hire which is usually somewhat higher than the nightly 'subsistence' cost for a driver. If a chauffeur cannot arrange free accommodation with your hotel he will, no doubt, sleep on the back seat and ensure a small extra profit. Ostensibly the reason for this slant towards chauffeur-driven hire is the danger of accidents and damage to hard-to-obtain vehicles. The standard of driving in Sri Lanka is decidedly on the hair-raising side. The major hire companies are:

Quickshaw's Ltd, 3 Kalinga Place, Colombo 5 (tel 83133-5, 82995); representing Hertz.

Mercantile Tours (Ceylon) Ltd, 51 Janadhipathi Mawatha, Colombo 1 (tel 28707-8); representing Inter-Rent.

Avis Rent-a-Car Service, Mack Transport Ltd, Mackinons Building, 11A York St, Colombo 1 (tel 29881, 29888)

Mack's are probably in the lead when it comes to providing self-drive rather than chauffeur-driven cars although they have both types available. Some of their self drive rates are:

	per day	plus per km	per week (unlim. km)
Daihatsu Charade	280	2.00	3500
Renault 12	400	2.60	4750
Mitsubishi Colt	500	3.00	5750
Mitsubishi Galant	600	4.00	7200

The Mitsubishis are both air-con. Their additional cost for a driver is Rs 100 per day.

Quickshaw's rates include a daily allowance of 50 miles or a weekly allowance of 250 miles. Some of their rates are:

	per day	per week	excess miles
Mitsubishi Colt	325	1650	5
Renault 12	400	2000	5.50
Mitsubishi Galant	475	2400	6.50

Quickshaw's are much less happy about letting their cars loose on a self-drive basis. Their daily 'subsistence' allowance for a driver is Rs 40 but overall it's cheaper to be driven than to drive yourself.

Driving Yourself

During the course of researching the third edition of this guidebook I rented a Daihatsu Charade from the Avis agent for 15 days during which time I covered 2710 km. A small car – a Charade is a handy little minicar comparable in size to a Honda Civic, Austin Metro, VW Polo or similar – is really all you need for Sri Lanka. The distances are not great and despite your slow speed you won't be cooped up in it for too long.

Finding your way round the country is no problem at all; there are milestones (or km markers) on all the major roads and Sri Lankan maps indicate where these are so you can always tell exactly where you are and how far to the next town or junction. You must obtain a temporary Sri Lankan driving licence while in Sri Lanka. This is issued by the Automobile Association on production of your International Driving Permit. If you hire a car the renter will obtain it for you. The Automobile Association of Ceylon (tel 21528-9), 40 Sir Macan Marker Mawatha, Galle Face, Colombo 3 can also supply information on road conditions and other driving queries.

Speed limits are 35 mph (56 kph) in built up areas, 45 mph (72 kph) in the country. Petrol is no problem, it's widely available and not excessively expensive by modern standards at Rs 13.50 a litre. Punctures seem to be a way of life – the roads are hard on tyres and the tyres are not always in A1 condition to start with. During our circuit of Sri Lanka we had three punctures, two of them through picking up nails. Every little village seems to have a puncture repair specialist who will do an excellent, though rather time consuming, repair using decidedly primitive equipment. A tube patch will be vulcanised on by attaching a metal container to the appropriate place, filling it with kerosene and setting the kerosene aflame!

Mechanical repairs, should you be so unfortunate as to need them, are likely to be equally ingenious. 'Our jeep broke down three times', wrote another wheeled-traveller. 'Twice with a broken axle! Every time there was willing, constructive help available. After 24 hours in one garage, plus welding, labour, etc, we were charged Rs 200 (less than US$10) for fixing the axle........ and it's still holding together!'

Driving in Sri Lanka is not really any great problem. Traffic in Colombo, up to Kandy and along the west coast 'beach strip' is fairly heavy, but elsewhere in the country it's usually quite light. You do not, however, travel at any great speed for the roads are narrow and potholed and there is often much pedestrian, bicycle and animal traffic to navigate around. Even on the odd stretch where the road is clear you still have to proceed cautiously and slowly because bumps, dips and severe potholes can appear almost anywhere. The one exception would have to be the superb stretch of road from near Ratnapura down to the south coast near Ambalantota, between Tangalla and Hambantota.

Although we saw a number of accidents during our time on the road, overall I think driving, if you take care, is fairly safe. Whenever you meet an oncoming car you have to slow right down because the road is simply not wide enough and each car will have to pull part way off. The main danger is the completely unpredictable nature of pedestrians and bicyclists. You should always be prepared for any bicyclist to suddenly decide to make a completely unannounced U-turn at any time and for no apparent reason. Don't have accidents, the basic Asian rule will always apply – you're the stranger here, therefore it's your fault.

Being Driven

The major advantages of being driven in Sri Lanka are that you have none of the responsibilities of keeping the vehicle together and avoiding the dangers on the road and that you have a guide always ready to hand. The major disadvantage is that you have another person to look after and no matter how helpful or unobtrusive your driver there are bound to be times when you don't want him around – or do want him around and he isn't! Plus, of course, you have less space in the car.

Several visitors have written to say how convenient a car and driver can be if your time is limited. There is no necessity to hang around waiting for transport and you can stop anytime, anywhere. 'There were other small but significant advantages', wrote one visitor. 'For example while we relaxed at dinner, our driver arranged for us to have front row seats to watch the Kandy dancers'.

It's wise to be cautious if hiring a car and driver from one of the small time operators without a reputation to uphold. A Swiss couple wrote recently of being simply dumped by their driver who decided he didn't want to go where they wanted to go any longer and hightailed it for Colombo!

Of course the biggest disadvantage of going by car (with or without a driver), even if the cost is not a consideration, is that you lose the day to day contact with Sri Lankan life and the Sri Lankans which public transport always provides.

Cars

With the easier import restrictions Japanese cars are beginning to appear in increasing numbers in Sri Lanka. Car imports are still, however, quite limited so cars tend to lead long and hard lives. Cars used to find their way into Sri Lanka by a rather fascinating process. There is no local manufacturing industry so most cars were imported second hand. Dealers would put ads in the papers announcing they were off to Singapore or the UK and expected to be able to bring back, say, '72 model Ford Escorts for Rs Y or '69 model Peugeot 404s for Rs X. Orders in hand they would then trot off to buy whatever was needed.

Apart from foreign exchange restrictions there is also a sliding scale import duty, based on the CIF price of the imported car, which often resulted in the duty being higher than the actual price of the car — over US$2500 the duty was 200%! Sri Lanka has many fine condition old cars on the road including an amazing number of pre-war Austin 7s and British sports cars of the '50s including MG-TCs and MGAs, frogeye Sprites, TR2s and the like.

MOTORCYCLES

Motorcycles can be a reasonable alternative for intrepid travellers. Distances are relatively short and some of the roads are simply a motorcyclist's delight. With far more Japanese motorcycles coming into the country it is now quite easy to hire bikes. Daily rental rates vary from around Rs 100 per day for a 125 cc machine to around Rs 200 for a 175 cc or larger bike.

There are lots of places renting bikes in Hikkaduwa or you can enquire at the Tourist Office in Colombo. Stafford Motors in Colombo are the Honda importers for Sri Lanka and they're a particularly good place to rent a motorcycle. Although their rates may be a little higher than smaller places, their bikes are reliable and if you do have any trouble they have a string of local dealers all over the island. Their rates also include helmets and comprehensive insurance. Stafford Motors (tel 580793) are at 514 Duplication Rd, Colombo 3 and they have 80 cc bikes at Rs 150 a day, 125 cc at Rs 175, 185 cc at Rs 225, and 250 cc at Rs 250.

BICYCLES

Keen round-the-world bicyclists will probably find Sri Lanka a joy, apart from the uphill sections of the hill country, but hiring a bike in Sri Lanka is often far from that. I've hired bikes in Anuradhapura, Polonnaruwa, Kalkudah, Hikkaduwa and Negombo and the bikes generally ranged from barely reasonable (the Negombo ones were an honourable exception) to diabolical.

Flat tyres come with alarming regularity and if one brake works with 25% efficiency you're doing well (one bike Maureen was handed in Polonnaruwa had absolutely no brakes at all; ever tried stopping a bike with your feet on the ground in an emergency?). Altogether bicycles show the Sinhalese total disdain for maintenance at its worst! Fortunately the opening up of imports to Sri Lanka seems to have brought more bicycles in and more spare parts for the ones already there. The situation has improved.

Bringing your own bicycle in to explore the country is quite a different story. The following account comes from Ian Anderson, England:

As a cyclist I would recommend Sri Lanka as a good place to visit because its size means it can easily be covered in six weeks or so. The usual advantages that a cyclist has in mobility and independence are emphasised when you look at crowded trains and minibuses.

There are disadvantages. Number one is the state of the roads which range from very poor to appalling, especially around the monsoon period. I was able to go on flooded roads that no four-wheeled transport could use but this required a combination of wading, swimming, wheeling the bike along handy railway lines and, when necessary, hiring a canoe! It all adds to the interest.

I would recommend bringing a good supply of spare tyres and tubes as these can suffer excessively from the poor road surface. The normal size bicycle tyre in Sri Lanka is 28" x 1½". Some imported 27" tyres for our 10-speed bikes are available but only in a few shops in Colombo and at high prices. Suriyages Ltd (tel 91505), 524 Maradana Rd, Colombo 10 is a possible source of parts.

A second problem with bicycling in Sri Lanka is the driving of some bus drivers, especially the minibus drivers. Few Sri Lankans can resist sounding their horns at every opportunity – it usually means 'look what a big vehicle I am' or 'I'm coming through regardless'! On the other hand, outside the towns traffic is very light and as long as you keep your wits about you and accept a certain lack of signals or predictable behaviour by other road users or pedestrians, you should be OK.

I recommend a good lock when your bike is out of sight or else constant vigilance, particularly in small villages. Early starts are essential due to the heat. The distances you cover will be limited by the state of the roads and a large amount of 'eyes down' cycling will be necessary. Brings lots of suncream – local brands are not effective and imported ones are very expensive. You can take your bike on the trains but at 'parcel rate' it costs about twice the 3rd class passenger fare.

LOCAL TRANSPORT

In Colombo there are taxis and auto-rickshaws. The taxis are all old British Morris Minors and instantly recognisable. Auto-rickshaws are a more recent innovation. These Indian-made vehicles are small three wheelers, powered by a motor-scooter engine and with a driver up front and room for at the very least two passengers in the back. Taxis and auto-rickshaws are metered and the drivers are almost always willing to use the meters – possibly because they spin round at a scarcely believable pace!

Outside of Colombo you will find taxis in the major towns; even quite small towns will probably be able to boast a single taxi. Don't expect meters outside Colombo, though. It's strictly a case of agreeing a fare in advance. Curiously bicycle rickshaws are nowhere to be seen in Sri Lanka.

FLYING

There are no regular domestic air services in Sri Lanka at present. A domestic carrier, Upali, was created to take over the internal air services of Air Ceylon at the same time as Air Lanka came into existence to operate internationally. But Upali soon disappeared and the only internal air services today are light aircraft and helicopter charters.

TOURS

Colombo has a great many travel agencies and tour operators with day or longer tours to all the main attractions. The tourist office can advise you on tours. The railway also operate Rail Tours from one to six days using their luxury air-conditioned coaches. They have an information office at the Fort Station in Colombo but the tours only operate at the height of the tourist season. Day tours include Hikkaduwa and Galle; Kandy; or Polonnaruwa, Aukana and Sigiriya.

Colombo

The easy-going capital of Sri Lanka is not a great attraction in itself – there is little of real interest here compared to the rest of the country – but it is a pleasant place to spend a few days in and makes a good base from which to start out into the real Sri Lanka. Colombo is the bustling commercial centre of Sri Lanka as well as the gateway for all arrivals by air yet somehow its size (around three quarters of a million population) is very far from overwhelming. Indeed the centre (known as 'Fort', although there is little sign of that today) is distinctly handy and very easy to get around on foot. The administrative capital of Sri Lanka is now Sri Jayawardenepura-Kotte and is situated just outside of Colombo; there's certainly a trace of presidential ego in that name!

Orientation

Once you've got a few directions down you'll find Colombo a relatively easy city to find your way around. If you're going to be spending any time in the capital a copy of the handy little *A to Z Colombo* street directory will come in useful. It is readily available from the Map Sales Office but unfortunately does not extend as far south as Dehiwala and Mt Lavinia. It does, however, include a very useful foldout map showing all the main bus routes. The airport tourist counter gives out free maps of Colombo.

From the visitor's point of view Colombo is virtually a long coastal strip extending 10 or 12 km south of the central Fort area. The spine of this strip is the Galle Rd – if you kept on along it you'd eventually leave Colombo far behind and it would take you all the way to Galle.

Travelling down the Galle Rd, south from Fort (Colombo 1) you come first to the Galle Face Green, inland from which is Slave Island, which isn't really an island at all since only two of its three sides are surrounded by water. This area and Kollupitiya, into which the Galle Rd runs next, are Colombo 3. Next up along the Galle Rd is Bambalapitiya, Colombo 4; followed by Wellawatta, Colombo 6; Dehiwala and finally Mt Lavinia. Finding places along the Galle Rd is slightly complicated by the numbers starting back at one as you move into each new district. Thus there will be a 100 Galle Rd in Colombo 3, again in Colombo 4 and again in Colombo 6. There are some quite reasonable stretches of beach along the coast by the Galle Rd, although Mt Lavinia is the nearest beach centre to Colombo.

Back in the central Fort business area, if you headed straight inland you'd quickly find yourself in the Pettah, Colombo 11. If you arrive in Colombo by rail you'll find yourself at the Fort Railway Station, which is at the south-west corner of the Pettah, very close indeed to the downtown Fort area. The central bus station is at the south-east corner and requires another bus ride or a short walk into the centre

Moving down the Galle Rd again, if you turned directly inland (east) at Dharmapala Mawatha in Kollupitiya you'd soon find yourself in Colombo 7 – home for the art gallery, museum, university and most of the embassies (but not the British and US embassies which are on the Galle Rd in Colombo 3). Continue down the Galle Rd to Bambalapitiya and turn inland at Dickman's Rd and you'd find yourself in Havelock Town, Colombo 5.

Information

The Tourist Board's Travel Information Centre is at 41 Glen Aber Place in Colombo 4 – just off the Galle Rd. That's supposedly a temporary address following the demolition of the convenient old office on the Galle Face. There's a small, and not so well equipped, centre at the Department of Information Building, Sir Baron Jayatilaka Mawatha, Colombo Fort – opposite Air Lanka. The Tourist Police (tel 26941, 21111) are at 12 Hospital St in Fort.

The Department of Immigration & Emigration (tel 29851, 21509) is on Galle Buck Rd. The Cultural Triangle Office (tel 587912), for Archaeological Permits, is in the Ministry of Cultural Affairs, 212 Bauddhaloka Mawatha, Colombo 7. You can get a Rs 225 pass which covers admission to Sigiriya, Polonnaruwa and Anuradhapura – but admission to each centre is Rs 75 so there's no saving. Entry charges for foreigners are being instituted at other centres so an all in pass may become better value at some point.

The Buddhist Information Centre (tel 23709) is at 50 Ananda Cumaraswamy Mawatha (Green Path), Colombo 7. At the Gangaramaya Bhikku Training Centre, Beira Lake Rd, Colombo 2, there is a museum of Buddhism. The nearby temple is very beautiful. Meetings are held on Saturdays at 5 pm at the Servants of Buddha, Maitriya Hall, Lauries Rd, Colombo 4.

Banks & Post Office Most of the main banks are located in the central Fort area. On the ground floor of the Bank of Ceylon on York St, just down from the Taprobane Hotel, there is a foreign exchange counter open 8 am to 8 pm every day of the week including weekends and holidays. You can also change money in the Bureau de Change in the Bank of Ceylon, York St from 8 am to 4 pm on weekdays, and in the Air Lanka office at 14 Sir Baron Jayatilaka Mawatha during the same hours.

American Express are at 11 York St, Colombo Fort. Thomas Cook (tel 22511-4) are at 17 Sir Baron Jayatilaka Mawatha, Colombo Fort.

The General Post Office is on Janadhipathi Mawatha in Colombo Fort. Ring 26203 for poste restante enquiries. They will forward mail on to you in other towns. Stamp collectors may want to visit the Sri Lanka Philatelic Bureau, 4th floor, Ceylinco House, Janadhipathi Mawatha, Fort. The Central Telegraph Office is on Duke St in Fort and international calls can be made from here. Book international phone calls by ringing 100.

Transport Information For flight arrival details or other airport information ring the airport – tel 030-2281. The Railway Tourist Office (tel 35838) is at the Fort Railway Station. For bus enquiries ring the CTB – tel 28081. The Automobile Association of Ceylon (tel 21528-9) is at 40 Sir Macan Markar Mawatha, Galle Face, Colombo 3.

Airlines Airline offices in Colombo are mainly in Fort, they include:

Air Lanka	14 Sir Baron Jayatilaka Mawatha, Colombo Fort (tel 21291) 660 Galle Rd, Colombo 3 (tel 81131-3)
Aeroflot	79/81 Hemas Building, York St, Colombo Fort (tel 25580, 33062)
British Airways	63 Janadhipathi Mawatha, Colombo Fort (tel 20231)
Gulf Air	11B & 11C York St, Colombo Fort (tel 29881-7)
Indian Airlines	95 Sir Baron Jayatilaka Mawatha, Colombo Fort (tel 23136)
KLM	61 Janadhipathi Mawatha, Colombo Fort (tel 26359, 25984-6)
Kuwait Airways	Ceylinco House, 69 Janadhipathi Mawatha, Colombo Fort (tel 20914)
Maldives International	see Indian Airlines
Pakistan International	432 Galle Rd, Colombo 3 (tel 29215, 25362, 25800)
Royal Nepal Airlines	434 Galle Rd, Colombo 3 (tel 24045, 28945)
Singapore Airlines	15A Sir Baron Jayatilaka Mawatha, Colombo Fort (tel 22711-9)
Thai International	16 Janadhipathi Mawatha, Colombo Fort (tel 36201-5)

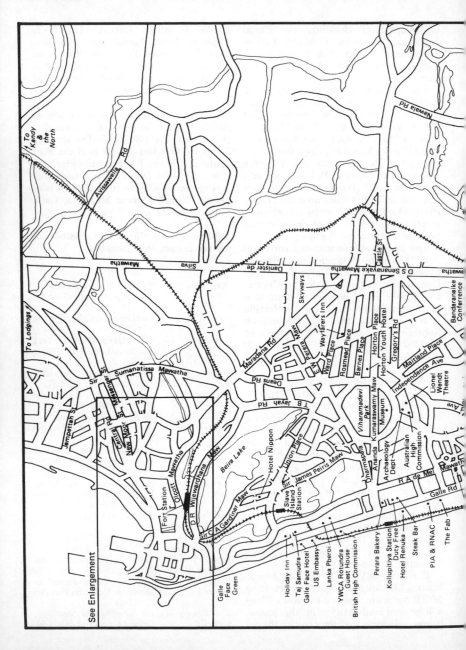

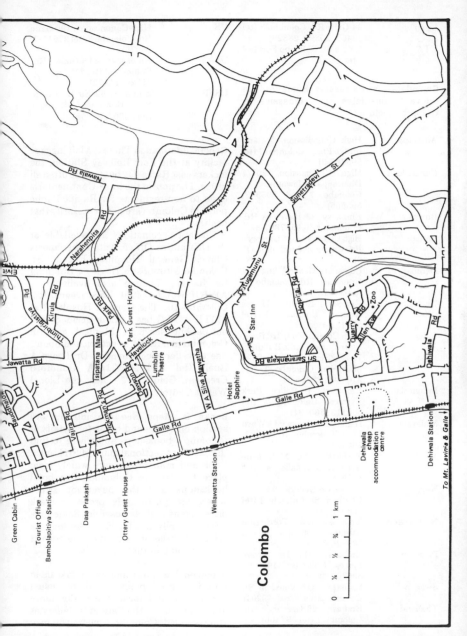

Colombo

Green Cabin
Tourist Office
Bambalapitiya Station
Dasa Prakash
Ottery Guest House
Wellawatta Station
Dehiwala cheap accommodation centre
Dehiwala Station
To Mt. Lavinia & Galle

Nawala Rd
Narahenpita Rd
Elvir
Thimbirigasiya Rd
Kirula Rd
Park Rd
Park Guest House
Jawatta Rd
Havelock Rd
Ispatana Maw
Bauddhaloka
Lumbini Theatre
Vajira Rd
Baudon Rd
Dickman Rd
Galle Rd
W A Silva Mawatha
Star Inn
Sri Saranakara Rd
Hotel Sapphire
Galle Rd
P. Rugemunu St
Hopple Rd
Sunetradevi St
Quarry Rd
Allen Ave
Zoo
Dehiwala Rd
Dehiwala

0   ¼   ½   ¾   1 km

| Upali | 34 Galle Rd, Colombo 3 (tel 20465, 29399, 28826) |
| UTA | 5 York St, Colombo Fort (tel 27605- 6) |

Consulates & Embassies Some of the relevant consulates and embassies in ' Colombo include:

Australia	High Commission, 3 Cambridge Place, Colombo 7 (tel 598767-9)
Bangladesh	High Commission, 207/1 Dharmapala Mawatha, Colombo 7 (tel 595963, 593565)
Burma	Embassy, 23 Havelock Rd, Colombo 5 (tel 587607-8)
Canada	High Commission, 6 Gregory's Rd, Colombo 7 (tel 595841-3)
Denmark	Consulate-General, 264 Grandpass Rd, Colombo 14 (tel 547806)
Germany (West)	Embassy, 40 Alfred House Avenue, Colombo 3 (tel 580431-4)
India	High Commission, 3rd floor, State Bank of India Building, 18-3/1 Sir Baron Jayatilaka Mawatha, Colombo 1 (tel 21604-5, 22788-9)
Indonesia	Embassy, 1 Police Park Terrace, Colombo 5 (tel 580113, 580194)
Malaysia	High Commission, 63A Ward Place, Colombo 7 (tel 94837, 596591)
Maldives	Embassy, 25 Melbourne Avenue, Colombo 4 (tel 86762)
Nepal	Consulate-General, 92 Chatham St, Colombo 1 (tel 26393)
Netherlands	Embassy, 25 Torrington Avenue, Colombo 7 (tel 589626-8)
Pakistan	Embassy, 211 De Saram Place, Colombo 10 (tel 596301-2)
Sweden	Embassy, 315 Vauxhall St, Colombo 2 (tel 20201, 20204)
Thailand	Embassy, 26 Gregory's Rd, Colombo 7 (tel 597406)
UK	High Commission, 190 Galle Rd, Colombo 3 (tel 27611-7, 20079)
USA	Embassy, 44 Galle Rd, Colombo 3 (tel 21271, 21520, 21532)
USSR	Embassy, 62 Sir Ernest de Silva Mawatha, Colombo 7 (tel 26262, 27855)

General Information There is a left luggage facility at the Fort Railway Station, the lockers cost Rs 5 a day but they're often all in use. The pool at the Inter-Continental is open to non-residents for Rs 50! Public pools in Colombo are not necessarily that healthy.

Cholera vaccinations are available at the Quarantine Office, Anti-Tuberculosis Clinic, General Hospital, Regent St, Colombo 8 (opposite Hayley's Building) for Rs 10. They're also available at APHOI (tel 597422), 385 Deens Rd, Colombo 10. The General Hospital (tel 91111, 93184) has 24 hour accident and out-patient services. Medical care in Colombo is nothing to get excited about, one traveller recommended Dr Theva A Buell (tel 92417), 31/2A Guildford Crescent, Colombo 7 – near the Lionel Wendt Centre.

Books & Maps See the introductory section on books and maps for details of Colombo's bookshops and where to find the excellent sectional maps of Sri Lanka. Book and map prices vary widely from place to place in Colombo. The hotel bookshops and the pavement street sellers are particularly prone to mark prices up as high as possible. Some low-priced, locally produced books may be priced at three or four times the correct price in some of the big hotels.

Shopping The government run Laksala in Fort is a good place for all the usual handicrafts and local items. For more unusual finds try the Serendib Gallery at 100 Galle Rd, Colombo 4 where you may find old maps and prints or rare books on Sri Lanka as well as modern handicrafts. A longer term resident recommended Kollupitiya as a good shopping area with lower prices than in Fort but better quality than in Dehiwala or Bambalapitiya. When the Pettah shops are closed on Sundays, Main St becomes an open air bazaar. Duke St in Fort is also a busy bazaar. The State Gems Corporation is at 24 York St in Fort.

Go to the Children's Bookshop, 20 Bogala Building on Janadhipathi Mawatha, near the clock tower in Fort, for cassettes of Sinhalese classical and folk music. There's a local version of western rock known as Baile. For unadulterated spices try the YWCA Spice Shop on Union Place.

Colombo's mad house Duty Free Shopping Centre is on the Galle Rd in Kollupitiya. There's a bus stop right out front. At the height of the Indian duty-free shopping spree you could 'sit outside and watch visitors from India staggering out balancing five video recorders on their heads!' To get in you need a passport, currency form and have to pay a Rs 25 entry charge but there are good bargains on cigarettes, whiskey, cameras, watches and electrical goods. The non-consumable goods are noted in your passport so you can't sell them in Sri Lanka. All the shops in the centre are closed from 1 to 2 pm for lunch.

There are several supermarkets around Colombo where, at a price, you can get all sorts of western goods from baked beans to disposable nappies (diapers). Cornell's, on the Galle Rd near the duty free centre, is one of the larger ones. The Tea Promotion Board has a store at 574 Galle Rd, Colombo 3.

Fort

During the Portuguese and Dutch periods 'Fort' was indeed a fort, but today it is simply the commercial centre of Sri Lanka. Here you'll find most of the major offices, some of the big hotels, and the majority of the department stores. Not to mention airline offices, the GPO, the immigration office, travel agents, restaurants, and countless street hustlers ready to sell you anything from a padded bra to a carved mask. The government run Laksala (in the Australia Building on York St) is a complete exhibition of Sinhalese handicrafts expertise; far more than just a shop.

A good landmark in Fort is the clock tower at the junction of Chatham St and Janadhipathi Mawatha (once Queen St), which 140 years ago was a lighthouse. It's almost exactly midway between the big Ceylon Inter-Continental Hotel and the GPO. Other sights in Fort include the busy port area, the President's house (known as 'Queen's House'), and the boulder in Gordon Gardens, inscribed with the Portuguese coat-of-arms, which marks the place where they first set foot on the island in 1505. Unfortunately it's not on public view since it's in the Presidential Gardens.

In the main, however, it's the street scenes and street life which attract attention in Fort. Here you'll see everything from briefcase toting city workers to Buddhist monks, apprentice snake charmers to uniformed young schoolgirls.

Galle Face Green

Immediately to the south of Fort is the Galle Face Green – a long expanse of open land back from the seafront. Life goes on around the clock on the green whether it's an early morning cricket match or a late evening stroll. Kite flying is a particularly popular pastime. Facing each other from opposite ends of the green are the delightful old Galle Face Hotel and the contemporary Ceylon Inter-Continental. Two new hotels, the Galadari Meridien and the Taj Samudra look out on to the Green. The State Assembly building is at the northern end of the Green.

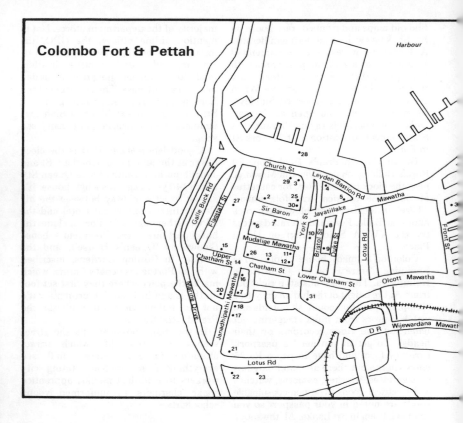

Colombo Fort & Pettah

1 Immigration Dept.
2 Singapore Airlines
3 Hotel Taprobane
4 American Express
5 Indian Airlines
6 GPO
7 Air Lanka
8 Ex-Servicemen's Institute
9 YMCA
10 Aeroflot
11 Nectar Cafe
12 Laksala
13 Pagoda Tea Room
14 Clock Tower
15 Thai International
16 Foriegn Currency Shop
17 Ceylinco House
18 British Airways
19 Fort Railway Station

20 Hotel Inter-Continental
21 Galdari Meridien Hotel
22 State Assembly
23 Old Secretariat
24 Bus Stand
25 Foriegn Exchange Counter
26 Nanking House
27 President's Residence
28 Passenger Harbour Terminal
29 Church of St. Peter
30 State Gem Corporation
31 Highway Dept (Map Sales)
32 Old Dutch Cemetery
33 Dutch Period Museum
34 Jami-Ul-Alfar Mosque
35 Old Town Hall
36 Sea Street Temples
37 The Wolvendaal Church
38 Courts of Justice

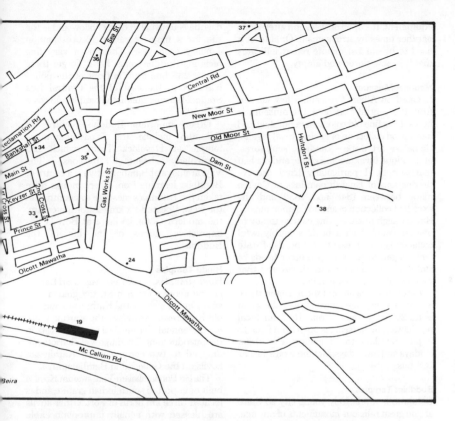

Pettah

Adjacent to Fort and immediately inland from it is the Pettah, the bustling bazaar area of Colombo. You name it and some shop or street stall will be selling it in the Pettah. Each street seems to have its own speciality. Unfortunately the Pettah was the worst hit part of Colombo by the events of 1983 and the damage was extensive. The word Pettah is a derivation of the Tamil word 'pettai' which literally means 'outside the fort'.

Mosques & Temples In the Pettah you can find a selection of Hindu temples and Moslem mosques including the decorative Jami-Ul-Alfar Mosque with its red and white, candy-striped brickwork which was built in 1909. Sea St has the Hindu temples from which the Vel Cart Festival commences – see the section on temples below. The Dutch Wolvendaal Church is also in the Pettah.

Museums The Dutch Period Museum is on Prince St in Pettah and has had a colourful history. At various times it has been the Dutch town hall, a gentleman's residence, an orphanage, a hospital, a police station and finally a post office. Now restored to its former glory it is open from 9 am to 5 pm, Monday to Friday.

The Fort Railway Station, which marks the southern boundary of the Pettah, has an interesting small museum of old railway equipment. It's open on weekend afternoons or other times by arrangement. Or at least it used to be – a last minute report indicates that it is now closed and empty.

National Museum

Located on Albert Crescent, a few km out from the central Fort area, the museum is housed in a fine old colonial-era building and has a good collection of ancient royal regalia; Sinhalese art work – carvings, sculptures, etc; antique furniture and china; and ola leaf manuscripts. I particularly liked the reproductions of English paintings of Ceylon made between 1848 and 1850 and the excellent collection of antique demon masks. But the high point, leaving culture totally to one side, would have to be the superbly awful collection of the presents that heads of state feel obliged to shower upon other heads of state. Unfortunately I later discovered that was only a temporary exhibit.

In the grounds around the museum there is a particularly fine banyan tree. Admission is Rs 20 for foreigners, only Rs 2 for local residents. The museum is open from 9 am to 5 pm, Sundays to Thursdays, closed on Fridays and Saturdays. Get there on a 114 or 138 bus.

Buddhist Temples

Colombo is a relatively young city so there are no great religious monuments of any age. The most important Buddhist centre is the Kelaniya Raja Maha Vihara about 11 km from Fort. The Buddha is reputed to have preached here on one of his visits to Ceylon over 2000 years ago. The temple, which was later constructed on the spot, was destroyed by Indian invaders, restored, destroyed again by the Portuguese and not restored once again until comparatively recently. The dagoba is unusual in being hollow and is the site for a major perahera (procession) in January each year. There is a very fine reclining Buddha image here. To get there take a 235 bus from in front of the police barracks to the east of the Central Bus Station. It terminates at the temple and costs Rs 2.50.

Other important Buddhist centres in Colombo include the Isipathanaramaya temple at Havelock Town, which has particularly beautiful frescoes. The Vajiraramaya at Bambalapitiya is a centre of Buddhist learning from where monks have taken the Buddha's message to countries in the west. Located six km east of the centre, the modern Gotami Vihara at Borella has impressive murals of the life of the Buddha.

Hindu Temples

Hindu temples, known as *kovils* in Sri Lanka, are numerous. On Sea St, the goldsmith's street in the Pettah, the Kathiresan and the old Kathiresan Kovils are the starting point for the annual Vel Festival (see Festivals in the introduction). The huge Vel chariots are dragged to two corresponding Kathiresan kovils on the Galle Rd in Bambalapitiya.

The Sri Ponnambalam-Vaneswaram Kovil is built of imported south Indian granite and is located three km north of Fort. Other kovils are blessed with equally unpronounceable names, such as the Sri Bala Selva Vinayagar Moorthy Kovil with shrines to Shiva and Ganesh; the Sri Shiva Subramania Swami Kovil on Kew Rd, Slave Island; or the Sri Muthumariamman Kovil on Kotahena St.

Mosques

Colombo also has many mosques, most important of which is the Grand Mosque on

A   Tea picking near Nuwara Eliya
B   Fishing boats on the beach at Hambantota
C   Planting rice beside the Colombo-Kandy road

New Moor St in the Pettah, where you'll also find the already mentioned Jami-Ul-Alfar Mosque. There are many mosques on Slave Island, which really was used for keeping slaves on during the Dutch era, but in the British days was the site for a Malay regiment's quarters; from which the name Kompanna Veediya – Company Street – derived.

Churches

Nor does Colombo neglect churches – Wolvendaal Church in Colombo 13 is the oldest Dutch church, it was erected between 1749 and 1757. Tombstones from an even older Dutch church now pave the floor. Right in Fort, near the Hotel Taprobane, St Peter's Church was once part of the Dutch Governor's residence – it was first used in 1804. The 1842 St Andrew's Scots Kirk stands a long way from the bonny Highlands on the Galle Rd, Kollupitiya; next to the Lanka Oberoi.

Dehiwala Zoo

One of Colombo's big tourist attractions is the zoo at Dehiwala, 10 km from Fort. By Asian standards it's a very fine zoo – in terms of the sort of treatment the animals get – although the big cats and the monkeys are still rather squalidly housed.

Major attraction is the 5.15 pm elephant show – they troop on stage in true trunk-to-tail fashion and perform a whole series of feats of elephantine-agility. They dance around with bells on their legs, stand delicately on little round platforms, balance momentarily on their front feet, one picks up his keeper in his trunk, and finally they all troop out, their leader tootling merrily on a mouth (trunk?) organ.

The zoo also has a fine collection of birds, a cage of siamese cats (!), and a gibbon who had obviously been studying the sub-continent too long. After a virtuoso slow motion performance for us, swinging around his enclosure, the gibbon swooped over to the front and stuck his open palm out through the bars, obviously looking for a little baksheesh.

The zoo also has an aquarium and is open from 8 am to 6 pm daily, entry cost is Rs 35 for foreigners. You can get there on a 132 bus from along the Galle Rd.

Other

At one time Cinnamon Gardens really was a cinnamon plantation but today it's simply the diplomatic quarter and Colombo's ritziest address – more commonly known as Colombo 7.

Colombo has a number of private and public art galleries including the public gallery on Ananda Cumaraswamy Mawatha (Green Path) in Colombo 7 and the more contemporary Lionel Wendt Centre on Guildford Crescent, Colombo 7. There's also Kalagaraya at 54 Ward Place, Colombo 7.

The Vihara Maha Devi Park actually occupies the site where the cinnamon plantation in Cinnamon Gardens used to be. It's notable for its superb flowering trees in March, April and early May. The nearby Planetarium on Bauddhaloka Mawath and Reid Ave has English shows on the last Saturday of the month at 2 pm, entry Rs 4.

The Bandaranaike Museum is in the Bandaranaike Building on Bauddhaloka Mawatha, Colombo 7, and tells the life of the late prime minister and the events of his assassination. It's open from 9 am to 4 pm daily except Mondays and poya holidays and entry is Rs 1.

A Dutch coat of arms at the 'old gate' in Galle
B Bathtime in the river
C Kandaswamy Kovil, Jaffna

Places to Stay

Although you'll find some of the cheaper hotels and the popular YMCA in and around the centre, Colombo's guest house bargains are mainly further out. See the Orientation information for where is where in Colombo. Basically you'll find the most expensive hotels in the centre or at the city end of Galle Rd – Kollupitiya, which is Colombo 3. As you move down Galle Rd you'll find cheaper places in Bambalapitiya (Colombo 4) and especially Dehiwala (Colombo 6 – more or less). Prices generally go down as you get further out, Dehiwala is about eight km (five miles) straight out the Galle Rd from the centre. After Dehiwala they climb again as you move into the beach resort of Mt Lavinia, although still more reasonably priced than in the centre.

Places to Stay – bottom end

There are a few cheap places smack in the middle of Colombo, but some of them tend to be perpetually full. The *Central YMCA* is at 39 Bristol St, only a short stroll from the Fort Railway Station. There are 58 beds here with fanless doubles at Rs 102, singles/doubles with fan at Rs 106/157 or doubles with bathroom for Rs 232. The rooms with fan are up on the top floor and tend to get hot. If you're sharing a room make sure your locker can be locked. There is an additional Rs 1 daily or Rs 2.50 weekly temporary membership charge. The Y also has a cafeteria; it's a good place for breakfast if you arrive in Colombo by an early morning train.

Virtually next door at 29 Bristol St, the *Sri Lankan Ex-Servicemen's Institute* has eight rooms at Rs 78/162.50 for singles/doubles. The bar has the cheapest beer in town. There are a couple of other cheap hotels in town along Mudalige Mawatha, beside the Nectar Cafe. The *Globe Hotel*, with doubles from around Rs 125, is typical but one angry woman wrote recently that the rooms have all been 'peepholed' so unless you like putting on a free show for the staff don't stay there.

The *Lodgings*, at 41 1/1 Mahavidyalaya Mawatha (formerly Barber St), Colombo 13,

has 18 rooms with doubles and attached bath, prices from Rs 75. It's 1½ km from the Fort Railway Station and close to the Central Bus Station and Pettah area. Rooms are reasonably clean and comfortable. To get there take a bus from Jayatilaka Mawatha to St Anthony's Church in Kochikade from where you take the road opposite the church, then third turn on the right, straight up to the top of the hill and left at the clock tower. It's next to the Bank of Ceylon. There are some good restaurants (like the Moslem *Iqbal*), a bakery (*Lion's Bakery*) and a milk outlet nearby.

There are some cheap hotels right across from the Fort Railway Station but this area was badly hit during the 1983 riots. Look for the *Maliban Hotel* (tel 21973) at 850 Olcott Mawatha for basic but reasonable rooms. Some of the hotels along here were really for emergencies only.

The *Scout Hostel* (tel 33131) at 131 Baladaksha Mawatha, Colombo 3 has just eight dorm beds but they also have camping facilities. There is a *Girl Guide Hostel* (tel 97720) for women only at 10 Sir Marcus Fernando Mawatha, Colombo 7. A bit further out at 50 Haig Rd, Bambalapitiya, Colombo 4 the *Youth Council Hostel* has 30 beds at Rs 20 for YHA members, Rs 25 for non-members. The *Horton Youth Hostel* has moved to Station Rd, Wellawatta.

There are a number of base price places further out along the Galle Rd in Dehiwala, the last Colombo suburb along the Galle Rd, although Mt Lavinia is really just another suburb of the city. It will cost you a couple of rupees for a bus this far out – take a 100, 101, 102, 105, 106, 133 or 134. Not all buses go this far along the Galle Rd. A three-wheeler will cost you Rs 30 to 50. Get off at St Mary's Church, the cheap accommodation here is all on the coast side of the Galle Rd. *Big John's* (tel 715027), at 47 Albert Place, is the mainstay of the Travellers' Halt network in Sri Lanka. Dorm beds here cost Rs 25 or there are singles from Rs 30, doubles from Rs 70. They have various overflow places in the locality.

The next street along is Campbell Place

and *Seabreeze* (tel 717996) at number 37 has rooms with and without bath from Rs 25 to Rs 75 plus a small dorm. It's a friendly, well-run place. Right by the railway line at 55 Vanderworth Place, four more streets down from Campbell Place, is the *Beach Spot*. The *Surf-In* at 2 Campbell Place and *Sea View* at 34 Albert Place are other guest houses in the area. *Gehan Villa* at 9 Second Lane, Dehiwala has had several recommendations from travellers who thought the food here was particularly good.

Tourist Rest (tel 714521) at 7 Park Avenue, off Waidya Rd, Dehiwala, near the zoo, is a nice place with a spacious verandah and bicycles for hire. Singles/doubles cost Rs 75/100. From Dehiwala it's only a short stroll along the beach to Mt Lavinia.

Places to Stay – middle

There are a great number of places in the middle price range including many guest houses listed in the Tourist Office's booklet. A popular place is the *Hotel Nippon* (tel 31887-8) at 123 Kumaran Ratnam Rd, Colombo 2. There are a variety of rooms with and without bathrooms, balconies and air-con. Prices, all including breakfast, start at Rs 125/175 for the bathless, non air-con rooms upstairs. With bath they're Rs 150/200 then with air-con as well they're Rs 200/250. Although most travellers reckon the Nippon is OK and good value for money, some have pointed out that it's not as clean as it could be and it can get rather noisy. Take a 138 bus from Fort or its about Rs 8 by three-wheeler.

Apart from the central YMCA there are also a couple of YWCAs in Colombo. The *YWCA International* (tel 24181, 24694) at 393 Union Place, Colombo 2 has 20 rooms at Rs 115/230 or at Rs 124/250 with attached bathroom, all rates include breakfast. This is a good place to stay – it's clean and well kept and since it's off the road it's fairly quiet. Meals at the YWCA are not only good but also excellent value

at Rs 30 per person. The *YWCA Rotunda Guest Rooms* (tel 23489) is at 7 Rotunda Gardens, Colombo 3 (Kollupitiya), off the Galle Rd just along from the Lanka Oberoi. They have doubles with bath at Rs 250 to 300, singles at Rs 90 and two five-bed dormitories at Rs 65 per person. All rates include breakfast.

Also fairly close to the centre at 15 Sea View Avenue, just off the Galle Rd in Colombo 3, the *Sea View Hotel* (tel 26516) certainly doesn't have a view of the sea but does have 23 rooms with doubles at Rs 275. Also in Colombo 3 at 265 Galle Rd the *Chinese Lotus Hotel* (see the Places to Eat section below) has large, spacious rooms with fan from around Rs 250. It's next to the Duty Free Shopping Centre.

Continue a little further along the Galle Rd to Bambalapitiya, where the *Ottery Inn* (tel 83727) at 29 Melbourne Avenue has eight rooms with singles/doubles at Rs 150/200 including breakfast. It's quiet and reasonably well kept. Melbourne Avenue is almost directly across the Galle Rd from Dickman's Rd. Down Dickman's Rd and to the right, the *Tourist Guest House* (tel 84005) at 8/1 Elibank Rd, has rooms from Rs 40 and 'apartments' for Rs 100.

In Dehiwala, almost out at the zoo, the *Star Inn* (tel 714030, 716999, 717523) has 22 rooms at Rs 150/175. It's at 73/22 Sri Saranankera Rd; to find it turn off at Canal Bank Rd or Hospital Rd, just after the Dehiwala Canal and a half km or so before the zoo turn-off.

Back towards the centre at 77 Rosemead Place in Colombo 7, the Cinnamon Gardens diplomatic quarter of the city, the *Wayfarer's Inn* (tel 93936) has rooms at Rs 250/325 or at Rs 350/425 with air-con. It has a pleasant garden and is located in a peaceful area of the city. A taxi into Fort from here will be about Rs 25.

There are a great number of private guest houses around Colombo, most of them with only one or two rooms. You can find more than 50 of them listed in the tourist office accommodation guide!

Places to Stay – top end

Colombo has a number of new top bracket hotels nearing completion including the 400 room *Taj Samudra* (tel 548633), due to open in 1984 at a site looking across the Galle Face Green. Also due to open in 1984 is the 493 room *Galadari Meridien Colombo Hotel* (tel 549874). It's right across the road from the Inter-Continental, up at the Fort end of the Galle Face Green. Rooms are expected to be in the US$70 to 90 range. The current 'big four' top end hotels are all clustered close to this central waterfront park area.

The *Ceylon Inter-Continental* (tel 21221), at 48 Janadhipathi Mawatha, is in Fort, looking along the Galle Face Green from its northern end. It has 250 rooms with prices from US$80/86 for singles/doubles. There's all the usual 'international standard' features like air-conditioning throughout, swimming pool, restaurants, night club and quite a good little bookshop.

Facing this relatively modern hotel from the other end of the Galle Face Green is a hotel from quite another era – the 1864 *Galle Face Hotel* (tel 28211). Now part of the Regent group the majestic old Galle Face was the superior establishment during the British colonial era and still has plenty of charm today. It also has antique and decrepit plumbing, the rooms on the Galle Rd side are noisy and during monsoon rains you'd better pick where you sit in the snack bar if you haven't brought an umbrella. Still if you like Raj-era hotels of the Raffles type (if I can afford it I certainly do!) you'll love the Galle Face. There are 87 rooms from $69 to 80 but the regular rooms are nothing special, if you're planning to fork out the big money to stay here splurge on the king-size rooms.

Just across the Galle Rd from the Galle Face Hotel is the *Lanka Oberoi* (tel 20001). The address is 77-83 Stewart Place but you can ignore that, it's on the Galle Rd in Colombo 3. The Oberoi has 600 rooms with singles/doubles at US$82/93. Externally the Oberoi is a rather unexciting looking cube, but internally it's a hollow atrium hotel with gigantic batik banners hanging from top to bottom of the airy lobby. Rooms are arranged in four levels looking out over the open space. Although the rooms are just modern hotel standard the Oberoi does have surprisingly good food. Breakfast here is a luxurious extravagance, well worth a treat trip. If you're staying across the road at the Galle Face it's a necessity since the breakfast there is dismal.

U-turn and head back towards Fort along the Galle Rd but turn right instead of left at the Galle Face Hotel and you'll find the *Holiday Inn* (tel 22001-9) at 30 Sir Mohamed Macan Markar Mawatha. There are 96 rooms here at US$52/60 but, like the prices, this is a step down from the top bracket hotels. All mod-cons but smaller and simpler.

Those are Colombo's current upper end hotels but others close to that bracket include the fine old *Hotel Taprobane* (tel 20391-3) at 2 York St, right in the middle of Fort and overlooking the harbour. It used to be known as the Grand Orient Hotel and is renowned for its high altitude Harbour Room restaurant with stunning views over the harbour activity. The 61 rooms cost Rs 625 for singles, Rs 750 to 850 for doubles.

Also right in the middle of Fort is the *Ceylinco Hotel* (tel 20431-2-3) at 69 Janadhipathi Mawatha. There are just 15 rooms here with prices from Rs 500 to 700.

A number of upper range hotels can be found strung out along, or close to, the Galle Rd. At 112 Galle Rd, Colombo 3 the *Hotel Ranmuthu* (tel 33986) has 54 rooms at Rs 925/1000 including all meals. Continuing down the Galle Rd the *Hotel Renuka* (tel 26901) at 328 Galle Rd, Colombo 3, has 43 rooms at Rs 882/921. Both of these hotels have swimming pools.

Just off the Galle Rd in Colombo 5 (Bambalapitiya) the *Havelock Tourinn* (tel 85251-3) is at 20 Dickman's Rd. Singles/doubles are Rs 650/750 including breakfast. It's air-con and there's a swimming pool.

In Colombo 6 (Wellawatta) the *Hotel Brighton* (tel 85211-3) is on Ramakrishna Rd, by the waterfront off the Galle Rd. It has 62 rooms with air-con singles/doubles at Rs 550/650 and it has a swimming pool. The Brighton is conveniently close to the Galle Rd yet pleasantly away from that busy thoroughfare's traffic noise and pollution. Also in Colombo 6 the *Hotel Sapphire* (tel 83306) is at 371 Galle Rd and has 40 rooms at Rs 550/650 – there's an additional charge for air-con here. The Sapphire is near a good stretch of beach.

Places to Eat

Around Fort Colombo has a better selection of restaurants than anywhere else in Sri Lanka and is also one of the better places for finding real Sri Lankan food. A Colombo favourite (mine and nearly everybody else's it would appear) is the genteel *Pagoda Tea Room* on Chatham St in Fort. It's a big, old fashioned, crowded place – definitely a mile away from your average run-of-the-mill Asian cheapie. White tablecloths (if they aren't at the wash) and hovering waiters are all part of the scene, but the food is of excellent quality and remarkably low in price. They have one of the best selection of short eats in Sri Lanka or for Rs 25 you could indulge yourself on fillet steak and vegetables. On hot days their Rs 4 lemon squash is knockout and so is their Rs 5 ice cream, but the Pagoda is mainly a lunchtime place as it shuts at 6 pm. Incidentally, rock music fans may have seen the Pagoda in a Duran Duran video film clip!

For a quick, cheap snack try the *Nectar Cafe* on the corner of York St and Mudalige Mawatha in Fort. It's a self-service cafe with very reasonably priced food and snacks. Their low priced ice cream is just one dish that packs in the

travellers. There are a number of very cheap places along Mudalige Mawatha offering vegetarian food, like south Indian thalis, for just a few rupees.

In this same central area *Cargill's* have good cold drinks and the *YMCA* on Bristol St has a cheap self-service cafeteria and is a good place for an early breakfast when most of Colombo is still asleep. Western-style fast food outlets are springing up around Fort – like *The Picnic* or *Gillo's*.

On the corner of Chatham St and Janadhipathi Mawatha the *Nanking Hotel* is a popular Chinese restaurant that has the commendable virtue of staying open late at night – well late night by early-to-bed Colombo standards anyway. The menu is Chinese standard (including delicious crab) and the prices are quite reasonable. At 70 Chatham St there is also the *Peony Restaurant*. On the north side of Upper Chatham St the *Taj Restaurant* is cheap and OK and seems to stay open later than most other restaurants around.

Out of Fort There are a number of other Chinese restaurants around Colombo including the *Hotel Nippon* at 123 Kumaran Ratnam Rd, Colombo 2 which does excellent Chinese food and also specialises in Japanese food. Ten to 15 minutes walk from the Nippon is the *Seafish*, behind the cinema on Kumaran Ratnam Rd. The seafood grill or Beach-comber Special is very good, as are desserts.

At 199 Union Place the *Fountain Cafe* is owned by Ceylon Cold Stores (bottlers of Elephant House soft drinks) and is something of a showcase. They do western and Sri Lankan meals from Rs 20 to 60 plus terrific ice cream and iced coffee. It's open 11 am to 11 pm daily plus there's a snack bar out back from 4.30 to 6.30 pm. Located midway between the Hotel Nippon and the YWCA this real find is cool, peaceful and surrounded by a garden.

Along the Galle Rd If you like the Pagoda then the *Green Cabin* at 453 Galle Rd, Colombo 3 will appeal just as much – because it's run by the same people. It's rather smaller than the Pagoda but the food is of equally high quality and you can also eat outside. Don't miss their excellent lamprai if it's available. The Green Cabin has one big advantage over the Pagoda in that it's open in the evenings.

Perera & Sons (Bakers) at 217 Galle Rd, Kollupitiya, Colombo 3, does cheap short eats but although there are a few chairs it's basically a take-away place. They have cold drinks and cakes too. The *Steak Bar*, on the Galle Rd in Colombo 3, is an air-con hamburger joint – good milkshakes but their hamburgers are not too exciting. Back up by the Galle Face Green the *Courtyard Restaurant* is in the Galle Face Courtyard, across from the Galle Face Hotel, and is a pretty reasonable sort of place.

There are also a number of Chinese restaurants along the Galle Rd. The *Chinese Lotus Hotel*, at 265 Galle Rd, Colombo 3, does good fresh crab; you can choose your crab in the kitchen. Opposite Dickman's Rd in Colombo 4, the *Chinese Dragon Hotel* at 231 Galle Rd has good, cheap food. The *Park View Lodge Restaurant*, at 70 Park St, Colombo 7, has good Chinese, western and Sri Lankan food.

Unfortunately the popular Greenlands Hotel was burnt out in the riots but you can get excellent Indian vegetarian food at *Dasaprakash* at 237 Galle Rd, Colombo 4, just before Dickman's Rd. It's a clean, modern place and the food, although not super-cheap, is excellent and their ice cream a real taste treat.

Top End Places If you want to move well up-market the big hotels all have restaurants and coffee bars. The *Harbour Room* on top of the Taprobane is well known for its superb view – indeed the view is a notch or two ahead of the food! The *Taprobane* also does a lunch time buffet but it seems to have gone down in the world – it costs Rs 70.

The food at the *Galle Face Hotel* is not all that exciting but morning coffee or afternoon tea is a splendid experience and the bar, although expensive, is a great place for a leisurely drink in superbly colonial surroundings. Across the Galle Rd the *Lanka Oberoi* does excellent food, especially there breakfast which is well worth the extravagance. If you're in Fort late in the evening when nothing seems to be open try the *Inter-Continental*, their Rs 50 lasagna is terrific.

On R A de Mel Mawatha (Duplication Rd) at the corner of Alfred Place, off the Galle Rd in Colombo 3, *Saras* does excellent, although rather pricey, Indian food. Count on Rs 200 and up for a good meal. It's air-con and specialises in Indian vegetarian food although they also do meat dishes including tandoori food. At 263 Duplication Rd the *Eastern Palace* has good, though not cheap, Chinese food.

The *Ceylinco Hotel* has the *Asa Kade* rooftop snack bar while local residents speak highly of the *Palmyrah* at the Hotel Renuka or *La Langousterie* for seafood, on the beach at Mt Lavinia.

Entertainment

Colombo is not the place to head for if you're after the excitement of Asia after dark – it's distinctly sleepy. Cinemas showing English language films are mainly along the Galle Rd. Western films tend to take quite a time to get to Sri Lanka and they're often not in great shape when they do – having been unreeled on the projection room floor a few times too many. Indian films and locally produced films in Sinhala are generally simple enough in their plot to make language comprehension unnecessary. And they're very cheap. The big hotels have night clubs or cultural shows such as Kandyan or low country devil dances most nights of the week.

There is quite an active Sinhala

language theatre, particularly at the Lumbini Theatre in Havelock Town and the Lionel Wendt Theatre at 18 Guildford Crescent, Colombo 7. The State Dance Ensemble puts on traditional and creative dances every Wednesday and Friday at 7 pm at the John de Silva Memorial Theatre, Ananda Cumaraswamy Mawatha, Colombo 7. Tickets are available at the door.

Getting There
Colombo is the gateway to Sri Lanka from abroad and also the centre of the bus and rail network. See the relevant regional sections for getting out of Colombo and around the country by bus or rail. The main railway station, Colombo Fort, is within easy walking distance of the city centre. If the station here is your first experience of a rail travel on the subcontinent beware of the porters who will grab your bags and then demand an extortionate fee if you're not careful. Either negotiate before you let go or carry them yourself.

The CTB bus station (tel 28081) is on Olcott Mawatha in the Pettah, just a short distance along the road from the railway station. Minibuses go from right in front of the railway station or from an open area beside the CTB stand. Go to the railway station stand for buses heading south. The main CTB services from Colombo are:

01 Kandy – almost round the clock, every 15 minutes during the day, express services every half hour.
02 Galle – almost round the clock, every 15 minutes during the day.
03 Ratnapura – every 15 minutes during the day.
03 Kataragama – once daily via Ratnapura.
04 Medawachchiya – twice daily via Putalam.
04 Anuradhapura – approximately 10 times daily.
05 Kurunegala – via Minuwangoda, during the day.
06 Kurunegala – via Warakapola, every 15 minutes during the day.

32 Matara – approximately 12 times daily.
32 Tissamaharama – via Galle, some continue to Kataragama, approximately eight times daily.

Getting Around
Train & Bus You can use the railway service for getting to the suburbs dotted along the Galle Rd – Bambalapitiya, Kollupitiya, Dehiwala and Mt Lavinia – although it would be much easier to take a bus. A bus route map is a wise investment if you're going to be doing much bus riding; they're readily available in Colombo. A timetable is not necessary, the buses can hardly be described as running to one. The CTB buses and the minibuses operate parallel services.

Use your elbows and keep a tight grip on your money and valuables, pickpockets are rife in Colombo public transport. They're particularly found on the crowded Galle Rd where they often work in pairs, one jostling you while the other robs you – often as you board the bus. Go to the police – you won't get your money back but they often jettison passports and tickets later. One Australian I met actually got her passport back from her embassy after the pickpockets had kindly (!) dropped it in a mailbox.

Taxis & Auto-rickshaws The Colombo taxis are still all old British Morris Minors They're all metered and, wonder of wonders, the meters work. And at a fairly stunning rate too! Auto-rickshaws, three-wheeler vehicles exactly like those in India, are somewhat cheaper. Flagfall is Rs 1.50 but the meters all seem to run faster than they should.

Colombo Airport
You can get to or from the airport by taxi, bus, minibus, airport bus or train. Sri Lanka's international airport is 35 km (22 miles) north of Colombo at Katunayake. It used to be named Bandaranaike International Airport but that name is definitely out of favour with the current government!

Taxi Taxis from the airport cost a standard Rs 250, you pay at a counter in the airport building and a taxi is then called for you. Going back to the airport you can use that price as a top end bargaining level.

Bus A 187 bus from the Central Bus Station departs for the airport every 20 minutes. The 45 minute journey costs Rs 5 but the CTB buses don't run beyond 9 or 10 pm. The minibus fare is the same.

Private minibuses to and from the airport are about the same price and run virtually 24 hours a day so there is now plenty of airport transport. From the airport simply walk straight out across the car park, veering slightly to the left and you'll see the bus stop. Ignore the touts who will intercept you on the way. Rs 15 may seem a lot less than the taxi or airport bus fare but it's three times what it should be! From Colombo you'll find the private buses along Chatham St all the way to the Pettah.

Airport Bus There is a bookable minibus service operating from outside the Taprobane Hotel to the airport and vice versa. This connects to all international flights and costs Rs 75 per passenger. Bookings can be made at the Taprobane Hotel or through travel agents. 'In the three times I've used it', reported a traveller, 'they have always been 30 to 45 minutes late'.

Train There is also a railway station right at the airport but the service is generally not too convenient – it's mainly used for airport workers going to and from work. Daily departures from Colombo Fort are at 5.10 and 5.26 am and at 3.20 pm. From the airport departures are at 7.56 and 8.30 am and 4.32 pm (or 5.57 pm?). The trip takes about 1½ to two hours and costs Rs 4.80 in 3rd class. The branch off to the airport is only about three km from the airport itself so at other times shoestring travellers could catch one of the regular Colombo-Negombo trains at that junction although these mainly operate before 10 am and after 5 pm. Train tickets must be purchased at the ticket counter in the airport building.

Negombo Transport Another route which some people use, particularly on departure from Sri Lanka, is not to go to or from Colombo at all but to Negombo, the beach resort/fishing village about 35 km north of the capital and only 13 km from the airport. See the Negombo section for details.

Airport Facilities After a bout of re-construction Colombo's Katunayake airport terminal is quite modern and efficient. At the airport there is a bank with facilities for changing money or re-exchanging your unspent rupees; a post office; a tea centre selling packaged tea; a tourist office counter; a railway reservations counter and, once you have cleared immigration on departure, duty free sales and a very expensive restaurant which only accepts foreign currency. If you feel like paying over a US dollar or nearly a pound sterling for a coke this is the place to go. If you need a last minute drink have it before immigration or buy it in the duty free shop!

A peculiarity of the airport is that you have to go through customs on departure as well as arrival, the check is fairly cursory, however.

Airport Accommodation There are a couple of hotels in the Free Trade Zone near the airport. *Hotel Goodwood Plaza* (tel 030-2561-3) is on Canada Friendship Rd and has 32 rooms priced from Rs 500. On the same road, and similarly equipped with a swimming pool, air-con, etc, the *Orient Pearl Hotel* (tel 030-2356, 2563) has 32 rooms from Rs 350/400. If you need to stay close to the airport at more economical rates you'll have to make the short trip to Negombo.

West Coast Beaches

The west coast is the major sea-and-sand tourist area of Sri Lanka and with very good reason. There can hardly be a strip of coastline anywhere in the world endowed with so many beautiful beaches. Round every bend you seem to come upon yet another inviting tropical vista – the appropriately beautiful palm trees, bending over the appropriately gold sands, lapped by the appropriately blue waves.

The accessible west coast region extends for about 270 km (170 miles) starting at Negombo (about 35 km north of Colombo) then running south of Colombo through Mount Lavinia, Beruwela, Bentota, Ambalangoda, Hikkaduwa, Galle, Weligama, Matara, Tangalla and Hambantota before finally turning inland towards the hill country. The road skirts around the Yala wildlife reserve before joining the coast again at Pottuvil near Arugam Bay, the southern end of the 'East Coast' beach strip. The west coast road also runs north of Negombo but this region is not of such great interest.

At present the bulk of Sri Lanka's beach resort development is concentrated on the west coast but beaches are not all the coast has to offer. You can visit the mask carvers at Ambalangoda, explore Sri Lanka's most historically interesting town (Galle) and find many other attractions. The coast is at its best from around November to April. In May the south-west monsoon means it is time to move across to the east coast. Although the main accommodation facilities are concentrated in a number of towns along the coast there are also many small guest houses and hotels scattered between the larger centres. Many of these quiet, secluded places are an ideal escape from the noise and hype of resorts like Hikkaduwa.

NEGOMBO

On our first trip to Sri Lanka, Negombo was our last stop and after the magnificent beaches of Hikkaduwa and Tangalla on the west coast or Passekudah and Nilaveli on the east, it was frankly a disappointment. Compared to those resorts Negombo's beach is not very attractive – but there's more to Negombo than a stretch of sand. It's picturesque and fascinating, both historically and in its everyday life. everyday life.

During the Dutch era this was one of their most important sources of cinnamon and there are still a number of reminders of the Dutch days. Close to the seafront you can see the ruins of the old Dutch fort with its fine gateway inscribed with the date 1672. There are several old Dutch buildings still in use, including the lagoon rest house (Negombo has two rest houses), plus the Dutch revealed their love of canals here, like nowhere else in Sri Lanka. The canals that run through Negombo extend south all the way to Colombo and north to Puttalam, a total distance of over 120 km. You can easily hire a bicycle in Negombo and ride along the canal-side path for some distance.

The Dutch did not find it too easy taking Negombo from the Portuguese, they first captured it in 1640, lost it again the same year, then captured it permanently in 1644; but the British took it from the Dutch in 1796 without a struggle. The people of Negombo, the *Karavas*, fisherfolk of Indian descent, remained totally unaffected by the colonial comings and goings. To this day they take their outrigger canoes, known as *oruvas*, out each day in search of the fish for which Negombo is famous. Fish auctions on the beach and fish sales in the market place are a common Negombo sight. The shark catch is brought in on the beach in the early afternoon. Nor is it all from the open sea, the Negombo lagoon is famous for its rich harvest of lobsters, crabs and (particularly) prawns. The fishing boats, sweeping into the lagoon after a fishing trip, are still a fine sight and Negombo also has a flourishing local boat building business.

The Negombo town centre is a bustling little place and all of Negombo is dotted with churches – so successfully were the Karavas converted to Catholicism that today the town is often known as 'little Rome'. The Fisherman's Festival is held here in late July. St Mary's Church in the town centre has very good ceiling paintings by a local artist. The island of Duwa, south of the lagoon and joined to Negombo by the lagoon bridge, is famed for its annual passion play which involves the whole village.

Small villages dot the coast to the north and south, you can easily reach them by bicycle. Just across the lagoon bridge there's a second fish market, a good place to visit in mid-afternoon or at sunset as the fishing boats return.

Negombo's European side also shows through – down by the lagoon mouth with its Dutch fort and cemetery and the magnificent banyan tree on the green, cricket matches are still a big attraction.

Places to Stay – bottom end

Almost all the places to stay in Negombo, top and bottom end, are stretched along the shoreline, starting about a km north of the town. There are several shoestring traveller places with rooms at under Rs 100. Lewis Place is the beach road and right at the start of this stretch, 2 Lewis Place, you'll find the *Negombo Guest House*, cheapest (and most basic) of the cheapies. The room dividers are just cane slats backed by a curtain and it's very plain and, from several reports, not as good as it once was. Singles/doubles are Rs 75/100.

If you take the other fork by the Negombo Guest House, then follow the road round to the right, you'll find yourself on Anderson Rd, which runs alongside the canal. *Dillwood* (tel 031-2810), at number 47, is one of the travellers' halt places and has seven well kept rooms, all with fans, and prices from Rs 75 for singles, Rs 125 to 175 for doubles. They also have beachfront places near the Bikini Beach Restaurant for Rs 200 to 250.

There is also the *Travellers' Halt* at 26 Perera Place – to get there continue about a km further along Lewis Place and turn right shortly before the big Brown's Beach Hotel. The Travellers' Halt is also friendly and well kept and has rooms with attached bathrooms and mosquito nets. Prices range from Rs 40 to Rs 75. A couple of other good guest houses close to the Negombo Guest House junction are the *Alpine Guest House*, just on the town side, and the *Sun Shine Guest House*, near the beach. At the latter doubles with bath, fan and mosquito net are Rs 65 to 125.

There are various small hotels along the beach strip in Negombo, interspersed between the more expensive places. The *Beach View Guest House*, next to the big Blue Oceanic Hotel on Lewis Place, has clean and pleasant rooms and very friendly staff. Doubles are Rs 200. Several travellers have recommended this place. A little south of the Beach View is the *Sea Sands Guest House* (tel 031-3154) which has very pleasant rooms with an outside verandah and similar prices. Don't confuse it with the similarly named Sea & Sands, much further south down Lewis Place. Also up at the northern end of the beach strip, and in this same price range, the *Windmill Beach Hotel* is clean, well run and reasonably priced and it has excellent food.

Scattered around Negombo there are also quite a few rooms in private houses – many of them have signs outside to advise you of their availability. Other smaller hotels and guest houses you could try include the *Ceylonica Guest House* (tel 031-2976) at 29 Lewis Place with 10 rooms at Rs 100/150. Opposite 74 Lewis Place is Carron Place where there are a couple of good places. The *Rainbow Guest House* (tel 031-2082) at 3 Carron Place has rooms at Rs 150/200. It's a friendly place with good food. At number 2 the smaller *Sea Drift Guest House* (tel 031-2601) is cheaper at Rs 125/150. The *Beach Bungalow* at 63A Lewis Place has been recommended by a couple of travellers. Away from Lewis Place the guest house at 96 St Mary's St, last street on the right before the lagoon bridge, has good food and rooms from Rs 40 and up. *Seaforth* at 31 Customs House Rd, near the Lagoon View Rest House, is another small guest house.

Also away from the beachfront hotel strip Negombo also has two rest houses – one close to the waterfront and one on the lagoon, rather closer to the town. The latter is the pleasant *Lagoon View Rest House*, by the lagoon bridge. Cost including all meals is Rs 250/350 for singles/doubles. The *Sea View Rest House* is Rs 220/250 room only and it also has more expensive air-con rooms.

Places to Stay – top end

In terms of number of hotels Negombo is the biggest beach resort in Sri Lanka although the hotels here are not as large as at some other 'European package resorts' in Sri Lanka. Biggest and best known of the bunch is *Browns Beach Hotel*. The hotels form an almost continuous strip along Lewis Place all the way to Ethukala, north of Negombo. Several of the big hotels have equipment and facilities for watersports – sailing, windsurfing and waterskiing.

There are a few places not on this beach strip. The two rest houses, see above, are not located there. Nor is the *Blue Lagoon Hotel*, which is north of the lagoon, about eight km from Negombo. If you cross the bridge over the lagoon you can continue along the small coast road beside the beach almost all the way into Colombo.

1 Morning Star Guest House
2 Sun & Sea Cottage
3 Sea Shells Hotel
4 Goldi Sands
5 Holz Loffel Restaurant
6 Blue Oceanic Beach Hotel
7 Oasis Beach Hotel
8 Jet Travels Hotel
9 Hotel Sea Garden
10 Beach View Tourist Guest House
11 Windmill Beach Hotel & Restaurant
12 Sea Side Restaurant
13 Restaurant Fish & Lobster
14 Sea Sands Tourist Guest House
15 Topaz Beach Hotel
16 4 Seasons Guest House
17 Dolphin Beach Guest House
18 Silva's Restaurant
19 Bikini Beach Restaurant
20 Sea Food Restaurant
21 Coconut Grove Restaurant
22 Samanalaya Tourist Guest House
23 Sea Fish Restaurant
24 Ocean Fish Restaurant
25 Green Cabin Restaurant
26 Santhi Guest House
27 Brown's Beach Hotel
28 Laksala
29 Goldi Steak Haus
30 Golden Beach Hotel
31 QK Beach Hotel
32 Sea View Restaurant
33 Melloins Restaurant

34 Restaurant Orient Grill
35 Paradise Restaurant
36 Sunflower Beach Hotel
37 Tharanga Restaurant
38 7 Hills Restaurant
39 Sunbeam Restaurant
40 Silvermine Guest House
41 Travellers' Halt
42 Silver Sands
43 Catamaran Gardens
44 Mandarin Restaurant
45 Starbeach & Dephani Guest Houses
46 Join Us Restaurant
47 Ocean View Guest House
48 Don's Beach Hotel
49 Galaxy Guest House
50 Sea Drift
51 Rainbow Guest House
52 Joy's Restaurant
53 Pamela Beach Guest House
54 Interline Beach Hotel
55 Beach Bungalows
56 Sea & Sands Guest House
57 Sea Queen Restaurant
58 Dilwood
59 Rino Inn
60 Ceylonica Guest House
61 Alpine Guest House
62 Milan Guest House
63 Silver Fawn Guest House
64 Negombo Guest House
65 Roman Garden Guest House
66 Fish Market
67 Sea View Rest House
68 Fort
69 Lagoon View Rest House
70 Coronation Restaurant

Negombo

Prices quoted below are generally room only but many of the hotels also have prices inclusive of meals. They include:

Aquarius Beach Hotel (tel 031-2120, 2448), 75 Lewis Place, 14 rooms, Rs 175. *Blue Lagoon Hotel* (tel 031-2380, 3004, 3005), Talahena, 64 rooms, singles/doubles Rs 350/375. *Blue Oceanic Hotel* (tel 031-2377, 2642), Ethukala, 70 rooms, singles/doubles Rs 650/700, air-con additional Rs 100.
Browns Beach Hotel (tel 031-2031, 2032, 2076, 2077), 175 Lewis Place, 133 rooms plus 10 bungalows, Rs 750.
Catamaran Beach Hotel (tel 031-2342, 2206), 89 Lewis Place, 46 rooms, Rs 350.
Dons Beach Hotel (tel 031-2120, 2448), 75 Lewis Place, 60 rooms, Rs 300. *Dons Palm Beach Hotel* (tel 031-2113, 2632), 159 Lewis Place, 50 rooms, Rs 350.
Golden Beach Hotel (tel 031-2113, 2632), 161 Lewis Place, 50 rooms, Rs 150 to 200.
Goldi Sands Hotel (tel 031-2021, 2348), Ethukala, 64 rooms, singles/doubles Rs 550/600.
Interline Beach Hotel (tel 031-2350), 65/3 Seneviratna Mawatha, off Lewis Place, 32 rooms, Rs 500.
Ranweli Holiday Village (tel 031-2136), Waikkal, Kochchikade, 84 rooms, singles Rs 400-600, doubles Rs 450-650.
Sea Gardens Hotel (tel 031-2150), Ethukala, 15 rooms, Rs 300.
Seashells Hotel (tel 031-2062), Palangaturai St, Kochchikade, 72 rooms, singles/doubles Rs 550/600.
Silver Sands Beach Hotel (tel 031-2402), 95 Lewis Place, 18 rooms, singles/doubles Rs 125/150.
Sunflower Beach Hotel (tel 031-2042, 2841), 143 Lewis Place, 66 rooms, singles/doubles Rs 300/350.
Thilanka Beach Hotel (tel 031-22821, 22833), Dungalpitiya St, 75 rooms, singles/doubles Rs 175/225.

Finally, and not in Negombo at all, but nor is it in Colombo so I might as well put it here, there is the *Pegasus Reef Hotel* (tel 070-205, 209) at Santha Maria Mawatha, Hendala, Wattala. This is between the airport and the capital, 29 km from the airport, 11 km from the city. It's on the beach, there are 144 rooms and you can start thinking from about US$60 for a double. Although it is normally reached by turning off the airport-Colombo road you can also get there by the narrow coastal road from Negombo.

Places to Eat

There are now quite a number of restaurants, including several seafood specialists, along Lewis Place. Other seafood specialists include the *Sea Food Restaurant*, the *Sea Fish*, the *Ocean Fish* and the *Green Cabin*; all opposite Brown's Beach Hotel.

Further north along Lewis Place at Ethukala, the *Windmill Hotel's* restaurant has great food including an all-you-can eat smorgasbord. By the Windmill Hotel is the *Sea Side Restaurant* which does excellent fried noodles and prawns.

On Lewis Place by Carron Place is *Joy's Restaurant* with good and reasonably priced food (rice and curry for Rs 22), pleasant surroundings and friendly service; don't miss their delicious fruit cocktail. The *Seven Hills Restaurant* at 142 Lewis Place is also pretty good although you have to check their addition on the bill. A little further north and on the beach side the *Tharanga Restaurant* is another place with good Sri Lankan food. The *Reef Valley*, opposite the Catamaran Beach Hotel, is quiet and the food OK.

In town you'll find quite a selection of the standard rice and curry places plus the *Coronation Hotel* which offers various rice dishes, excellent short eats and lots of baked goodies. And 'the cheapest arrack on the whole island'! Down an alley opposite the Coronation is *John's Hotel* where you can get an excellent and cheap rice and curry.

Getting There

One of Negombo's most useful roles is as a transit point for getting to the airport since transport is much cheaper between the airport and Negombo than to Colombo. A minibus to the airport costs Rs 2.50. A taxi will cost about Rs 80 from the bus stand, Rs 125 from the middle of the hotel strip. See the Colombo section for more details on airport transport.

You've got a choice of bus or train to make the 35 km trip from Colombo. Minibuses cost Rs 4.50. Buses from Colombo to Negombo stop at 9.30 pm on Sunday night. By train it costs Rs 5.50 in 3rd, Rs 12.50, but the trains are much slower than the buses.

Getting Around
If you want to have a look around Negombo, particularly the ride along the canal bank, then hire a bicycle from places on Lewis Place. The bicycles here are in quite good condition. A taxi from Lewis Place to the minibus station should be around Rs 25; you'll have to pay more from the hotels.

MT LAVINIA
Only 11 km from the centre of Colombo, Mt Lavinia is the closest beach resort to the capital but beware of the sometimes severe undertow. On weekends it can get very crowded. It can be a convenient place to stay when in Colombo although nearby Dehiwala is better for low-budget accommodation. Apart from the beach and associated activity, Mt Lavinia's main attraction is the magnificent Mount Lavinia Hotel, which at one time was the ostentatious residence of the British governor. There's a free cultural show here almost every night – Kandy dancers and the like.

Places to Stay – bottom end
There are an enormous number of private rooms and guest houses at Mr Lavinia although it is not a particularly good place for very cheap accommodation. You can find a number of them listed in the Ceylon Tourist Board Accommodation Guide. They're particularly found along the Galle Rd, Sri Dharmapala Rd and De Saram Rd.

Recommendations have been made for Joe Silvas at 27C De Saram Rd with bed

and breakfast available at Rs 100. Mrs A H Seelladasa at 10/3 Lillian Avenue, near the Mt Lavinia Hotel, is clean, friendly and very well kept. Three immaculate rooms at Rs 150 for bed and breakfast. At 26/2 Sri Dharmapala Rd the Thilanka Beach Bungalows (tel 712090) have five cabanas with attached bathroom at Rs 100. A B Ratnayake (tel 717394) at 24/1 Huludagoba Rd has a nice double for Rs 150 but it's hard to find.

You can get good food at reasonable prices in the Mount Grill on the Galle Rd.

Places to Stay – top end
The magnificently colonial Mt Lavinia Hotel (tel 715221-9) is by the waterfront and very close to the Mt Lavinia railway station. It has 275 rooms, all with air-con and prices from Rs 650 to 950 for singles, Rs 800 to 1150 for doubles. Their weekly evening buffet is terrific value.

Other places include the 50 room Palm Beach (tel 717484, 712771-3) at 52 De Saram Rd, where singles/doubles are Rs 600/700. Also on De Saram Rd the Ranveli Beach Resort (tel 717385) at 56/9 has 28 rooms at Rs 250/300. At 50/2 the Rivi Ras Hotel (tel 717786, 717731) has 50 rooms from Rs 375. The Sea Breeze Tour Inn (tel 714017-8) has 23 rooms with singles/doubles at Rs 225/250 including breakfast.

Tilly's Beach Hotel (tel 713531-3) at 20 De Soysa Avenue has 69 rooms at Rs 550/600. The Mount Royal Hotel (tel 713030, 714001, 714003) at 36 College Avenue has 60 rooms from Rs 550. There are a number of smaller hotels and guest houses in Mt Lavinia. They include:

Estoril Beach Resort (tel 715494), 5/2 Lillian Avenue, 25 rooms singles/doubles Rs 150/175.
Lavinia Beach Inn (tel 714028), 8 rooms, singles/doubles Rs 125/150.
Marina Nivasa (tel 717337), 30 Sri Dharmapala Rd, 15 rooms, singles/doubles Rs 250/275 including breakfast.

Mt Lavinia Holiday Inn (tel 717187, 712681), 17 De Saram Rd, 7 rooms, singles/doubles Rs 200/225.

Ocean View Tour Inn (tel 717200), 34/4 De Saram Rd, 23 rooms, Rs 100 to 175.

KALUTARA

Immediately south of the Kalu Ganga Bridge, and on the coast side of the road, is the Gangatilaka Vihara which has a hollow dagoba with an interesting painted interior. By the roadside there's a small shrine and bo tree where drivers often stop to make offerings to ensure a safe journey.

Kalutara, which is 43 km south of Colombo, was once an important spice trading centre; controlled at various times by the Portuguese, Dutch and British. Today it has a reputation for its fine basketware (visit Basket Hall) and for growing the best mangosteens in the island.

Places to Stay

The *Hotel Merivierre* (tel 042-2339, 2536-7) on St Sebastian Rd, has 105 rooms, some of them air-con, with prices from Rs 650 and up. *Hotel Mermaid* (tel 042-2613, 2663) has 51 rooms from Rs 220/250. *Sunset Cabanas* (tel 042-2522-4) are at Pothupitiya, Wadduwa with 25 rooms from Rs 225. At 62/9 Sri Sumangala in Kalutara North the *Garden Beach Hotel* (tel 042-2380) has rooms from Rs 150, extra for air-con.

BERUWELA

Close to the coast 58 km (36 miles) south of Colombo the first recorded Moslem settlement on the island took place here in 1024 AD. The Kechimalai Mosque is situated on a headland just after the coastal road forks off from the main road through the town. The mosque is said to be built on the site of the first Moslem landing and is the focus for a major festival at the conclusion of the fast of Ramadan.

Places to Stay

There is nothing really to attract the independent traveller at Beruwela, it's mainly for package tourists. There is a *Rest House* situated on the coastal road a short distance after it forks from the main road at the Colombo end of town. It doesn't enjoy the usual rest house advantages of a beautiful situation nor is it any way a very special place to stay – but it is rather expensive.

A little further south you come to the complex of new tourist hotels. They are all very much aimed at the package tourists who come to Sri Lanka from chilly Europe for the sun, sea and sand. The *Barberyn Reef* consists of a whole series of individual little cottages/cabanas in a variety of styles but the other hotels are rather more architecturally conventional. Bed and breakfast prices in these hotels are generally in the US$40 to 70 bracket but the vast majority of the guests here will be on all-inclusive packages. The Beruwela hotels are:

Barberyn Reef (tel 048-5220, 5582), 84 rooms (14 with air-con), singles/doubles Rs 500/600.

Beach Hotel Bayroo (tel 048-5297), Moragalla, 65 rooms (some air-con), Rs 800, additional cost for air-con.

Confifi Beach Hotel (tel 048-5217, 5317), Moragalla, 68 rooms, from Rs 1000, additional cost for air-con.

Neptune Hotel (tel 048-5218, 5219, 5301), Moragalla, 104 rooms, all air-con, singles Rs 600 to 1000, doubles Rs 800 to 1300.

Palm Garden Hotel (tel 048-5263), Galle Rd, 126 rooms, all air-con, singles/doubles Rs 1100/1350.

Pearl Beach Hotel (tel 048-5117, 5118), 40 rooms, Rs 250.

Riviera Beach Resort (tel 048-5245), Moragalla, 48 rooms, singles/doubles Rs 200/250.

Hotel Swanee (tel 048-5208, 5209, 5213), Moragalla, 52 rooms, Rs 300 to 400. *Wornels Reef Hotel* (tel 048 5430, 5431), Moragalla, 105 rooms, Rs 350.

Beruwela also has a few smaller guest houses like the *Berlin Bear* (tel 048-5525)

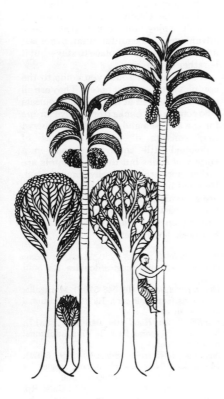

at Maradana with rooms at Rs 175/225. Or the *Dinara Guest House* (tel 048-5466) at 269 Galle Rd with rooms at Rs 125/175.

Getting There
See the Bentota section below for information on getting to Beruwela.

BENTOTA
Beruwela and Bentota are so close they almost run together; between the two you pass through Alutgama which serves as the main railway station for both centres and also has a raucous fish market. The Bentota River divides Alutgama from the Bentota tourist complex and a few km inland, on the south bank of the river, is the old Galpota Temple, said to date from the 12th century.

Bentota village itself is a little inland from the coast – the Bentota which overseas visitors experience is a totally new construction built solely as a place to attract tourists. The 'Bentota National Holiday Resort' consists of four major hotels plus its own small shopping complex, bank, police station and even its own modern little railway station – where not all the trains bother to stop. Naturally other shops and facilities, including a few cheap places to stay, have also sprung up around the main complex. Bentota enjoys a double attraction for tourists – on the coastline they've got a fine beach while the Bentota River curves inland behind the coast and offers calm water for sailing, windsurfing and water skiing. Non-residents can use the pool at the Bentota Beach Hotel for Rs 15.

West coast
A Inside the Fort, Galle
B Dutch-built canal in Negombo
C Lighthouse-clock tower in Colombo fort

Places to Stay – bottom end

Outside the resort complex there are some cheaper places such as *Palm Beach* while the area south of the resort, close to the beach, was a popular area for campers in the days when hordes of VW Kombis used to be driven overland. Closer to the Bentota railway station is the *Susanta Guest House* while about 100 metres down the main road towards Ambalangoda and Hikkaduwa is the *Thewalauwa Guest House*, a very fine old building. On the south edge of town the *Silkoga Inn* is a friendly and moderately priced place not too far from the beach. You'll find some guest houses in Alutgama too.

Induruwa is a quiet fishing village eight km south of Bentota. At the *Ripples Tourist Inn* there are eight rooms in what was once a private villa. The manager is an excellent fish chef who worked for the Australian High Commission for many years. Travellers report that the food is 'astoundingly good' and the place is 'a real find'. Doubles are Rs 100 with bath. There's a secluded, palm-fringed beach, toddy tappers and a small fishing colony. The *Venus Tourist Beach Hotel* is also in Induruwa.

Places to Stay – top end

Although there are some cheaper places to stay here the emphasis is, like Beruwela, very much on the package tour visitors. Independent travellers will generally keep on heading south towards Hikkaduwa. The big hotels here are part of the National Holiday Resort complex.

The top hotel, and one of the biggest beach hotels in Sri Lanka, is the 135 room *Bentota Beach Hotel* complete with everything from air-conditioning, a swim-ming pool and discotheque to a full-sized elephant for the amusement and edification of guests – and a half-size baby one. The resort is built on the site of an old Dutch fort and is modelled after the star fort pattern. Other hotels include the *Serendib Hotel*. The *Lihiniya Surf Hotel* is to the north of the complex as is the *Hotel Ceysands* at the end of the peninsula bounded by the ocean and the Bentota River. There is also a small, two-room *Holiday Cottage* in the resort complex.

Bentota Beach Hotel (tel 048-5266, 5177), 135 rooms, all air-con, singles/doubles Rs 1100/1200.
Hotel Ceysands (tel 048-5073), 84 rooms, all air-con, singles/doubles Rs 800/900. *Kosgoda Beach Resort* 150 rooms, all air-con, singles/doubles Rs 1000/1100.
Lihiniya Surf Hotel (tel 048-5126), 92 rooms, all air-con, singles/doubles Rs 950/1150.
Hotel Serendib (tel 048-5353, 5248, 5313), 90 rooms, singles/doubles Rs 1000/1400 including all meals.

Places to Eat

In the Bentota resort shopping centre, close to the main road, the *Tharanga Hopper Bar* offers a variety of snacks at very reasonable prices – considering the sort of resort it's attached to. The *Goldi Steak House* is also in the resort centre.

Getting There

Beruwela and Bentota are both on the main road and rail route south from Colombo through Galle but Alutgama, the small town sandwiched between the two resort areas, is the main bus and rail terminus. Alutgama is a rail terminus for trains heading south or north – at certain times of the day if you are coming north

A   Unawatuna Bay
B   Kustaraja figure at Weligama
C   Weligama Bay & Taprobane Island

from Hikkaduwa towards Colombo you will have to change trains at Alutgama. Bentota's small railway station is not a stopping point for all express trains.

It's a 1½ to two hour train trip from Colombo Fort to Bentota, cost is Rs 8 in 3rd, 19.60 in 2nd. From Bentota to Hikkaduwa takes an hour on the express but note that this route tends to be quite crowded on the trains. CTB buses and minibuses run through Bentota, any bus going to or from Galle will get you there.

AMBALANGODA

South from Bentota the road and railway run close to the continuously beautiful coast. There are a handful of guest houses and small hotels dotted along this stretch should the urge to stop become overpowering. Ambalangoda is a fair size, but sleepy little town, considerably overshadowed by its more glamorous neighbour Hikkaduwa, 13 km (eight miles) further south. Despite which it is a very pleasant stop as Ambalangoda has a beautiful sweep of sandy beach to the north of the town centre, an interesting little rocky islet surrounded by coral, straight off from the town centre and the (as usual) beautifully sited Rest House.

Ambalangoda is most famous for its mask carvers and you will find them concentrated on the northern edge of town, around the point where the road doglegs in from the coast. From the bus or railway station you have got a couple of hundred metres walk back up the road. See the Things to Buy section for more information on masks and mask carving.

Good mask carvers in Ambalangoda include M H Mettananda at 142 Patabendimulla Rd (the main road), not far from the centre. I bought a mask here when researching the first edition of this book and was pleased to find, on subsequent trips, his masks were even better. Right on the corner, a little further on, is the house and shop of the famous mask carver Ariyapala. About 50 metres further towards Colombo is his son's (also

Ariyapala) place. Hand-woven cotton is another Ambalangoda craft.

Only a couple of rupees from Ambalangoda by bus the Karandenir Temple has a huge, painted reclining Buddha but the building is in a state of near collapse. It overlooks jungle and rice paddies.

Places to Stay

Right by the seashore the *Rest House* (tel 097-299) has nine rooms and costs Rs 250/275 for singles/doubles. Meals are also available and one traveller wrote that the hoppers here were particularly good. As usual the rest house has nabbed the best location in town, with its own little rock-protected bathing pool right in front and beautiful views to the north and south. Unfortunately, according to some reports, the Rest House is not as well kept as it should be.

The *Blue Horizon Tour Inn* (tel 097-475) is at 129 High Beach Rd, right next to the Rest House, and singles/doubles are Rs 125/175. It's a friendly, family run place with excellent food.

There are a couple of other hotel-style places and a couple of guest houses in Ambalangoda – plus the usual mob of terrible touts. At 738-740 Galle Rd the *Randomba Inn* (tel 097-406) has singles at Rs 90, doubles at Rs 100-200. In Randomba the *Lalanika Beach Hotel* (tel 097-366) has rooms from Rs 60 to 150.

Brooklyn (tel 097-359) on New Galle Rd is a guest house with a very well kept garden and singles/doubles at Rs 125/180. *Shangrela Beach Inn* (tel 097-342) on Sea Beach Rd is another popular guest house with singles/doubles at Rs 125/175, but it is not as good value as the rest house. *Darshana*, at 14/1 Sea Beach Rd, has been recommended as cheap, clean and friendly. It's right on the beach, north of the town centre, and has rooms at Rs 50 plus good food. The *Maliya Guest House* at 7 Vilegudia Rd is also said to be good as is the *Sea View* at 14 Hirewatha which has good food and arranges trips out to the coral islands.

Places to Stay – Near Ambalangoda

There are places to stay along the coast both to the north of Ambalangoda and to the south, between Ambalangoda and Hikkaduwa. North at Ahungalla the *Luxury Tourist Guest House* is opposite the 48 milestone, near the big Triton Hotel. The *Triton Hotel* (tel 097-218, 228) has 125 rooms starting at Rs 1600 for a bed and breakfast single.

The *Sirini Guest House* in Akurala is 11 km north of Hikkaduwa and is quiet, peaceful and has a good beach. There are several other places in Akurala including the *Beauty Coral Hotel*, which is very pleasant and close to the beach. They have snorkelling gear, a boat and bicycles at this very friendly place.

At Kahawa, just six km from Hikkaduwa, the quiet *Sun Island Village* has cabanas for Rs 125 and excellent food. At Watugedera, five km from Ambalangoda, the *Greenlands Tourist Home* on Kohilawagaura has doubles at Rs 50. Get there on a 390 or 394 bus for Erawawila Junction, getting off at the Watugedera post office.

Getting There

Ambalangoda is only a couple of rupees from Hikkaduwa by bus.

HIKKADUWA

Situated 98 km (61 miles) south of Colombo, Hikkaduwa is the most varied and probably the most popular of the beach centres. It's the variety that attracts people – there are a handful of 'international standard' hotels and literally dozens of smaller guest houses and hostels backed up by an equally varied selection of restaurants, snack bars and cafes. Plus there's an equally varied choice of beach and sea. Hikkaduwa is famed for its 'coral sanctuary', a large shallow area enclosed by a reef, carpeted with multicoloured corals, populated by countless colourful tropical fish. Yet only a short distance south of the centre the reef fades out, the beach widens and

you've got a sandy-bottomed surfing beach with good waves for board surfing (the Aussie surfing freaks are here en masse) or just body surfing.

The coral sanctuary is just that – a sanctuary for fish where no fishing or spear fishing is allowed. It starts with a very shallow and calm area right in front of the 'Coral' hotels – it's really too shallow for anything but the most lethargic dabbling around. Further over by the Coral Gardens Hotel a deeper reef runs straight out from the shore to the Rocky Islands Sanctuary, a conglomeration of tiny islets surrounded by beautiful coral formations. It's an easy swim out to the islands, a couple of hundred metres from the shore. The water over the reef is never more than three or four metres deep and the fish are as varied as you could ask for. Large turtles also circulate around the reef, I once came across one which must have been three metres long. They lazily glide away from you if you try to pursue them.

If you've not got your own mask, snorkel and fins there are plenty of places which will hire them out to you – around Rs 35 for a set for the day. You can also hire scuba equipment, arrange lessons, organise diving guides and charter boats to get out to wrecks in the area. Or you can simply hire a glass bottom boat for around Rs 75 to 100 for a half hour (the whole boat) or an outrigger canoe with a glass viewing box for rather less – say Rs 60 to 75 for an hour.

On the other (southern) side of the Coral Gardens Hotel the reef ends and the long sweep of surfing beach starts. Several of the places along here hire out surf boards and windsurfing equipment (Rs 100 an hour with a little bargaining). There's usually a good break off the reef further out. Another couple of hundred metres south there's a sandy area good for body surfing. The beach here is wider, better for sun bathing than in front of the coral sanctuary. Take care at Hikkaduwa though, the currents can be tricky and

Railway Station

98 kms.

Hikkaduwa

25

99 kms.

1 Commercial Bank of
   Ceylon
2 People's Bank
3 Dolphin Restaurant
   & Hotel
4 Tony's Cool Place
5 Bank of Ceylon
6 Market
7 Bus Stand
8 Petrol Station
9 Post Office
10 Sandamali Cream House
11 Saradaj Cafe
12 The Lobster
13 Parrot's Paradise Restaurant
14 Chinese Dragon Rest-
   aurant
15 Beach Kabin & Restaurant
16 Nanking Restaurant
17 Hikkaduwa Beach Hotel
18 Poseidon Diving
   Adventures
19 Lovely Guest House
20 Police Station
21 Rainbow Beer Garden &
   Co-Op Restaurant
22 School
23 Dharshana Guest House
24 Hotel Sundek
25 Pink House Travellers Halt
26 Starfish Restaurant
27 Hotel Coral Sands
28 Hotel Blue Corals
29 Hotel Coral Reef
30 Restaurant Seashells
31 Hotel Seashells
32 Hotel Sun Sea Sand
33 Hotel Coral Reef Beach
34 Restaurant Das Abbas

35 White House Tourist
   Rest
36 Greenlyn Cottage
37 Sirimedura Tourist Nest
38 Vithana Guest House
39 Ganymed Restaurant
40 Coral Front Inn
41 Coral Centre Tourist Inn
42 Mama's Hotel & Rest-
   aurant
43 Siri Holiday Home
44 Coral Rock Hotel
45 Coral Seas Beach Resort
46 Silver Sands Inn
47 Coral View Hotel
48 Hotel Sea View
49 Swiss Hotel & Skandia
   Restaurant
50 Pizza House
51 George Guest House
52 Coral Rock Hotel
53 Tourist Library
54 Jewel Garden Guest
   House
55 Reef Coolspot
56 Rising Sun Guest House
57 Coral Gardens Hotel
58 Buddhist Monastery
59 Walkinn Guest House
60 Curry Bowl Restaurant
61 Wijitha Tourist Inn
62 Ozone

63 Lotus Guest House
64 Farm House Restaurant
65 Udula Restaurant
66 Udula Guest House
67 Hotel Wewela Beach
68 JLH Beach Restaurant
69 Hotel Lanka Supercoral
70 Hotel Reefcomber
71 Hotel Paradiso
72 New Dragon Restaurant
73 Saman Tourist Guest
   House
74 Sydney Tourist Restaurant
75 Shyan's Living Kitchen
76 Sandagiri Cream House
77 Holiday Inn
78 Rendezvous
79 Francis Hotel & Restaurant
80 Rangith's Snacks
81 Hotel Summer Breeze
82 Beauty Spot Restaurant
83 Blue Fox Cool House
84 Surfer's Rest Guest
   House
85 Richard & Son's Beach
   Inn

kerosene. Occasionally an elephant even lumbers lazily by. Plus, unfortunately, there's a fair amount of heavy traffic streaming through at far too fast a pace – any western cop with a radar speed trap would have a field day in Hikkaduwa, I've seen a TV commercial in Sri Lanka indicating that the local police are getting them! One thing the local cops have been getting into though is dope raids. Take care.

Just up the road from the post office there are no life saving facilities. There have been a few drownings here.

Of course life at Hikkaduwa isn't only sea and sand – although it may often feel that way. There are countless shops selling everything Sri Lanka has to offer – masks, gems, jewellery, batik, antiques. Plus clothes shops making all the usual travellers' gear – skirts, light cotton trousers, caftans and so on. Hikkaduwa's really just one long road, hardly a town at all, and there's always something happening along it. Ox-carts rumble by carrying wood, coconuts or tanks of there's an interesting Buddhist temple with lots of the locally popular 'comic book' paintings. One man has been working on it for seven years and is nearly finished. There are also a couple of beautiful peacocks here. Several other temples and monasteries are within easy bicycling reach of Hikkaduwa.

Information

If you're just passing the time you can borrow books from the 'Tourist Library'

Continued Next Page

86 Big Budde's
87 Lion's Paradise Guest House
88 Juppiter Restaurant
89 Blue Note Cabanas
90 Villa Paradise
91 Tandem Guest House
92 Migavilla – Homely Guest House
93 Dewa Siri Cafe
94 Surfing Beach Guest House & Restaurant
95 Wekunagoda Guest House
96 Catamaran Curry Centre
97 Casalanka
98 Robin's Nest
99 Ranjith's Beach Hut
100 Brother's Spot
101 Hansa Surf Guest House

102 Golden Sands Beach Hotel
103 Aeybbekay Guest House & Restaurant
104 Surfing Beach Snacks
105 Lakmal Hotel
106 Lak Ajantha Guest House
107 Stilt Fishing Beach Restaurant
108 Living Lobster Restaurant
109 Bobby Restaurant
110 Third World Restaurant
111 Munchee Restaurant
112 Funki Corner Restaurant
113 Silta's Restaurant

114 Brother's Spot
115 Rita's Guest House
116 Seethani Guest House
117 Sea Lion Guest House
118 Paradise Guest House
119 Sea Flower Guest House
120 Copa Cabana Restaurant
121 Milkiway Restaurant
122 Misty Restaurant
123 Cassiopeia Guest House & Restaurant

(see the map) where a local watchmaker lends out paperbacks. You have to leave a refundable Rs 15 deposit but one writer suggested it would be a 'nice idea to donate your deposit'. Hikkaduwa used to be a terrible place to change money – there was only one bank and the crowds and queues were always bad but there are now several banks. Only post mail in Hikkaduwa at the post office, it's likely to disappear from mailboxes.

There are all sorts of shops in Hikkaduwa including many places selling clothes at very low prices and often of quite reasonable quality. Opposite the big Coral Sands Hotel there's a new shopping arcade where you can get good leather bags.

Hikkaduwa can be surprisingly pleasant during the monsoon. Prices drop, the crowds disappear, the weather is often OK and within the reef, swimming is still possible. Unhappily, however, Hikkaduwa has in recent years become a less pleasant place to stay at any time of the year. It's another case (like Kuta Beach in Bali) of pure over-development. There are simply too many places crammed in too close together without any planning or thought at all. The shoulder to shoulder group of more expensive 'Coral' places are a pure eyesore. Even worse this development is eroding the beach and the locals have been tearing up the coral at a terrible rate in order to burn it to make lime for building construction.

Although it is all spoken of as Hikkaduwa the tourist development here has spread far beyond the boundaries of the village. Moving south towards Galle you'll find places to stay and eat through Narigama, Tiranagama and Dodanduwa.

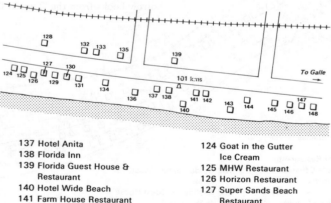

137 Hotel Anita
138 Florida Inn
139 Florida Guest House & Restaurant
140 Hotel Wide Beach
141 Farm House Restaurant
142 Tiranagama Beach Hotel
143 Little Lion Restaurant & Guest House
144 Dinky Gardens Cabana
145 Champa Restaurant
146 Sub Post Office
147 Star Restaurant & Guest House
148 Pearl Island Beach Hotel

124 Goat in the Gutter Ice Cream
125 MHW Restaurant
126 Horizon Restaurant
127 Super Sands Beach Restaurant
128 Cabana Gardens
129 Seeluft Restaurant
130 Hotel Harmony
131 Rainbow Restaurant
132 Priyanee Restaurant & Guest House
133 Gilbert's Restaurant
134 Sunil's Beach Hotel
135 Sunbeam Restaurant
136 Ranmal Restaurant & Travellers Halt

Places to Stay – bottom end

Virtually all Hikkaduwa's places to stay are strung out along the main road. It's certainly not the cheapest place to hang out in Sri Lanka, particularly at the height of the season, but there are plenty of places and a wide variety of costs and standards. You're bound to find something to suit although the best way to find it is probably simply to stroll down the road and look at a variety of rooms. In season you can find rooms for as little as Rs 50, although they tend to be rather basic. When you add on mosquito nets, fans, bathrooms, a bit of extra space, a verandah area outside with some shade, and so on, the prices soon start to climb. Plus prices are very dependent on demand – a Rs 70 room can soon become a Rs 150 room when it's the last one left. In the off season prices tumble and you can stay in Rs 500 places for only Rs 100; cheaper places don't tend to drop in price quite so dramatically.

In the past couple of years the already over-crowded scene at Hikkaduwa has become even more so. The tightly packed area of the strip now extends another km or two down the road towards Galle while in the centre of the strip dozens more places have been squeezed into the gaps between already existent places. Starting from the railway station/bus halt/banks/post office end of the town the places that follow are just a sampling of the wide choice along the strip. If mosquitoes are in season you may find fewer of them on the beach side of the road.

On the beach side the more expensive *Poseidon Diving Adventures* (tel 09-3294) is at the top end of the guest house price scale. Across the road and back over the railway tracks the *Lovely Guest House* has pleasant doubles with fans and bathrooms, but again at the top of the guest house scale. Back on the sea side of the road, and still in the more expensive category, the *Dharshana Guest House* has had a number of good reports from travellers.

Prices rapidly start to drop with the *Pink House*, back over the railway tracks. This very popular travellers' centre is a good place for a long stay. Up the road opposite the big Coral Reef Hotel is the *White House*, a friendly and well run place with a beautiful garden and similarly low prices. Two other popular cheapies are side by side a little further down – the *Hotel Seashells* and the *Sun Sea Sand Hotel*. Both have pleasant verandahs and are at the upper end of the cheap scale with rooms in the Rs 100 to 150 bracket. The *Coral Front Inn*, still on the railway side of the road, has a variety of rooms, the better ones open out onto the verandah and garden.

At the *Coral View Hotel* rather bare doubles are Rs 125. There are a series of places back around the creek. The *Rising Sun Guest House* is pretty good value and well away from the noise of the road – but right by the noise of the railway! Comfortable doubles with bathroom and mosquito net, looking out onto a cool, shady verandah, cost Rs 100 at the *Udula Guest House*. Across the road and right on the beach the *Lotus Guest House* has nice rooms but again more expensive – Rs 250 for a bed and breakfast double.

Prices go down as you move further along the beach. At places like the *Surfers' Rest Guest House* rooms are as cheap as you'll find them. *Hotel Francis* is a notch up market from these places with doubles around Rs 150. The relatively new *Blue Note Cabanas* are pleasant at Rs 150. The *Homeley Guest House* is a fine looking old building run by a very friendly lady. Rooms cost from Rs 70 for doubles and it's lovely inside and has lots of space and pleasant gardens. Then there's the *Wekunagoda Guest House* with rooms from Rs 50, the *Lakmal Hotel*, where doubles cost Rs 150 with their own bathroom, and quite a few others further along the road.

In fact these days you'll find places to stay almost all the way to Galle including a number of good places in Dodanduwa, four km south of Hikkaduwa. They include the friendly *Anoma Guest House* and the *Kusum Tourist Inn*.

Apart from the many guest houses it is also quite easy to get cheaper rooms in village houses. Just wander along looking hopeful and somebody will descend on you! Of course you may have to do without mod cons like running water but if the well is OK by you then you can get very good accommodation. Down at the southern end of the strip, or on the many little lanes that run inland, are the places to look. One travellers' experience:

Most of the 16 days we spent in Hikkaduwa we spent in a rental house which we shared with another couple. We looked at three houses. All of them were Rs 1000 for two weeks. One was a half km from the beach, had four rooms with one large bedroom and was relatively new. Another was about a half km from the beach, had five rooms, had an outside squatter, and was an older building. The one we rented was a km from the beach, had eight rooms with three bedrooms and inside squatter, and was nearly brand new. All three houses had electricity but didn't have running water or any kitchen appliances. All in all it was a most pleasant way to enjoy the area if one was planning on an extended stay.

Places to Stay – top end

There are quite a few guest houses which bridge the gap between the bottom end and top end at Hikkaduwa but basically the top end consists of a number of hotels. The *Coral Gardens*, Hikkaduwa's biggest hotel, was being totally rebuilt from the ground up in early '84 to make it even bigger. It's more-or-less the mid-point between the coral beach and the surfing beach and has by far the best setting at Hikkaduwa – right by where the reef starts and runs out to the coral sanctuary.

There are a number of top end places side by side on the coral diving beach – just to ensure that you get them nicely confused they all have the word 'coral' in their names. Rooms in these hotels are typically in the Rs 350 to 650 bracket although they can be much cheaper in the

off-season. Starting from the *Coral Gardens Hotel* end they include the newer *Coral Seas Beach Resort* (tel 09-3248). Then there's the *Coral Rock Hotel* (tel 09-2021) with 40 rooms and the *Hotel Coral Reef Beach* (tel 09-2197) with 50 rooms. The *Hotel Blue Corals* (tel 09-2679) has 52 rooms while the *Hotel Coral Sands* (tel 09-2436) has 58 rooms. The Blue Corals is probably the nicest of this group; there's some landscaping and palm trees on the beach front here. Unfortunately most of this strip of hotels has been so overbuilt that from the beach all you see is a solid facade of building and from the road virtually the only way to the beach is through one of the hotels. Across the road from the coral-hotel group is the *Hotel Sea View* at Rs 400 for doubles with breakfast.

On the other side of the Coral Gardens is the more recent *Hotel Lanka Supercoral* (tel 09-2897) with rooms at Rs 500 to 700. South towards Galle at Narigama, *Sunils Beach Hotel* (tel 09-2016) has 53 rooms at Rs 425 to 550.

Places to Eat

You'll find all the standard travellers' menu items in Hikkaduwa's many eating places. Jaffles, pancakes, fruit salad, milk shakes, banana and pineapple fritters, fruit drinks, ice cream and all the other necessities of life to turn a place into a food trip. In a few days at Hikkaduwa an awful lot of money seems to get spent on just dropping into some place or other for a quick curd and fruit salad, or something similar.

Many of the travellers' restaurants are remarkably similar, even down to the misspellings on the menus. They're also rather variable – they'll fix you something fresh and beautifully prepared for one meal and then serve up something tired and stale for the next. While we were having one of our best meals in Hikkaduwa somebody at the next table was complaining that his food was terrible.

Seafood figures large on the menus of

course – Hikkaduwan crab, whether it is boiled, roasted, served with chips, salad or ginger sauce, is a taste treat not to be missed. All sorts of fish (although it is usually fairly anonymous) are also popular. You can get good ice cream at Hikkaduwa and many of the restaurants have excellent cake (I really liked the iced ginger cake) always ready by the slice.

Up at the northern end of the strip good places to try include the pricier *Starfish Cafe*. The *Lobster*, also up at the northern end of the beach, is a very popular mid-range place with excellent food.

Possibly the longest running place at Hikkaduwa, and still as popular as ever, is the tiny *Reef Coolspot*, opposite the Coral Gardens Hotel. It seems to be packed out at almost any time of the day or night, but most particularly at breakfast time. Low prices and friendly service are part of the answer here.

Moving south, *Udulu's* and the *Farmhouse* next door are two popular places to eat. The *Sydney Tourist Restaurant*, *Shyan's Living Kitchen* ('undoubtedly the best restaurant on the strip' reported one traveller) and the slightly more expensive *Paradiso* also pack them in. On the beach side of the road the *Curry Bowl* has excellent food and relatively quick service. They even have brown rice and delicacies like pineapple chutney.

Restaurant Francis has a good reputation for some of the best food along the beach strip, but also for very slow service. Just beyond Francis is the *Beauty Spot Restaurant* with a wide variety of cheap and tasty curries.

Further south the *Blue Fox* is a good place for drinks and ice creams and they have great banana-pineapple fritters. The *Catamaran Curry Centre* is also very good. Fast service and excellent value food at *Big Budde*, on the beach side of the road. *Rangith's Snacks* has positively the best ice cream (and milkshakes if milk is available) in Hikkaduwa – the crowds sitting outside at night bear witness to that.

Still further south *Brother's Spot* is a pleasant beachfront place. Next door is *Silta's* – good, friendly and not too expensive. The *Ranmal Restaurant* is also nicely situated on the beach while the *Little Lion* is not only on the beach but also has Italian food.

Getting There

There are usually seven trains daily to Hikkaduwa from Colombo, less on Sundays. The trip takes around two to three hours and costs Rs 30.80 in 2nd class, Rs 12.50 in 3rd class. There is no 1st class on this route. Go to counter 10 for 2nd class tickets, counter 14 for 3rd, at the Fort station. This is a route that can sometimes be very crowded.

There is also a daily, one class Inter-City Express service operating Colombo-Galle with stops at Ambalangoda and Hikkaduwa.

There are frequent buses from Colombo, both CTB and private buses with fares from Rs 12.50 to 16. Buses also operate frequently to nearby Ambalangoda and Galle, the fare for the short trip to Galle is just Rs 2.75. Several operators have minibuses direct from Hikkaduwa to the airport so you can depart straight from the beach. The usual fare is Rs 100 and there will be signs announcing the departure times for each day.

Getting Around

It's very easy to hire bicycles in Hikkaduwa and there's quite a lot of interest in the vicinity. Daily charges are Rs 20. Motorcycles are also readily available in Hikkaduwa both for local use and further afield.

GALLE

The port of Galle is 115 km (72 miles) south of Colombo and very close to Hikkaduwa. Galle is Sri Lanka's most historically interesting city still functioning today. Although Anuradhapura and Polonnaruwa are far older they are effectively dead cities – the modern towns

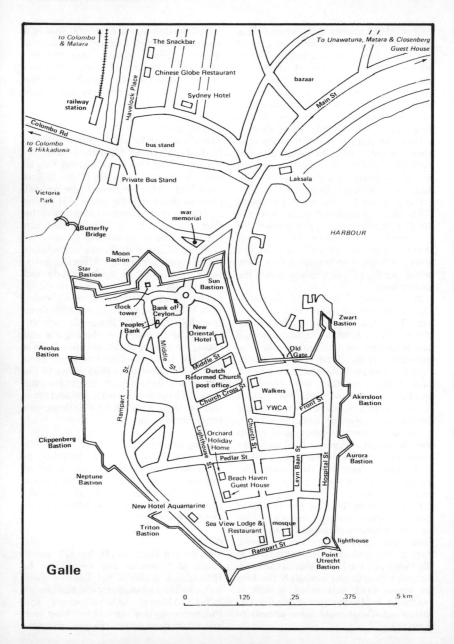

to Colombo
& Matara

The Snackbar

Chinese Globe Restaurant

Sydney Hotel

To Unawatuna, Matara & Closenberg
Guest House

bazaar

Havelock Place

Main St

railway
station

Colombo Rd

to Colombo
& Hikkaduwa

bus stand

Laksala

Private Bus Stand

Victoria
Park

war
memorial

HARBOUR

Butterfly
Bridge

Moon
Bastion

Star
Bastion

Sun
Bastion

clock
tower

Bank of
Ceylon

Peoples'
Bank

Zwart
Bastion

Aeolus
Bastion

Middle St.

New
Oriental
Hotel

Rampart St.

Old
Gate

Middle St

Dutch
Reformed Church
post office

Church Cross St

Walkers

YWCA

Front St

Akersloot
Bastion

Clippenberg
Bastion

Lighthouse St.

Orcnard
Holiday
Home

Church St.

Leyn Baan St.

Hospital St.

Aurora
Bastion

Pedlar St

Neptune
Bastion

Beach Haven
Guest House

New Hotel Aquamarine

Sea View Lodge &
Restaurant

mosque

Triton
Bastion

Rampart St.

lighthouse

Point
Utrecht
Bastion

Galle

0   125   .25   .375   .5 km

are quite divorced from the ancient ruins. Until the construction of breakwaters at Colombo harbour was completed, only a hundred years ago, Galle was the major port in Sri Lanka and still handles shipping today. You may also see western cruising yachts here. If you're trying to find a crew position on a yacht sailing from Sri Lanka enquire at the Port Office, Ocean Cruising Club, 6 Closenberg Rd.

Historians believe that Galle may be the Tarshish of Biblical times – from where King Solomon obtained gems, spices and peacocks, but it assumed real importance only with the arrival of the Europeans. In 1505 a Portuguese fleet, bound for the Maldives, was blown off course and took shelter in the harbour at dusk. Hearing a cock ('gallus' in Portuguese) crowing they gave the town its name although another story relates that it is derived from the Sinhala word 'gala' meaning rock, of which the harbour has plenty. At first the Portuguese made little use of the port but in 1589, involved in one of their periodic squabbles with the Kingdom of Kandy, they built a small and primitive fort which they named Santa Cruz. Later they extended this with a series of bastions and walls but the Dutch, after their takeover of the island, destroyed almost all traces of the Portuguese presence and burnt their records. Galle fell to the Dutch in 1640 after a four-day siege.

In 1663 the Dutch built the 36 hectare (90 acre) fort which stands in almost perfect repair today and encompasses all the older part of Galle. Later Galle passed into British hands but by this time commercial interest was turning to Colombo and Galle has scarcely altered since the Dutch left. It's a delightful little place, quiet and easy-going within the old fort walls and with a real sense of being steeped in history.

The Fort

One of the most pleasant strolls you can make is the circuit of the fort walls at dusk. As the daytime heat fades away you can, in an easy hour or two, walk almost the complete circuit of Galle along the top of the wall – only once – at Akersloot, just beyond the old gate – is it necessary to leave the wall. The main gate into Galle is a comparatively recent addition – it was built by the British in 1873 to handle the heavier flow of traffic into the old city. This wall, the most heavily fortified since it faced the land, was originally constructed by the Portuguese with a moat and later substantially enlarged by the Dutch. In 1667 they split this section, originally named the 'Sea Bastion', into separate 'Star', 'Moon' and 'Sun' bastions.

Following the fort wall clockwise you soon come to the original gate, now known as the 'Old Gate'. On the outer side the British coat of arms tops the entrance while inside the letters VOC are inscribed in the stone. They stand for the Dutch East India Company and are flanked by two lions, topped by a cock and bear the date 1669. Just beyond the gate is the 'Zwart' bastion or 'Black Fort' which is thought to be the oldest of the fort bastions and to have been originally constructed by the Portuguese. Today it houses the police station.

The eastern wall ends at the Point Utrecht Bastion, close to the powder magazine. The modern 18 metre high lighthouse stands atop this bastion. The lighthouse keeper *may* magically materialise when visitors arrive and, for a few rupees, will show you up to the top.

The rocky point at the end of the next stretch of wall was once a Portuguese Bastion and from here the Dutch signalled approaching ships to warn them of dangerous rocks – hence its name 'flag rock'. Pigeon Island, close to the rock, was used as a signal post and a musket shot was fired from here to alert ships to the danger. On the Triton Bastion there used to be a windmill which drew up sea water to be sprayed from carts to keep the dust down on the city streets. There are a series of other bastions and the tomb of a Moslem saint on the way back.

Inside the Fort

Most of the older buildings within the fort date from the Dutch era and many of the streets still bear their Dutch names or are direct translations – thus Mohrische Kramer Staat became the Street of the Moorish Traders and Rope Walk Street has remained as Leyn-Baan Street. The 'Groote Kerk', or Great Church, was originally built in 1640 but the present church dates from 1752-55. Inside, the floor is paved with gravestones from the old Dutch cemetery. The old bell tower stands opposite the church. There are two other churches within the old town but they date from the British era.

On the corner opposite the Dutch church is the old Dutch Government House, now used as offices by Walker & Sons. Over the doorway a slab bears the date 1683 and the figure of a cock. The old Dutch ovens are still inside and the building is said to be haunted by more than one ghost! The Dutch also built an intricate sewer system which was flushed out daily by the rising and falling tide. With true colonial efficiency they then bred musk rats in the sewers which were exported for their musk oil.

Close to the lighthouse on Hospital St there's a small group of interesting little shops including a seashell shop at number 34.

Outside the Fort

Just to the west of the esplanade, in front of the fort, the picturesque Butterfly Bridge spans the river to the Victoria Park. In the new town there is a bustling market place and a variety of shops – there are very few in the old town. The small stretch of beach just outside the Old Gate is a busy scene late in the afternoon as fishermen sell their catch. There are some fine old traders' homes close to Galle including Closenberg, now a guest house, which was the residence of a British P&O captain.

Places to Stay – bottom end

It's a question of in-the-fort or outside-the-fort in Galle and fortunately most of the cheaper places are inside. Actually most cheap accommodation here is of the rooms in private homes variety – you can't walk down any street in Galle, carrying a bag, without someone trying to grab you and haul you away to their house – although there are also some hotels. Take care with the Galle touts though – some of the places they'll try to take you to are distinctly second rate.

Popular guest houses include Mrs Wijenayake's immaculately kept and very friendly *Beach Haven* (tel 09-2663) at 65 Lighthouse St, where rooms cost Rs 125 single or 150 double. These more expensive rooms have attached bathrooms but there are also three cheaper, but still perfectly adequate, rooms at Rs 50. Meals are also available here and the food is very good.

There are quite a few other guest houses around Galle which are listed in the tourist office guide. *R K Kodikara's* guest house (tel 09-2351) at 29 Rampart St is also 'friendly and cheap' though perhaps not as well kept as it could be – singles/doubles cost just Rs 25/40 or Rs 35/55 with fan. 'Kodi is very sociable, loves to sit and chat and share an arrack on the house', wrote one visitor. Another reported that: 'the atmosphere is very colonial – they have an antique houseboy called Edmond!'

Recommendations have also come in for *Mrs Mashoor's*, 8 Parawa St, which is 'a pleasant place to stay'. Several travellers have recommended *Mrs Khalid's* guest house at 106 Pedlar St, where rooms cost around Rs 75 and food is good, although not too cheap. *Mrs Saheed's Guest House* at 79 Lighthouse St has large airy rooms with fan and mosquito nets. There are other guest houses at 71 Lighthouse St and the *Faikas Guest House* at 40 Middle St.

The *Orchard Holiday Home* (tel 09-2370) at 61 Lighthouse St is a popular small hotel. There are seven spacious rooms, each with its own bathroom at a cost of Rs 100 single or Rs 150 double. Prices are lower out of season. The *New Hotel Aquamarine* on Rampart St replaced the old Hotel Aquamarine but it's rather more basic and not so good as the old place. Singles are Rs 50 to 85, doubles Rs 75 to 125.

On the corner of Rampart and Church Sts, near the lighthouse, the *Sea View Lodge & Restaurant* is a rather decrepit looking place although it's housed in an elegant old Dutch building. There's a fine balcony overlooking the sea and a variable restaurant. Rooms range from Rs 40 to 100, the higher priced rooms have attached bathrooms and there are fans and mosquito nets. The YMCA does not appear to take guests anymore but there is said to be a YWCA behind Walker's.

Right beside the bus stand and near the railway station, outside the fort, the *Sydney Hotel* is dirt cheap with singles at Rs 50 or less. It's also as basic, dull and dingy as you'd expect from the price. There are 11 *Railway Retiring Rooms* (tel 09-2271) at Galle Station costing Rs 110. There are also some guest houses outside the fort, such as *Lucky Cottage* at 86 S H Dahanayake Mawatha (used to be Richmond Hill Rd).

Places to Stay – top end

The delightfully olde worlde *New Oriental Hotel* (tel 09-2059) is at 10 Church St in the fort, right next to the Dutch Church. It has all the old, but very well kept, Victorian flavour you could ask for and has singles/doubles at Rs 200/375 or single suites from Rs 300 to 350, doubles from Rs 450 to 500. Breakfast costs Rs 30, lunch or dinner around Rs 70. It's a fine old place, the only upper notch hotel actually in the fort at Galle, and everybody seems to like it – 'best value for money in Sri Lanka – space, antique opulence and cheerful service' wrote one obviously satisfied customer. The New Oriental has 36 rooms, an atmospheric old bar and has recently added a swimming pool. It was originally built in 1865 as officers' barracks.

About three km from the fort on the Matara side of Galle, the *Closenberg Hotel* (tel 09-3073) once had its own little bay until it was filled in for a land reclamation project; there's still a fine sweep of sand to the south of it. It was originally built by a P&O captain in the heyday of British

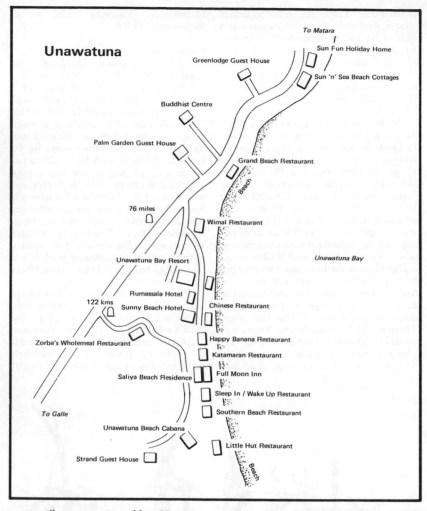

Unawatuna

To Matara

Sun Fun Holiday Home

Greenlodge Guest House

Sun 'n' Sea Beach Cottages

Buddhist Centre

Palm Garden Guest House

Grand Beach Restaurant

Beach

76 miles

Wimal Restaurant

Unawatuna Bay Resort

Unawatuna Bay

Rumassala Hotel

122 kms

Sunny Beach Hotel

Chinese Restaurant

Happy Banana Restaurant

Katamaran Restaurant

Zorba's Wholemeal Restaurant

Full Moon Inn

Saliya Beach Residence

Sleep In / Wake Up Restaurant

Southern Beach Restaurant

To Galle

Unawatuna Beach Cabana

Little Hut Restaurant

Strand Guest House

Beach

mercantile supremacy and has 22 rooms, priced from around Rs 250 to 350 for a double, room only – meals are also available.

Continue a little beyond Closenberg and a steep road leads off and up to the *Harbour Inn Rest House* (tel 09-2899), from where you can look across the bay to Galle, far below. You definitely need transport to get here! There are only four rooms here with rooms at Rs 275 or including all meals at Rs 415 for a single, Rs 630 for a double.

Places to Eat

The *New Oriental* is certainly the best place for a meal in Galle. The food is pretty good, the service excellent and the surroundings can't be beat. Next door the *New Oriental Hotel Bakery* does short eats or rice and curry. You can also eat in the *Sea View Hotel*.

Otherwise almost all the places to eat are outside the fort. Near the grubby Sydney Hotel, across from the fort and by the CTB bus stand, is the excellent *South Ceylon Restaurant* with the South Ceylon Bakery downstairs and the restaurant upstairs. The food is delicious (cashew curry, pineapple curry, good breakfasts) and drinks are good too. Plus it's cheap and the service is friendly. You can hire cars or vans here.

Around the corner at 30 Havelock Place, the road running parallel to the train line and canal, the *Chinese Globe Restaurant* is excellent value – a huge fried rice for Rs 10 to 16. A couple of doors further along the *Snackbar* is a clean, quiet place for a cold drink. You can get curd at the town end of the market.

Getting There

Trains from Colombo cost Rs 36.50 in 2nd class, Rs 14.90 in 2nd. The trip can take 2½ to four hours although most trains complete the journey in around three hours. There are seven trains daily Colombo-Galle, four of them continue on to Matara, another one to two hour trip.

In addition the new, one class Inter-City Express departs Colombo daily at 3.45 pm and arrives in Galle two hours later. It stops only at Bentota, Ambalangoda and Hikkaduwa and the fare to Galle is Rs 40. Departure from Galle on the return trip is at 7.50 pm.

There are also plenty of minibuses and CTB buses running down this busy coastal strip. Minibus fare from Colombo is Rs 15.

It's only 20 to 40 minutes from Hikkaduwa to Galle and only a couple of Rs by bus. Unawatuna, the next popular beach centre along the coast, is only 15 minutes away. A bus on to Matara will cost Rs 6.

UNAWATUNA

Just a few km south of Galle, Unawatuna is a wide, curving bay with a picturebook sweep of golden beach. The main road joins the coast almost at the southern end of the bay and there are a number of small hotels and guest houses scattered along the road or at the beachfront, back from the road. There's only one 'top end' hotel although a big new project is underway at the north end of the beach which may alter the feel of the place.

Unawatuna is fairly quiet and easy going, still a small fishing village with a sprinkling of visitors; the development has not swamped the village like Hikkaduwa. It is, however, unplanned development just like Hikkaduwa – the only access to the main beach area is by sandy tracks and hotels, restaurants and tourist shops are thrown up, higgledy piggledy, all over the place. Fortunately there aren't too many of them and the beautiful beach, clear water, good reef and relatively calm and peaceful atmosphere make this one of the most pleasant beaches in Sri Lanka.

Places to Stay

Until the completion of the big Aldiana Club resort at the end of the beach the 30 room *Unawatuna Beach Resort* (tel 09-2065, 2456) is the only top end place. It's modern but rather tackily cheap and unimaginative – although quite comfortable. Rooms at ground level are Rs 250, upstairs they're Rs 350 facing the beach, Rs 325 facing away. There's a beachfront restaurant here and you can hire snorkelling gear (Rs 25 half-day, Rs 40 all day) or wind-surfing equipment (Rs 70 an hour).

A little beyond is the cheaper *Sunny Beach Hotel*, with pleasantly comfortable rooms, especially those upstairs with the big verandah area. Rooms are typically in the Rs 100 to 250 bracket. Right in front of it, and right on the beach, is the *Chinese Restaurant*, which has really excellent food, some of the best food I've had in Sri Lanka. Between the resort and the Sunny Beach is the *Rumassala Hotel*.

Other places further along the beach include the *Full Moon Inn* with doubles at Rs 150, *Saliya Beach Residence* and on the road running back from the beach the *Unawatuna Beach Cabanas* and the *Strand Guest House*. There are lots of homes back here with signs out when they have rooms to rent and for cheaper or long term accommodation this will be your best bet.

There are more possibilities along the main road, where it meets the coast. Although the places here are not as secluded and not always as close to the beach as some of the bayfront places they do generally have better fresh water. A drawback of some of the bayfront places is the water tends to be salty. *Greenlodge Guest House* has nice doubles with bath for Rs 150. On the beach side of the road the *Sun 'n Sea Beach Cottages* has doubles at Rs 150.

Recently opened, though in a very old house, *Nooit Gedacht* (tel 09-3449) is a guest house in an elegant 17th century Dutch administrator's residence. It's a 10 minute walk from the beach and has singles/doubles, all with bath and verandah, at Rs 100/175 in season. There's also a three room family unit for Rs 400 and meals are available.

Places to Eat

There are a number of places to eat in Unawatuna, particularly along the beach where you can sit outside, try the fresh local seafood, wash it down with a cold beer and watch the water lap on the beach. Sounds idyllic doesn't it? The *Chinese Restaurant* in front of the Sunny Beach Hotel does terrific food. There's also a beachfront bar and restaurant in front of the Unawatuna Beach Resort.

Just beyond the Chinese Restaurant is the *Happy Bananas Restaurant*, again with very good fresh seafood. Crab and chips costs Rs 60, fish and chips Rs 20 to 25. Continuing along the beach in that direction you come to the *Katamaran Restaurant*, the *Sleep In/Wake Up Restaurant* (depending which side you approach it from), the *Southern Beach Restaurant* and the *Little Beach Restaurant*. Going along the beach in the opposite direction, beyond the Unawatuna Beach Resort, you come to the *Wimal Restaurant* and the *Grand Beach Restaurant* – OK if you can fight the flies off.

Finally, on the back road into the bay area, there's the Rajneesh restaurant *Zorba's Wholemeal Restaurant*. Slightly pricier but excellent food in extremely neat and tidy surroundings. And you can admire the pictures of the Bhagwan in his Rolls-Royce while you eat.

Getting There

It's only 15 minutes or so from Galle to Unawatuna – take a Matara bus or any bus heading east along the coast.

TALPE & KOGGALA

Beyond Unawatuna the road runs close to the coast most of the way to Matara and beyond. There are numerous beautiful stretches of beach, picturesque coves and tiny bays. This is also the part of the coast where you will see stilt fishermen, if the sea is running right for them. From Unawatuna onwards you can expect to see them anytime.

Just before Koggala a small road turns inland beside the WW II airstrip and leads to a huge lake. There are a series of islands

---

A   On the inner harbour, Trincomalee
B   Entrance to the lagoon, Negombo

in this large tank and from December to April great numbers of birds flock here. Outriggers can be hired to paddle you out for a look. Plans to re-open the airport commercially may affect the birds' habits.

At Koggala, near the international resort hotels and a little inland from the coast road and railway line (a sign directs you), there's the Martin Wickramasinghe Museum of Folk Art and Culture. It's open 9 am to 12 noon and 1 to 5 pm except on Mondays and poya days when it is closed.

There's the interesting old Purvaramaya Temple, with some recently restored wall murals, just beyond Koggala. The turn-off is in Kataluwa – past the 82 mile and 132 km posts and across the river, at the Shining Star Beach Inn sign. You have to go a couple of km off the road and take the right turn – ask directions. A monk, they're very friendly here, will open the building up if you ask. Some of the Jataka scenes painted here are said to be 200 years old and have been featured on a series of Sri Lankan stamps. Notice the European figures in their 19th century attire.

In recent years more and more places to stay have sprung up along the coast. Leaving Unawatuna you'll find places dotted along the road through Talpe, then there is a big international resort at Koggala and more places between there and Weligama.

Places to Stay

At Talpe, between the 125 and 126 km markers and three km beyond Unawatuna, is the *Beach Haven Hotel* (tel 09-2663). Opened in 1981 it's run by the friendly people who operate the Beach Haven Guest House in Galle. It's right by the beach, has a swimming pool and the 21 rooms cost Rs 325/350 for singles/doubles room-only. Meals are also available at Rs 30 for breakfast, Rs 55 for lunch or dinner. Stilt fishermen fish from right in front of the hotel.

It's only about five km further down the road to Koggala (also referred to as Habaraduwa) where the *Hotel Horizon* (tel 097-2528, 2597) has 70 rooms with prices from Rs 670. The *Koggala Beach Hotel* (tel 09-3280) has 204 rooms at Rs 900/1100 for all-inclusive singles/doubles. The *Tisara Beach Hotel* (tel 09 2017) has 180 rooms with all-inclusive prices of Rs 800/1000.

In Kotulawa, just beyond Koggala, there is the smaller *Shining Star Beach Inn* and the *Sagara Guest House*.

WELIGAMA

About 30 km south of Galle, the town of Weligama has a fine sandy sweep of bay – just as its name, which means 'sandy village', might suggest. Very close to the shore, so close in fact that you could walk out to it at low tide, is a tiny island known as Taprobane. It looks like an ideal artist's retreat, which indeed it has been at one time. Currently it is owned by an Australian.

Along this stretch of coast, and particularly at Ahamgama, you're likely to see stilt-fishermen. Each fisherman has a pole firmly embedded in the sea bottom close to the shore. When the sea and fish are running in the right direction they perch upon their poles and cast their lines out. Stilt positions are passed down from father to son and are highly coveted.

A Stilt fishermen near Weligama
B Swami Rock at Trincomalee
C The beach at Tangalla

The road through Weligama divides just as it enters the town. One road runs along the coast, the other a short distance inland. Take the inland route and just by the railway crossing there is a small park with a large rock-carved figure known as the *Kustaraja*. It's been variously described as a king who was mysteriously cured of leprosy or as Avalokitesvara, a disciple of the Buddha. Weligama is also famous for its lacework; some local entrepreneurs are bound to rush out to try and sell you some.

Places to Stay – bottom end

At 484 New By Pass Rd, at the Matara end of the town, just where the road along the coast and the road through the town meet again, *Sam's Holiday Cabanas* are right by the beach. Singles/doubles cost Rs 100/150 with breakfast and it's a very pleasant, unhurried place. The owner used to run a place in Hikkaduwa.

The *Weligama Bay Tourist Inn* and the *Udula Guest House* are close to the Weligama Bay Inn. Other places include *Eden's Rest* and *Leela Lace Industries* (tel 0415-201). The latter is on the main coast road and directly behind it there is a small three-room guest house with rooms at just Rs 50. The *Holiday Rest* is at 245 Main St. *Raja's Guest House* is a pleasant and reasonably priced place at Paranakade. Rooms cost Rs 30 to 50 with fan and mosquito net. From the bus stand walk back towards Galle, past the petrol station and take the small track.

Places to Stay – top end

The attractive *Weligama Bay Inn* (0415-299) has a wide, open balcony, pleasant green gardens and a fine view across the beach. There are 12 rooms with costs of Rs 150/200 for singles/doubles and meals are available. Although it's name doesn't indicate it this is a rest house and Weligama also has a second *Rest House* on the Galle side of the Weligama Bay Inn. Rooms in the new Rest House, which is quite OK although not as elegant as the Bay Inn, cost Rs 125/150.

Back from the coast, behind the

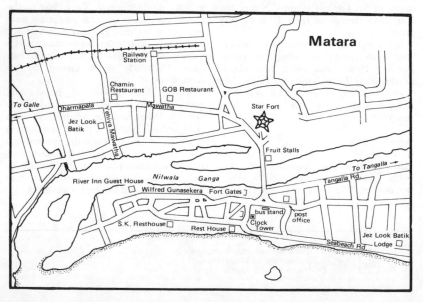

Weligama Bay Inn, is the *Ruhunu Guest House* (tel 0415-228) on D M Samaraweera Mawatha. It's another pleasant and relaxed place with singles/doubles at Rs 175/225 including breakfast.

Or there's the 60 room *Bay Beach Hotel* (tel 0415-201). It's further back towards Galle and has a view looking right along the beach. There are 56 rooms here costing Rs 550. There's a swimming pool and other mod cons and the shallow beach beside it is good for swimming.

MATARA

Exactly 100 miles (160 km) from Colombo, this town marks the end of the southern railway. Matara has two fine Dutch forts, the larger one contains much of old Matara including the excellent Rest House which is said to be built on the site where captured elephants were corralled. The other fort, the small 1763 Star Fort, is now used as a library and has a most attractive and unusual gateway. It's about a hundred metres from the main fort gate – on the other side of the road and heading towards Colombo.

It's an easy-going town with horse carriages clip-clopping by and a long stretch of beach, although you can also head a few km back towards Colombo and turn off to Polhena. Here you'll find a shallow swimming area with a pleasant little beach.

Matara is famous for its curd and treacle so you should not fail to try it here. Curd is a favourite delicacy all along this stretch of coast. If you're interested in batik drop into Jez Look Batik at 12 Yehiya Mawatha.

Places to Stay – Matara

Matara has quite a variety of places in the lower price category. In the Matara Fort, the entrance is only about a hundred metres from the bus station, you will find the *Matara Rest House* which, as usual, is beautifully situated right by the beach with a wonderful view in both directions. Although the original building is quite old

there are two recently added new wings with very comfortable rooms. Singles/doubles range from Rs 50/100 to Rs 75/130, all with attached bath. You can get doubles in the old building for less than Rs 50, a real bargain. Meals cost from Rs 12 to 25 for breakfast. Rs 30 to 40 for lunch or dinner although rice and curry is just Rs 25. The restaurant here has a much more extensive and reasonably priced menu than that usually found in rest houses – great fruit salad.

Further in to the fort the *River Inn Guest House*, by the river at 96A Wilfred Gunasekera, has singles/doubles at Rs 125/150. At 38 Wilfred Gunasekera the *Blue Ripples Guest House*, is 'lovely, with fantastic rooms right over the river'. 'Quiet, beautiful and excellent value' wrote another traveller. There are two large rooms with fan and bath at Rs 50. Other guest houses in the fort can be found at 6 Middle St, 16 Middle St and Mrs de Silva's at 90 Wilfred Gunasekera. There are no signs at most of these fort guest houses.

There are several other possibilities along the coast road towards Tangalla – the main road to Tangalla is a block inland from the coast. The *Jez Look Beach Lodge* (tel 041-2142) at 47 Beach Rd, has dorm beds at Rs 25, singles/doubles at Rs 75/150. It's run by the Jez Look Batik centre in Matara which was once a popular place to stay in its own right. Other places to stay along the coast road include the *Beach Lodge, Alaha's Rest, Beach Inn* and *Lakmini Rest*. The *Maheeka Tourist Inn* (tel 041-2131) is at 363 Meddawatha and has singles/doubles at Rs 75/150.

Other Matara cheapies are on the way out of town towards Galle. If you follow the road from the bus stop it crosses the wide river and bends round to follow the coast. The turnoff to the railway station is about a half km along and a block beyond that you will find the *Chamin Restaurant & Guest House*, which has clean, functional rooms at Rs 60.

Places to Stay – Polhena

As if the plethora of cheap places to stay in Matara wasn't enough there is also Polhena Beach about three km west (the Galle side) of Matara. It is just a short bus ride from Matara but there are only a handful of buses right to the beach each day – otherwise you will have to get off at the main road junction and walk the half km down to the beach.

The excellent *TK Travellers' Halt* has dorm beds and also rooms from Rs 50 to 125, the more luxuriously equipped rooms have attached bathrooms. The cheaper rooms have mosquito nets and fans though, so they are no hardship. TK consists of two separate houses about a hundred metres apart, they're signposted as you come in to Polhena from the Matara-Galle road. It has a good menu too. There are one or two other small guest houses around Polhena Beach including one opposite the Polhena School

Polhena also has the sole upper bracket hotel at Matara/Polhena – the pleasantly sited *Polhena Reef Gardens Hotel* (tel 041-2478). The 20 rooms cost Rs 350 to 400 room only. Snorkelling and skin diving equipment is available from the hotel and there is a relaxing garden by the waterside.

Places to Eat

There are a number of good places to eat along Dharmapala Mawatha including the *Chamin Restaurant*, which has a long menu of the Chinese regulars plus really excellent fish and chips. Further back towards the bus station there's the *GOB Restaurant* and right by the bridge, on the Galle side, the *Richcurd Bakery* has good short eats and cakes.

On the other side of the road, just on the Galle side of the bridge, there's a string of fruit stalls selling a wider variety of tropical fruit than I've seen anywhere else in Sri Lanka – even mangosteens and custard apples when nowhere else seemed to have them. And right across the road there's a whole bevy of signs calling out to my fellow curd and treacle lovers. What a food trip!

Getting There

Matara is the end of the railway line from Colombo. Fares from Colombo are Rs 50.30 in 1st class, Rs 20.50 in 2nd. Only four of the daily Colombo-Galle trains continue to Matara. From Colombo it takes four to five hours.

The minibus fare from Colombo is Rs 20, from Galle Rs 6. From the Matara bus stand a 350, 356 or 460 bus will take you to Polhena Beach.

MATARA TO TANGALLA

There are several places of interest along the 30 km of coastal road from Matara to Tangalla. Including two superb examples of what one visitor labelled 'neo-Buddhist kitsch'; he went on to extoll the virtues of Sri Lankan pop music which 'plumbs the depths of dreadfulness'!

Weherehena Temple

Just as you leave Matara a turn inland will take you to the Weherehena temple where there is an artificial underground cave decorated with comic book-like illustrations of scenes from the Buddha's life. There's also a huge Buddha figure here. You can get there on a 349 bus.

Every year during the full moon at the end of November/beginning of December there is a perahera held at the temple. During the evening there's a big procession of dancers and elephants from all the surrounding villages. There's also a smaller 'preview' procession on the day before. This festival, held to celebrate the anniversary of the founding of the temple, is becoming better known and accommodation can be difficult to find in Matara at that time.

Dondra

Only five or six km out of Matara you come to Dondra, the southernmost point of Sri Lanka. It's a pleasant walk out to the lighthouse which marks the actual southern extremity of the island. From there you get a superb view of the fishing boats riding the waves.

Wewurukannala Vihara

If the Weherehena temple in Matara is 'Marvel Comics meets Lord Buddha' then here it's Walt Disney who runs into him. At the town of Dikwella a road turns inland towards Beliatta. About a km and a half along you come to a huge, 50 metre high, seated Buddha figure – the largest Buddha in Sri Lanka. The temple has three parts – the oldest is about 250 years old but is of no particular interest.

Larger and newer, a second shrine room has a quite amazing collection of life size and vibrantly coloured figures depicting the Buddha doing everything from taking his first steps, (immediately after birth), through leaving his family to seek enlightenment, finding it, passing on the message and finally achieving nirvana. There are also models of devils, monsters, Veddahs, disciples, 24 of the Buddha's previous incarnations, larger seated, standing and reclining figures and everything else you could ask for. I particularly liked the figure of the Buddha while still a prince, riding away from his family on what looks like a horse from a fair ground merry-go-round.

Finally there is the gigantic seated figure which was constructed only in the late '60s and is still not finished. As if to prove that it really is as high as an eight-storey building, what should be right behind it but (you guessed it) an eight-storey building. You can climb up inside to look over his shoulder at the surrounding rice paddies or on up to his head where you can look through a little glass panel to see what there is inside a 50 metre-high Buddha's head. Answer? – all the Buddhist scriptures, a small dagoba and a circle of small Buddha figures. 'I couldn't work out the significance of the ice cream cone on his head', wrote one highly impressed visitor.

Furthermore the walls of the backing building are gradually being painted with yet more comic strip representations of events in the Buddha's lives. 'Our favourites', two travellers wrote, 'were a man in combat with a Gonzala styled ape and a man questioned, then whipped, then arms and legs sawn off and then going to nirvana. So far they're only down to the fourth floor so the lower three have yet to reveal their stories'. It is all quite a contrast to the supremely tasteful Buddhist art of the ancient cities. There's one other thing to see here, an interesting clock in the adjoining building – made by a prisoner 65 years ago.

Mawella

About six km beyond Dikwella, at the 117 milestone, a path leads off the road to the spectacular Ho-o-maniya blowhole on the coast. During the south-west monsoon (June is the best time) high seas can force water through a natural chimney in the rocks 23 metres up and then spout out up to 18 metres in the air.

Places to Stay

A new and expensive, though very pleasant, place stands on a headland on the Matara side of Dikwella. The Italian built *Dikwella Village Resort* (tel 041-2961) has 44 rooms with prices from around Rs 500. It should be a good place for a spaghetti!

Further on towards Tangalla at Kamagoda the *Hotel Country Comfort* (tel 041-2962) has 20 rooms with prices including breakfast of Rs 500/600 for singles/doubles.

TANGALLA

Situated 195 km (122 miles) from Colombo, Tangalla (also spelt Tangalle) is one of the nicest places on the coast – particularly if you just want somewhere to laze and soak up the sun. The town itself is an easy going place with several reminders of Dutch days including the old Rest House which was once home for the Dutch administrators.

It's Tangalla's series of bays which are the modern attraction, however. To the east of the Rest House there is a long stretch of white sand shimmering away into the distance while to the west you've got a choice of a whole series of smaller bays. Some of them shelve off very steeply and the resulting waves make them dangerous for poor swimmers if there is any sort of sea running, compounded by the nasty rocks which punctuate the shore line. If the sea is calm they are just fine.

The bay just on the town side of the *Tangalla Bay Hotel* is probably the most sheltered although right beside the Rest House there's a tiny bay which is very shallow and generally flat calm. By the Peace Haven and Palm Paradise developments there are two very picturesque and fairly secluded bays which are popular for seekers of an overall suntan.

Mulkirigala

North of Tangalla the Mulkirigala rock temple has a little of Dambulla and Sigiriya about it. Steps lead up to a series of cleft-like caves in the huge rock. Like Dambulla they shelter large reclining Buddha figures together with wall painting and other smaller sitting and standing figures. You can then continue on your barefoot way to a dagoba perched on the very top of the rock, from where there is a fine view over the surrounding country.

Manuscripts discovered here in a monastic library by a British official in 1826 were the key which scholars used to translate the *Mahavamsa* from the Pali script.

Getting There

Mulkirigala can be reached from Tangalla either via Beliatta or Wiraketiya. By bus take a Middeniya bus (check that it will go via Beliatta) and ask to be let off at the Mulkirigala junction. Or you can take a bus just to Beliatta and from there a minibus. You could even get there by bicycle from Tangalla although it's a rather rough ride at times.

Places to Stay – bottom end

There are a number of cheap places in Tangalla including quite a few guest houses in the centre of town. Tangalla has plenty of very persuasive touts waiting for travellers at the bus stop. Avoid them if possible. Most of the places that follow are an easy walk from the stop.

About a half km out of town on the Matara side, before you get to the big Tangalla Bay Hotel, is the *Tangalla Beach Hotel* (tel 0416-294) (a discreetly different name huh?) where there are dorm beds and rooms going all the way up to Rs 100. It's certainly a long way from luxurious and prices are definitely negotiable depending on demand and how much you look likely to pay!

The very popular *Magic Circle Guest House* used to be only a hop, step and a jump away but it is now much further down the road towards Matara and when I was last there it was no longer taking guests. You could always check. The owner is a keen magician and guests could brush up on their rabbit-out-of-a-hat tricks while staying there!

Between the Tangalla Beach (the cheap one) and the Tangalla Bay (the expensive one) is the *Seaview Tourist Inn*, which is somewhat more luxurious, but not too much more expensive. It's clean, has good outside toilets, showers and wash basins. There is also the *Tourist Guest House* (or Touristen Gasthaus for German visitors) which is next door and run by very friendly people. The rooms have mosquito nets and attached bathrooms.

Back in the town centre the *Diana Travellers Lodge* is another member of the Travellers' Halt chain and is very popular with travellers. It's about seven minutes walk uphill (there's only one hill) from the bus station – just follow the main road towards Colombo. Coming from Matara you can ask the bus to stop right outside, thus avoiding the touts at the bus station! A well furnished double is just Rs 50. The rooms even have kitchen facilities and there's a big garden.

You can also find a string of guest houses along Beach Rd, towards the Rest House, and along Samuel Mawatha off Beach Rd. The *Beach Inn Guest House* (with rooms from Rs 50 to 100) is typical. The *Sethsiri Tourist Rest House* has doubles with fan and mosquito nets and it's a 'lively, friendly, warm little place'. It's down the lane beside the *Deepa Tourist Inn*, which is also good value with 'lovely rooms for Rs 50 and superb food – lots of plants, balconies and a pet monkey'. 'A shame about the monkey', wrote another traveller. In this same area the *Santana Guest House* has also been recommended – 'friendly, well located, extremely clean, varied menu and a wonderful young owner'.

Hijara at 347 Matara Rd, on the edge of town, is a recently opened guest house with very good rooms. Or there's the *Sonagiri Tourist Rest House* on the Hambantota side of town. *UP Uposera*, Bargolawatta, Medilla Rd is very cheap – left from the bus station and first right after the bridge. You can also find several guest houses along the road to Medaketiya Beach on the Hambantota side of town. The *Gayana Guest House* is right on the beach off this road. The *Ranjith Guest House* is 10 minutes walk from from the bus stand and right by the beach. Rooms, all with bathroom, cost from Rs 100. *A P K Sonnie* at 26 Medaketiya has pleasant rooms from Rs 30, good food and they won't pay touts!

Places to Stay – top end

There are several top end places and a rest house in Tangalla. You'll find the *Tangalla Rest House* right in the middle of town, pleasantly situated on the promontory at the start of the beach, which seems to stretch endlessly to the east. It's one of the oldest rest houses in the country as it dates back to the Dutch days – a small plate on the front steps indicates it was originally constructed in 1774. Accommodation costs Rs 150/250 for singles/doubles with breakfast. The seafood here

has an excellent reputation – it should certainly be fresh, the fishing boat harbour is right by the Rest House. Dinner is available from Rs 50 to 75, lobster is Rs 175. Not everybody, however, is impressed with it – one traveller wrote that his room had no water, a too small mosquito net and a fan 'like a hurricane'.

The other places are on the Matara side of town, starting about 1½ km out. The *Tangalla Bay Hotel* (tel 0416-246) has 36 rooms with prices of Rs 700/900 including all meals. Situated on a rocky promontory between two small sweeps of sandy bay, it blends in quite well with each room having its own balcony on top of the room below. The central complex has been designed to look like a boat – or at least that is the intention, it doesn't work too well. Non residents can use the pool here for Rs 20.

The pleasant *Peace Haven Guest House* (contact phone 95455) is on the next promontory along. There are 12 rooms either in the central building or in a number of separate cabanas scattered around the promontory. Nightly costs range from Rs 200 to Rs 350 in season. The cheapest rooms are bare and fanless. Meals cost Rs 40 for breakfast, Rs 65 for lunch or dinner. It's a peaceful place with two superb little beaches just beyond it.

The beaches are shared with the superb *Palm Paradise Cabanas*, a small development which you can admire on the cover of this edition. There are just a handful of delightful individual cabanas scattered around a green and shady grove of palm trees. Each one has a verandah where you can sit out front, a sleeping-living area with a mosquito-netted bed and enough simple furniture to make it quite comfortable, and a bathroom. They're simple, functional, attractive and very well designed. In fact I'd have to say they were amongst the best rooms of this type I've seen anywhere in Asia. In season they cost around Rs 400 a night. There's also an open restaurant and bar but, at least as this was written, there was no electricity.

Oil lamps provide a glimmer of light at night.

Another cabana complex, to be called *Bikini Beach*, is being built between Peace Haven and Palm Paradise.

Places to Eat

There are quite a few small cafes and restaurants around town – the usual rice and curry and nothing terribly special. *Gamini's Hotel* has been recommended as a good rice and curry specialist. Tangalla has a fine little market place right next to the bus station, you'll find stalls around here selling curd (Rs 9) and honey should you wish to add to your curd pot collection. *Southern Bakeries*, up the hill from the bus stop towards Matara, just beyond the Diana Lodge, has good snacks and short eats – it's clean and friendly.

Down the road towards the Rest House, which is a good place to eat in its own right, is the pleasantly breezy *Maxim's Harbour Inn*. Good food but only open in the season. Out of town towards the Tangalla Bay Hotel is the small *Turtle Landing Restaurant* by the beach.

Getting There

The railway line terminates in Matara but there are regular buses and minibuses on along the coast from Matara.

HAMBANTOTA

Between Tangalla and Hambantota you move from a wet zone to a dry zone; the dry zone continues right across the Yala wildlife park. Between Nonagama and Ambalantota the road from Pelmadulla, near Ratnapura, meets the coast road. For

much of its nearly 100 km distance this is one of the smoothest, widest and fastest roads in Sri Lanka.

At Hambantota the road turns inland from the coast, 237 km (148 miles) from Colombo. You can continue inland and rejoin the coast at Arugam Bay (Pottuvil); or head up to the hill country through Haputale or Ella; or double back to Colombo through Ratnapura. Hambantota is not the best place along the coast if you are in search of sand and sea although there are magnificent sweeps of beach both east and west of the small promontory from the town. Eastward there's often a large collection of outriggered fishing boats beached on the sands.

A major industry in Hambantota is the production of salt by the age old method of evaporating sea water from shallow salt pans. You will see these pans alongside the road as you turn inland from the coast. A few km out of Hambantota, or just before you reach it if you are coming down to the coast, is the last (or the first) of the coastal curd specialists. There are a number of small roadside stalls selling delicious curd and honey – definitely worth a stop if you can manage it.

Places to Stay

The *Hambantota Rest House* is nicely situated on top of the promontory overlooking the town and the long sweep of beach. It is a fairly modern (by rest house standards) place, quite large, and costs Rs 100/200 for singles/doubles with breakfast. Lunch or dinner costs Rs 45.

About a half km from the centre of town and the bus stop, on the Tangalla road, you will find the small *Joy Rest Home* at 48 Tangalla Rd – just a handful of rooms from Rs 30 (for a cheapie with mosquitoes) through Rs 40, 60 and up to Rs 75 with attached bath. It's a good place to stay. Next door is the *Hambantota Guest House*. At 9 Terrace St *Mrs M S M Nihar's* guest house has doubles at Rs 60, excellent food and a view from the front room of the sea, just 20 metres away.

The *Sea Spray Guest House* (tel 0472-212) is in Galwala, about a km from the bus stand – a well maintained place with its own large beach and rooms at Rs 200 with air-con and bathroom, a bit less without air-con. Also on the Tissamaharama side of town the *Yehiya Tourist Inn* at 27 Tissa Rd, Galwala has doubles at Rs 100.

Nearby the large new *Peacock Beach Hotel* (tel 0472-277) should be open in 1984. It has 80 rooms with prices from around Rs 700 including all meals.

WIRAWILA

From Hambantota the road runs virtually due north to Wellawaya where you have a choice of turning east towards Arugam Bay at the southern end of the east coast road or heading into the hill country by continuing north or turning west. Thirty km along this route, just before the Tissamaharama turn-off, the road runs on a causeway across the large Wirawila Wewa. This extensive sheet of water is a bird sanctuary and there are several places to stay around here. You may also see crocodiles and monkeys.

Places to Stay

There are several small guest houses and hotels around the tank. *Mike's Sanctuary Inn* has a good atmosphere and is conveniently situated close to the road and tank. Close by is the *Sanasuma Holiday Resort* (tel 717472) with 50 rooms costing Rs 460/570 all-inclusive. The *Ibis Safari Lodge* (contact tel 82069) has six rooms at Rs 210/265 for singles/doubles including breakfast.

TISSAMAHARAMA

There are turn-offs to Tissamaharama to the north and south of the Wirawila tank. The tank in Tissa, the Tissawewa, is credited to the brother of Devanampiya Tissa of Anuradhapura and is thought to date from the 3rd century BC. There is also a large restored dagoba which was

originally built by the father of Dutugemunu, who liberated Anuradhapura
from the Indians in the 2nd century BC.
The tank is notable for its very active bird
life.

On the coast, about 10 km south of
Tissa, the small village of Kirinda has a
fine beach and a small Buddhist shrine on
the rocks. Next to the dagoba in Tissa
there is a statue of Queen Vihara-
mahadevi who, according to legend,
landed at this place after being sent to sea
by her father King Kelanitissa as a
penance for injuring or killing a monk. The
daughter landed unharmed and subse-
quently married the local King Kavantissa.
Their son was to become the famous King
Dutugemunu.

Kirinda was used as a land base by
Arthur C Clarke's party when diving for
the Great Basses wreck – see Clarke's *The
Treasure of the Reef*. The Great and Little
Basses reefs have some of the most
spectacular scuba diving around Sri
Lanka but only on rare occasions are
conditions suitable for diving. For much of
the year fierce currents sweep across the
reefs. A lighthouse was erected on the
Great Basses in 1860.

Places to Stay

There are quite a number of places to stay
in Tissa since it is used by many people as
a departure point for trips into Yala
National Park. The *Tissamaharama Rest
House* (tel Tissamaharama 231) is
delightfully situated right on the banks of
the Tissawewa tank and has a pleasant
open air bar. There are 43 rooms with
singles/doubles at Rs 275/325.

Just beyond and opposite the rest
house is the *Anumpa Guest House* with
singles/doubles at Rs 50/75. The *Hotel
Singha* is also near the rest house.
Another good low-priced place to try is the
friendly *Village Tissa Guest House*.

The *Priyankara Guest House* (tel
Tissamaharama 95) has 12 rooms with
singles/doubles at Rs 175/200. Further
up the road towards Kataragama (all these
places are on the Kataragama side of
town) is the new *Hatari Inn* at Rs 125 and
the *Traveloque Inn* with rooms at Rs 225/
250.

The *Yala Safari Beach Hotel* is at
Amaduwa near Kirinda. Room only cost in
the 54 room hotel is Rs 300. *Brown's
Safari Beach Hotel* is also at Kirinda on
the coast and has eight rooms with
singles/doubles at Rs 250/300.

Getting There

Buses run to Tissa from Matara. If you're
continuing on to the Yala Park you catch
another bus here which will take you to the
park entrance.

KATARAGAMA

A further 15 km from Tissa is Kataragama,
the most important religious pilgrimage
site in Sri Lanka. Although it is a holy
place to both Buddhists and Hindus it is
the latter who flock here each July and
August. See the introductory festivals
section for more details on the fire-walking
and other acts of ritual masochism which
takes place here.

Places to Stay

The 45 room *Kataragama Rest House* (tel
Kataragama 27) has rooms from around
Rs 100. The *Surenie Inn* in New Town,
Kataragama has 25 rooms.

The *Bank of Ceylon* has an excellent
guest house with twin-bedded rooms for
Rs 75 – very clean with shower, etc. You
must arrive by 4.30 pm if you want dinner
and you're supposed to have booked
ahead in Colombo.

The Hill Country

The hill country in the centre of Sri Lanka is totally different to anywhere else in the island. Due to its altitude the often sticky heat of the coastal regions or the dry central and northern plains becomes a cool, perpetual spring. Everything is green and lush and much of the region carpeted with the glowing colour of the tea plantations. This is also the most Sinhalese part of the country for the Kingdom of Kandy resisted European takeover for over 300 years after the coastal regions had succumbed.

Kandy remains the cultural and spiritual centre of the island and is one of the top attractions in Sri Lanka. It's a relaxed and easy-going town with a delightful lakeside setting – a place where it's very easy to find the days just drifting by. There are many other hill country towns worth a visit and an abundance of pleasant walks and climbs, refreshing waterfalls and historical sites.

COLOMBO TO KANDY

There are a number of interesting places along the road from Colombo to Kandy. Near Gampaha, off the Colombo-Kandy road about 30 km from Colombo, the Henerathgoda Botanical Gardens are overshadowed by the the better known Peradeniya gardens at Kandy. They're of interest because it was here that the first rubber trees planted in Asia were carefully grown and their potential proved. Some of those original rubber trees are still there today. Admission to the gardens is Rs 5, Rs 2.50 for students.

Continuing on there's a memorial to Solomon Bandaranaike at Nittambuwa, 40 km from Colombo. You pass through areas of coconut, pineapple and cashew plantations and rice is grown in paddies along the road. At Radawadunna there are a whole host of little shops selling baskets, chairs, tables and other cane products at very cheap prices.

At Ambepussa, 54 km from Colombo, there is a very pleasant six room *Rest House* (tel Warakapola 544) with singles/doubles at Rs 150/200. There is another rest house a little further along at Kegalle. At Ambanpitiya there are tea and rubber factories close to the road – tours are available.

Elephants

There are a couple of tourist-oriented elephant villages near Kegalle where you can see elephants bathing and working or take an elephant ride. The Elephant Village has 11 or 12 elephants and entry costs Rs 30 – it's not as good value as the government run Pinnewala Elephant Orphanage, three km south of Rambukkana Station, which has about 15 elephants and only costs Rs 10. Some of the baby elephants here are surprisingly small; it must be one of the few places where an elephant can step on your foot and you can walk away with a smile! Bath time for the babies is between 10 am and 12 noon and 2 and 4 pm. Meal time (the little ones get a bottle of milk!) is 1 pm. At the Randeniya Elephant Baths the Rs 25 entry fee includes a ride.

Also near here are some clay pottery works and a couple of interesting temples. At Kadugannawa there is another rest house and also a memorial to Dawson, the English engineer who built the Colombo-Kandy road.

Getting There

To get to the elephant orphanage from Kandy take a 662 bus to Kegalle. From there take a bus from the stop at the Maya Photo Centre, near the minibus halt. The trip from there to the orphanage takes about 15 minutes.

KANDY

Only 115 km (72 miles) inland from Colombo, but climatically a world away due to its 500 metre altitude, Kandy is the relaxed, easy-going 'capital' of the hill country. It's also the cultural centre of Sri Lanka and in many ways the country's spiritual centre. Kandy was the capital of the last Sinhalese kingdom. After three centuries of defying the Portuguese and the Dutch, it finally fell to the British in 1815. In actual fact the Portuguese briefly captured the city on three occasions and the Dutch once, but it was not until the arrival of the British that the final spark of Sinhalese independence was extinguished.

Kandy is particularly famed for the great Kandy Esala Perahera held each year over the full moon in the month of Esala (July or August by our calendar), but it has attractions enough to justify a visit at any time of the year. The countryside around Kandy is lush and green and there are many pleasant walks both from the town itself or further afield. The central town is a delightful jumble of old shops, antique and gemstone special-ists, a bustling two-storey market and a good selection of hotels, guest houses and restaurants.

Information & Orientation

Kandy is dominated by its lake and the Temple of the Tooth. The town is surrounded by hills and many of the places to stay are perched up in these hills, looking down on the town. The main streets of the town are situated to the north of the lakeside with the bus and train stations just a short stroll down the main street from the lake.

The Temple of the Tooth is beside the lake, a little further along this same main street, past the large Queen's Hotel. Around the lakeside road, a short distance from the temple, is the small Tourist Office and the Kandy Arts Centre. The Tourist Office used to be in the library building by the lake and the new location may only be a temporary one. They are very helpful here but note that the office is closed on Saturdays and Sundays.

The manager of the arts centre, reported an art-collecting visitor, 'can find

an artisan to recreate anything one sees at the museum'. As well as the arts centre Kandy also has a Laksala crafts shop. Wooden souvenirs are available very cheaply at the Lankatilaka Temple, outside of Kandy.

The British Council, in the centre of Kandy opposite the clock tower, has a library. There's also a US Information Centre opposite the Hotel Casamara. You can buy and/or exchange books at Cindy's Bookstall in Torrington Lane, a side street between the Cold Store and the market. K V G de Silva on D S Senanayake Vidiya is probably the best bookshop in Sri Lanka, outside of Colombo. *Kandy* by Dr Anuradha Seneviratna is an excellent and authoritative guidebook to the temples and monuments of the city. It's published by the Ministry of Cultural Affairs. If you're interested in books on Buddhism visit the Buddhist Publication Society, known as 'The Wheel', by the lakeside.

It costs Rs 20 for non-residents to use the pool at the Hotel Suisse (including a towel). They can also play snooker or billiards on a 'big, well kept table in a room redolent of port, cigars and pompous conversations for Rs 20 per half hour'. At the Lakeside Cafe there's also a laundry service; cheaper than by-the-piece rate for laundry at hotels. The Bank of Ceylon in Kandy is also open on weekends for foreign exchange. The 'foreign package window' in the post office will wrap packages.

Kandy Esala Perahera

The big night of the year in Kandy actually comes as the culmination of 10 days of increasingly frenetic activity. A perahera is a parade or procession and Kandy's perahera peaks at the time of the full moon in Esala and is held to honour the sacred tooth enshrined in the Dalada Maligawa, the Temple of the Tooth.

The procession is actually a combination of five separate processions from the four Kandy *devales* – shrines to deities who protect the island and are also devotees and servants of the Buddha. There is Natha – a Buddha-to-be and of special importance to Kandy. Vishnu – the guardian of Sri Lanka and an indicator of the intermingling of Hindu and Buddhist beliefs since he is also one of the three great Hindu gods. Skanda – the god of war and victory; and Pattini – the goddess of chastity. But the most splendid perahera is that of the Dalada Maligawa, the Temple of the Tooth.

The procession is led by thousands of Kandyan dancers and drummers beating thousands of drums, leaping with unbounded energy, cracking noisy whips and waving colourful banners. Then comes long processions of elephants, 50, 60 or more of them. The brilliantly caparisoned Maligawa Tusker is the largest and most splendid of them all – decorated from trunk to toe he carries a huge canopy which shelters, on the final night, a replica of the sacred relic cask. A carpetway of white linen is laid in front of the elephant so that he does not step in the dirt.

The Kandy Esala Perahera is the most magnificent annual spectacle to be seen in Sri Lanka and one of the most famous in Asia. It has been an annual event for many centuries and is described by Robert Knox in his 1681 book *An Historical Relation of Ceylon*. There is also a smaller procession on the full moon day in June and special peraheras may be put on for important occasions – such as the Queen's visit to Sri Lanka in late '81.

It's essential to arrive early for roadside seats for the perahera – by 2 pm on the final night. Earlier in the week you can get seats about half-way back in the stands quite cheaply. Midway between the Temple of the Tooth and Queen's Hotel is a good place to take photographs because there's an area floodlit for Sri Lankan TV.

Kandyan Dancers

The famed Kandyan dancers are not principally a theatrical performance but you can see them go through their athletic

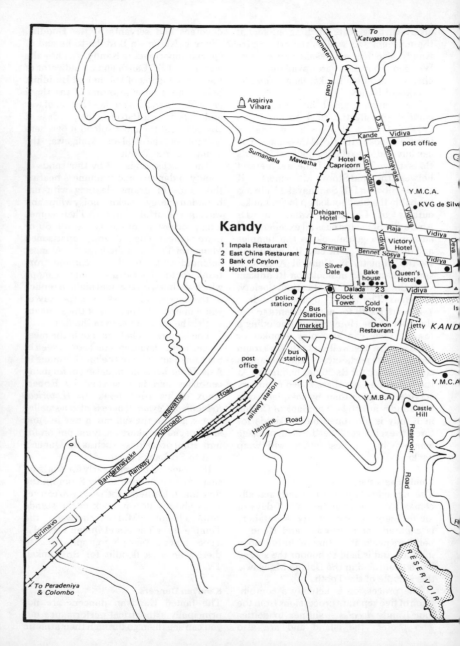

Kandy

1 Impala Restaurant
2 East China Restaurant
3 Bank of Ceylon
4 Hotel Casamara

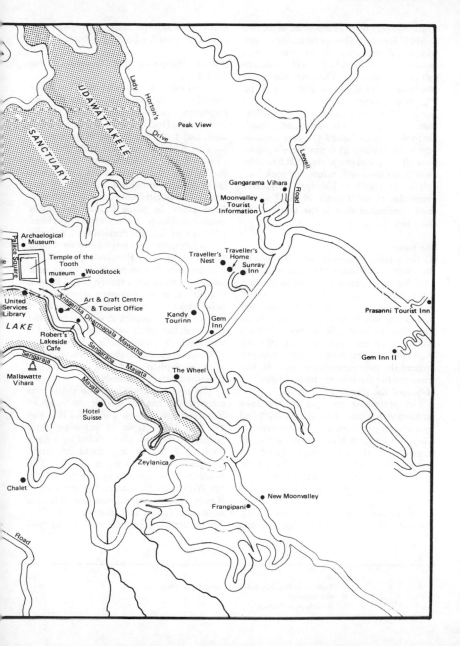

routines every night at one or more locales around Kandy. The performances are widely advertised – either your guest house or the Tourist Office will be able to tell you where to go. They last one to 1½ hours and cost Rs 75 to 100 for tickets. The performance now ends with a fire dance. The Keppetipola Hall performance is said to be particularly good. Ditto the Kandy Lake Club performance where on Fridays at 6 pm there's a free rock (?) band and magic show! 'It has to be seen to be believed', wrote one rock fan.

You can also hear Kandyan drummers every day at the Temple of the Tooth – their drumming signals the start of the daily *poyas*.

The Lake

Kandy's lake, a pleasant centre-piece to the town, is artificial and was only built in 1807 by Sri Wickrama Rajasinha, the last ruler of the Kingdom of Kandy. The island in the centre was used as his personal harem – to which he crossed on a barge. The less romantically inclined British used it as an ammunition store although they did add the fortress-style parapet around the perimeter of the lake. All the trees around the lake are named – you can play spot the mango or raintree.

The perimeter road around the lake makes a very pleasant stroll – it's also used by a steady procession of learner drivers, all in old English Morris Minors and all displaying L plates in very proper British fashion. On the far side of the lake, right by the lakeside in front of the monastery, there's a circular enclosure which is the monks' bathhouse. They'll invite males inside to see how a monk takes a fully clothed bath! From the bridge you can make a 20 minute tour of the lake and island by boat for Rs 35 per boat.

Dalada Maligawa (the Temple of the Tooth)

Located close to the lake the Temple of the Tooth houses Sri Lanka's most important Buddhist relic. The sacred tooth of the Buddha was said to have been snatched from the flames of his funeral pyre in 543 BC and was smuggled into Ceylon during the 4th century AD, hidden in the hair of a princess. At first it was taken to Anuradhapura but with the ups and downs of Sri Lankan history it moved from place to place before eventually ending at Kandy. For a short period from 1283 it was actually carried back to India by an invading army but was brought back to Ceylon by King Parakramabahu III.

Gradually the tooth came to assume more and more importance in Ceylon but the Portuguese, following one of their brief captures of Kandy, and in one of their worst spoilsport moods, assert that they took the tooth away and destroyed it with Catholic fervour in Goa. Not so is the Sinhalese rejoinder, they were fobbed off with a replica and the real incisor remained safely in Kandy.

The present Temple of the Tooth was constructed mainly during the reign of Kandyan kings from 1687 to 1707 and 1747 to 1782. It is an imposing pink-painted structure, surrounded by a deep moat, but not of any particular architectural significance in itself. The octagonal tower in the moat was built by Sri Wickrama Rajasinha, the last king of Kandy, and houses an important collection of ola-leaf (palm leaf) manuscripts.

The temple is open from dawn to dusk

Kandy
A   Temple of the Tooth illuminated for a perehera
B   Market stall
C   Bicycle repair shop

and there are morning and evening *poojas* (5.30 to 6.30 am, 9.30 to 10.30 am and 6.30 to 7.30 pm) when the heavily guarded room housing the tooth is open to devotees – and tourists. Of course you do not actually see the tooth – just a gold casket which is said to contain a series of smaller and smaller caskets and eventually the tooth itself. Or perhaps a replica, nobody seems to be too sure. The casket is behind a window and two decidedly mean-looking monks stand heavily on either side so there is no chance of any more sneaky Portuguese carting the sacred relic away. There's a Rs 25 charge to tape record the pooja, Rs 15 to take photographs.

Also within the temple precincts is the Audience Hall used by the kings of Kandy and the site for the convention of Kandyan chiefs which ceded the kingdom to the British in 1815. It is notable for the tall pillars which support the roof and for a time was used for ceremonial sittings of the Supreme Court. The courts around the back of the Temple of the Tooth are open to the public, even when in session. Sometimes you can see lawyers openly bargaining with each other to reach a settlement for their clients.

Kandy Museum

Behind the Temple of the Tooth you'll find Kandy's excellent small museum with much royal regalia and reminders of Sinhalese life prior to the arrival of the Europeans. It was once part of the palace complex and is open from 9 am to 5 pm except on Fridays and Saturdays. There is also an Archaeological Museum within the Temple of the Tooth, open 8 am to 4 pm except Tuesday. Admission Rs 25, student discount available.

Monasteries

As the cultural centre of Sri Lanka, the principal Buddhist monasteries have considerable importance – the high priests of the two best known monasteries, the Malwatte and the Asgiriya, are the most important in Sri Lanka. They also play an important role in the administration and operation of the Temple of the Tooth. The Malwatte monastery is directly across the lake from the Temple of the Tooth while the Asgiriya is on the hill off Trincomalee St, to the north-west of the town centre, and has a large reclining Buddha image.

Elephant Bath Time

At Katugastota, about four km from the centre of Kandy on the banks of the Mahaweli Ganga, elephants are brought down to the river by their *mahouts* for a midday bathe. There is usually quite a crowd of elephants enjoying a refreshing splash down here during the heat of the day – but note that it is quite a tourist scene these days and the *mahouts* are adept at demanding payment for photographing their noble steeds. If you decide to indulge in an elephant ride make sure you've specified how far the ride is going to be! They've become so commercial here that they generally want Rs 50 to 100 before they'll even talk to you. Best time to come is between 10 am and 12 noon or 2 pm and 4 pm. A 625 bus will take you there from the centre. Around perahera time elephant races are held here.

Scenic Walks

There are many walks almost in the centre of Kandy such as up to the Royal Palace Park overlooking the lake. There is a

---

Hill Country
A Elephant bath time at Katugastora, Kandy
B Ella Gap from Ella Rest House
C Adam's Peak – the shadow at dawn

cannon here, captured from the Japanese in Burma and donated by Lord Mountbatten. Further up the hill on Rajapihilla Mawatha there are even better views stretching over the lake, the town and the surrounding hills, which disappear in a series of gentle ranges stretching far into the distance.

On the other side of the lake you can take a longer stroll around the cool and pleasant Udawattakele Sanctuary. There is much birdlife and more than a few monkeys in the sanctuary but visitors are advised to be a little careful in this secluded woodland if they're alone. Muggers may be fairly rare in Sri Lanka but they're not unknown.

Arts & Crafts

The Kandyan Arts and Crafts Association has a good display of local lacquerwork, brassware and other craft items at their showroom beside the lake. The beautiful, miniature 'batik' elephants make good little presents for children back home. There is also a government-run Laksala arts and crafts shop in Kandy but it has nothing on the big one in Colombo. Kandy is packed with antique shops, particularly along the central lakeside road. Antique (and instant-antique) jewellery, silver belts, and other items are available in abundance.

Kandy also has a number of batik manufacturers – I particularly liked those at Fresco Batiks at 901 Peradeniya Rd, towards the Botanical Gardens. Travellers have also recommended Presar Batiks and Kjreil's Batiks, near the Gem Inn.

Botanical Gardens

The Peradeniya Botanical Gardens are six km out of Kandy towards Colombo; the Peradeniya railway station is the last stop before Kandy. Prior to the arrival of the British this was a royal park and it is today the largest Botanical Garden in Sri Lanka. The gardens cover 60 hectares (147 acres) and are bounded on three sides by a loop of the Mahaweli River – the longest river in Sri Lanka, which has its source close to Adam's Peak and runs into the sea at Trincomalee.

The gardens had some of the original rubber trees smuggled out of Brazil – until they were wiped out by a storm in 1980. There is also a fine collection of orchids and a stately avenue of royal palms which were planted in 1905. Admission to the gardens is Rs 15 for foreign visitors, Rs 7.50 for students, Rs 1 for local residents – another case of the Sri Lankan two-tier system when it comes to entry charges. A bus 652 will take you to the gardens.

There is a Royal Gardens Cafeteria about a hundred metres from the entrance, to the left. Shoestringers can find a cheaper canteen for garden employees, you won't be turned away. Outside the garden people will rent you bicycles to take inside for Rs 0.50.

A Temple Loop from Kandy

There are many temples scattered around Kandy – they are not really terribly interesting unless you're a real temple freak but on the other hand they do make a pleasant trip out into the country. It's a chance to see a little rural life with some culture thrown in. A particularly pleasant loop will take you from Kandy to three of these temples and back via the Botanical Gardens.

The first stop is the Embekke Devale, for which you need a bus from near the railway station. The bus only runs about once an hour and the village of Embekke is about seven twisting and turning km beyond the Botanical Gardens – it seems a lot further. From the village you've got a pleasant countryside stroll of about a km to the temple. The 14th century temple is said to have the best examples of wood carved pillars to be found in Kandy. They are thought to have come from a royal audience hall in the city. The carvings include swans, double-headed eagles, wrestling men and dancing women. There's a Rs 10 entry charge to the temple. A miniature version of the Kandy perahera is held here in late August.

From here to the Lankatilaka Temple is a km and a half stroll along a path through the rice paddies until the temple looms up on the left. From Kandy you can go directly to the temple on a 644 bus. Built on a rocky outcrop the temple is reached by a long series of steps cut directly into the rock. The brick structure houses a fine Buddha image and Kandy period wall paintings while outside there are stone elephant figures. It's considered to be one of the best examples of Sinhalese temple architecture.

It's a further three km walk from here to the Gadaladeniya Temple, or you can catch a bus – a 644 amongst others will take you there. This temple too is constructed atop a rocky outcrop and dates from a similar period to the Lankatilaka and Embekke Devale. There are definite signs of Hindu influence in the stone construction. A moonstone marks the entrance to the main shrine. This temple also has a Rs 10 entry charge.

From here the main Colombo-Kandy road is only about a km away; you reach it close to the 65th milestone. It's a pleasant stroll and from the main road almost any bus will take you to the Botanical Gardens or on into Kandy. The complete loop from Kandy costs about Rs 6 by bus – one bus out to Embekke, another from Lankatilaka to Gadaladeniya and finally from the main road junction to the Botanical Gardens and on into Kandy.

Other Temples around Kandy

Not far beyond the Gem Inn and Travellers' Nest, only a five or 10 minute walk, turn off the road to the Gangarama Temple with its six metre high Buddha statue.

Other temples in the vicinity of Kandy include the 14th century Degaldoruwa, about 2½ km north-east of the Lewella ferry crossing (also a suspension bridge) and 10 km from Kandy itself. It is famous for its recently restored frescoes illus-

trating scenes from the Jataka. They reflect everyday life in Kandy at the time of the temple's construction. The Galmaduwa is architecturally unique and was probably built, during the Kandy period, on the site of a much older dagoba. It is off the Kandy-Kundasale road, about six km to the south-east of Kandy. To get there take a 655 bus from the market bus stand to the end of line at the river. Walk across the footbridge and straight on to the temple.

At Medawala, 10 km to the north-east of Kandy, the Medawala Vihara dates from the 18th century and has a pleasantly rustic design with a tiled roof and a frieze illustrating mythical animals composed of parts of a variety of species. The antechamber is vividly painted with demons. A 603 bus from the market bus stand will get you there.

The Hindagala Temple is picturesquely situated and has rock carvings dating back to the 5th and 6th century. The 14th century Dodanwela temple houses the crown and sword of the Kandyan King Rajasinghe, presented after he defeated a Portuguese invasion force.

Those interested in the study of Buddhism can visit a couple of places, each about an hour out of Kandy. They offer 10 day courses each month. The Rockhill Hermitage is at Wegirikanda, reached via Gampola on a bus 645. The Nilambe Meditation Centre is near the Nilambe Bungalow Junction, reached via Galaha on a bus 633. From the junction you have a steep 1½ km walk through the tea plantations. Regular 10-day courses are held here, costs are around Rs 50 a day, the food is all vegetarian and most people seem to like it. When there are no courses anyone is free to come and stay and learn on an individual basis. They have a large library of books on Buddhist meditation and related subjects as well as a tape library.

Veddah Settlements

If you are interested in visiting a Veddah

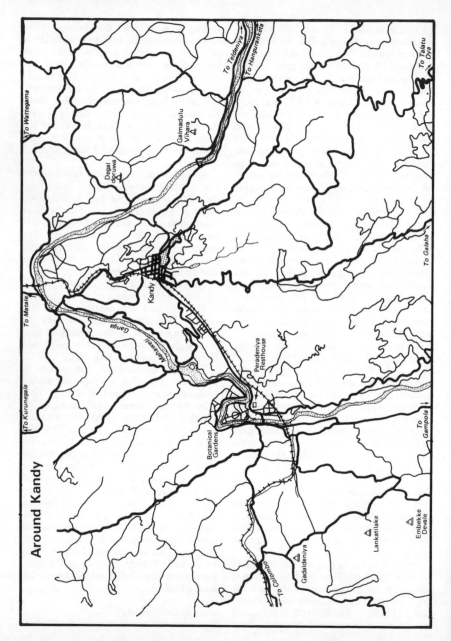

Around Kandy

village the best place to do it is Dambena, where there is a settlement of about 30. The Veddah's are the original, pre-Sinhalese peòple. You can get there by bus from Mahiyangana, about 80 km east of Kandy and the same distance north of Badulla. This is a long trip, about 3½ hours each way by bus. The village headman can be identified by the axe which is always balanced on his left shoulder as a mark of authority. Tour operators may already be including this settlement in their itineraries so it may not survive long in its present form.

Places to Stay

Kandy is the guest house capital of Sri Lanka and at the low budget end of the scale there are a great number of popular places. Kandy is also the capital of the touting business and unless absolutely necessary you should avoid them for all you are worth. They'll end up costing you much more for your room as they demand 50 to 100% of your first night room costs from the hotel operator.

Kandy Accommodation Warnings Touts

are pushier and greater in number in Kandy than anywhere else – if you know where you want to go then ignore them, they'll only push prices up for you. The Kandy touts are so persistent they'll actually go down to Colombo in order to intercept you on the train to Kandy. They befriend you and before you know it they're taking you to 'their place' in Kandy – where the price you pay will be hiked up to pay a healthy commission to them. Quite a few places in Kandy will pick you up from the station, or pay your taxi fare, to avoid having to pay off the touts.

At the time of the Esala Perahera prices in Kandy go nuts – if you can find a room at all that is. If you're intent on coming to see the perahera then be prepared for what it will cost you.

Places to Stay – bottom end

Guest Houses & Cheap Hotels Three of the most popular Kandy cheapies are in a small cluster about a km beyond the town centre – only a couple of minutes walk off the road to the left, down in the rice paddies. Here you'll find the *Travellers' Nest* (tel 08-22633) at 117/4 Anagarika Dharmapala Mawatha, which is so popular that a host of imitators with 'nest-like' names have sprung up. They now have 26 rooms – the basic rooms cost Rs 30/50 for singles/doubles, then there are rooms with fan and bath for Rs 75/100, fancier rooms at Rs 125 to 150 and upstairs larger doubles with attached bath and hot water for Rs 250 including breakfast. There's also a second building of 'economic' rooms. There's a pleasant balcony where you can sit and watch the monkeys and the food here is very good.

Next door is *Traveller's Home* (tel 08-22800) with similar sorts of prices. Third in this group is the *Sunray Inn* (tel 08-23322) with 18 double rooms from Rs 60 to 300. All three of these places are just far enough off the beaten track to be pleasantly quiet yet not too far from the town centre. Food is available at all of them too. A 654 or 655 bus will take you to them from the town but if you're lightly laden it's just a pleasant stroll uphill from the lakeside. If you phone from the station they'll probably arrange transport or pay for a taxi, to avoid dealing with the touts.

Another very popular place is the *Gem Inn* (tel 08-24239) at 39 Anagarika Dharmapala Mawatha. This is on the main road, just a short walk back towards the town centre. Rooms cost Rs 50 and 75 with common bath or Rs 100 for a double with bath. It's five minutes' walk above the Temple of the Tooth, or you can get there on a 654 or 655 bus, as for the Travellers' Nest. There are only a handful of rooms at the Gem Inn but there is a second Gem Inn which is superb if you're planning a longer stay. It's a little further out of town and high up on a ridge with a fantastic view stretching far across the hills to the north. The *Gem Inn II* is a very pleasant, spacious and relaxed house with excellent doubles with attached bathroom for Rs 150. You can walk down along the ridge to the town or a taxi will cost your Rs 30 to 40.

Take the steep road up behind the Kandy Museum and the Temple of the Tooth, veer left up the steep dirt path and at the top of the path and some steps you'll find *Woodstock*. It's a straightforward and simple place which has, according to one traveller, 'the best location in town, you get a wonderful breeze and a nice view of the temple and lake'. There are a variety of rooms with prices of Rs 30, 50 and 60 plus an octagonal room at the front for Rs 100. There are common bathrooms and toilets.

A place which has become very popular in the last year or so is the *Prasanna Guest House* (tel 08-24365) at 53/29 Hewaketa Rd. To find it continue on beyond the Travellers' Nest group until you see the steep downhill turn off to the left of the road. Basic rooms are Rs 40, no bath, or rooms with bath cost Rs 50 to 75. It's clean, neat and well equipped and several travellers have written to comment on the exceptional helpfulness of the owner. Further down the steep road at the river is a good swimming spot and also a non-commercial elephant bathing place.

Kandy has a great number of other places to stay and the tourist office by the lakeside will provide you with more information on smaller hotels and guest houses. Many of these small guest houses will only have a couple of rooms. Those that follow are just a limited selection, most of which have been recommended by travellers:

Mrs De Silva's guest house at 15 Malabar St (sometimes known as 'Doctor's House') is pleasant and friendly with rooms from Rs 75. The *Mawilmada Tourist Rest* (tel 08-23250) at 16 Mawilmada Rd has five rooms from Rs 30 to 75. The *New Moonvalley* has rooms at Rs 75 with

bath – it's plain but OK, quite a way up the road from the lake and opposite the Frangipani Guest House.

Several people have written to recommend *Lucktissme* (tel 08-22725) at 125 Pitakanda Rd, Mahayaya where singles/doubles are Rs 75/150. It's up the hill from the Katugastota road, near the elephant baths, but they'll pick you up from the station. 'A lovely place to stay, nice people and good food'. Several letters have also recommended *Jingle Bells* at 26 Sangamitta Mawatha. 'I checked it out because of the silly name', said one visitor, 'but the rooms (from Rs 60 to 125) were good and the family very friendly and helpful. The cooking was the best I had in Sri Lanka'. There are several other places up this road, including the more expensive *Kandy Tourinn* and the *Hotel Thilanka*.

Other places which have been recommended include *Lakshmi*, uphill (follow the Lake Inn signs) just before the Suisse. It's spotlessly clean and has rooms from Rs 50 to 100. Right in the centre, at 31 King St, the *Charlton Guest House* (no sign but the Charlton Shopping Centre is next door) is Rs 50 to 75 for a double. Also conveniently central *Mrs Wadugodapitiya's* guest house is at 74 Peradeniya Rd, about due west of the market across the foot bridge. The large rooms cost from Rs 50, there are modern bathrooms and it's pleasantly run.

Next to the YMCA at the lake, *Victoria Cottage* at 6 Victoria Drive is a beautiful house with doubles with bathroom for Rs 50 to 70. Somewhat more expensive, the *Sunrock Holiday Home* (tel 08-24137) is at 195 Heerassagala Rd and has rooms at Rs 150/200. At 30/61 Bangalawatta, Lewella Rd the *Linton Lodge* is on the edge of town, a 15 minutes walk to the temple. You can get there on a 655 bus. The rooms cost from Rs 35 and are very clean, the food is OK. *St Michael's Guest House* at Ampitiya is easy going and has good music – rooms are Rs 75/150 including breakfast.

There are *Railway Retiring Rooms* (tel 08-22271) at the Kandy station with rooms at Rs 143 and 163. Finally, close to the Temple of the Tooth, the *Olde Empire* (tel 08-24284) is one of the cheapest hotels in Kandy and it's a pretty good place. Rooms cost Rs 80 to 100, cheaper at the back although the singles there are a little cramped and dingy. There are fine views from the balconies and the place has a 'wonderful colonial feel'. A number of travellers have written to recommend it.

Ys & Hostels Kandy also has a number of Ys. Probably the best value of the lot is the *YMBA* (Young Men's Buddhist Association) at 5 Rajapihilla Mawatha – overlooking the lake and close to the Royal Palace Park. Costs here range from Rs 25 per person. Also on this side of the lake is the *YMCA* at 4 and 4a Sangaraja Mawatha. It has 10 rooms and is similarly priced but is only open to men and is rather run down.

There is a second *YMCA* (tel 08-23529) on Kotugodella Vidiya very close to the town centre. There are singles at Rs 23, fancier doubles with bath at Rs 84.50, share rooms (men only) are Rs 17.50 each or a dorm (again men only) at Rs 9.25.

Also centrally located, the *Kandy City Mission* is at 125 Trincomalee St, a few blocks up from the Queen's Hotel. It's very reasonable, clean and comfortable with rooms around Rs 75 to 150. The food here, both Sri Lankan and western, is good and they make their own cheese and dark bread.

There's a small *Boy Scout Youth Hostel* at the Boy Scout Headquarters, back across the lake again and further up the hill on Keppetipola Rd. At Katugastota the *Travellers' Halt* is 'one of the nicest youth hostels in Asia' according to a traveller. Ask directions for the railway bridge at Katugastota, cross the bridge and the YH (which has no sign) is the second house on the left.

Places to Stay – top end
Kandy has a couple of well kept top end places in the inimitable Sri Lankan, colonial-era-English style. *Queen's Hotel* (tel 08-22121, 22122) has been taken over by the Oberoi chain but the only change they have made appears to be a general rise in the price levels. It's right in the town centre and right beside the lake and has 120 rooms with singles/doubles at Rs 300/425. And hard beds, so I'm told! The Queen's also has an excellent restaurant, recommended for a splash out even if you're on a shoestring, and a beer garden.

Across the lake at 30 Sangaraja Mawatha, the *Hotel Suisse* (tel 08-22637, 22671) has a swimming pool (Rs 20 for non-residents), 96 rooms and costs from Rs 525/575. It's rather more secluded and quiet than the centrally located Queen's but not too far to stroll around the lake. Balcony rooms are very clean, spacious and restful.

Back in the town centre the *Hotel Dehigama* (tel 08-22709) is at 84 Raja Vidiya. It's a modern building with 35 rooms at Rs 300 – pleasant, friendly and with a 'charming little beer garden'. The recently opened *Hotel Hantana* (tel 08-23155, 23067) is on Hantana Rd, 1½ km from the centre of Kandy. It has 100 rooms priced from Rs 400.

The *Mahaweli Reach* (tel 08-22611, 23047) is at 35 Siyambalagastenne Rd, close to the Katugastota bridge, and also has a swimming pool. It has 50 rooms with rooms at Rs 400 or singles/doubles at Rs 600/750 including all meals. The pleasant *Ladyhill Tourist Hotel* (tel 08-22659) is high above the Peradeniya road, almost out at the Botanical Gardens. There are 40 rooms and nightly costs are Rs 350/400.

The *Chalet* (tel 08-24353) at 32 Gregory's Rd overlooks the lake across from the town centre and the 30 rooms cost from Rs 400 to 600 including all meals. 'The views are magnificent, the food and service excellent – better value than the Suisse or Queen's', reported one visitor. Also overlooking the lake, the *Castle Hill Guest House* (tel 08-24376) is at 22 Rajapihilla Mawatha and rooms cost from Rs 500. Good for a luxury stop reported one visitor – 'the immense rooms with their low art deco-like furniture, French doors to the gardens and stylised flower arrangements could almost be hotel stage-sets from a Fred Astaire movie!'

In Anniewatte, way up on top of a hill overlooking Kandy, the *Hotel Topaz* (tel 08-23062, 24150) has 70 rooms with prices from Rs 600. Or there is the small *Frangipani Guest House* (tel 08-23210) at 80 Ampitiya Mawatha, uphill from the end of the lake with singles/doubles at Rs 280/310 including breakfast. The *Riverdale Tourist Guest House* (tel 08-23020) is at 32 Anniewatte Rd and has 15 rooms from Rs 290/330 for singles/doubles. The *Kandy Tourinn* (tel 08-22790) is rather cheaper, it's on 17 Sangamitta Mawatha, uphill towards the Udawattakele Sanctuary. The *Peak View Motel* (tel 08-24241) is even further up the hill at 102 Dharmasoka Mawatha.

There are many other better quality hotels and guest houses which the Kandy Tourist Office can advise you about. The small *Chateau* (tel 08-23608) at 20 Rajapihilla Mawatha has just three rooms, each with its own bathroom. The friendly owners, the Abeywikremas, charge Rs 175/250 for this excellent little place. The clean and relaxed *Blue Star* (tel 08-24392) at 30 Hewaheta Rd has rooms, cabanas and fantastic food and nightly costs of Rs 160/220.

The *Windy Cot Guest House* (tel 08-22052) at 66 Riverdale Rd has rooms at Rs 240/270. At 2 Mahamaya Mawatha the *Zeylanica Guest House* (tel 08-24388) is more expensive at Rs 300/500 including breakfast but it's an attractive place, very well kept and conveniently located. The owners are 'knowledgeable, witty and cosmopolitan'. The *Hotel Gardenia* (tel 08-25430) at 108 Riverdale Rd has rooms

from Rs 250 and up – 'pleasant and much better value than Queen's Hotel'.

Kandy also has a *Rest House*, situated directly across from the main entrance to the Botanical Gardens at Peradeniya – get off the train at Peradeniya station if you're going there, don't continue in to Kandy.

Finally Kandy's most modern and expensive hotel is 27 km out of Kandy, higher up in a tea estate at Elkaduwa. The *Hunas Falls Hotel* (tel 31894, 35978) has 28 very modern rooms with air-con and all other mod-cons including swimming pool, tennis court, a well stocked fish pool above the Hunas waterfalls and plenty of walks in the surrounding hills. For this luxury count on around Rs 750 for a double, Rs 1250 with all meals.

Places to Eat

Cheaper Restaurants There are a number of popular cheaper places around Kandy but all of them seem to get mixed reports. None of them would rate culinary raves but they seem to yo-yo between acceptable and awful! Two of them are on the main road, virtually opposite each other. The *Bake House* is a big, two-level place with good short eats and a comprehensive menu although it's now quite expensive and a number of travellers have reported the food here can be very variable.

The *Ceylon Cold Store*, across the road, is not open in the evenings but is good for lunch and popular for quick snacks, drinks or ice cream ('delicious strawberry ice cream' reported one traveller). Good take-aways and ice cream from out front too. Like the Bake House it's now moderately expensive; meals generally cost from Rs 20 or 30 and up.

The rather scruffy *Impala Restaurant* (biriyanis a speciality) also does a really refreshing mixed fruit drink. On the left side of the Peradeniya road, just past the main roundabout in Kandy, the *Lyons Cafe* is clean, has quick service and good, cheap food.

Other cheaper restaurants include the *East China* (painfully slow service and the food is not very good when it finally arrives) on the Bake House side; the very popular *Devon* ('good and cheap') on the Cold Store side and the *Silver Dale* round the corner. At the latter the food can be very variable – some people find it terrible, others excellent.

The *Olde Empire*, between the Queen's Hotel and the Tooth Temple, may look a little grey and dreary, but the food here is surprisingly good. Come here for a good rice and curry and try their excellent ice cream. The *Kandy City Mission* at 125 Trincomalee St has good short eats plus their own cheese and brown bread. The *Jayananda Hotel*, nearly opposite the mission, has good rice and curry and also cheap western food.

The newly opened *Robert's Lakeside Cafe* is a pleasant outdoor snack place. Drinks are Rs 7.50 to 10, sandwiches Rs 12.50 to 27.50. And each table comes with a bell to ring for service! The *Victory Hotel* on Srimath Bennet Sosya Vidiya has a good variety of food and you can get a good beer at the *Sosya Irdeega* (loose beer shop!), just down from it.

Good food, pleasant surroundings but rather higher prices can be found at the *Royal Park Cafeteria* in the Botanic Gardens – lunch times only of course. The Rs 55 set lunch is good but here too the service can be slow. Note that there is also a cheaper employees' cafeteria in the gardens.

More Expensive Restaurants If you want to flash out in the evenings the dining rooms of the *Queen's Hotel* or the *Hotel Suisse* would be good places to do it. With service the fixed price dinners will come to around Rs 100 per person – you dine in 'olde English' style and surroundings but nobody has had a lot good to say about the Queen's food recently. Another splash out place is the restaurant at the *Hotel Thilanka*, 3 Sangamitta Mawatha, only five minutes from the Tooth Temple on foot. They have excellent Moghul, Chinese and Sri Lankan specialities.

Getting There
There are six direct trains to Kandy daily, the first service at 5.55 am from Colombo Fort and the last at 8.15 pm. The trip takes about three hours and costs Rs 60.50 in 1st, Rs 38.70 in 2nd, Rs 15.80 in 3rd. On most of the services there is only 2nd and 3rd class. The new Inter-City Express departs Colombo at 7 am daily. This one-class train takes just two hours and costs Rs 40. The only stop is at the Peradeniya Junction.

Some people say the right hand side has the best views, others the left, either way it's a nice view. The rail fare on to Nanu Oya, from where you take a bus or taxi into Nuwara Eliya, is Rs 31.70 in 2nd class, Rs 13 in 3rd.

You can also get to Kandy by CTB bus from Colombo for Rs 16 or by private minibus for Rs 20. There is a daily direct bus between Kandy and Katunayake airport. It departs from the airport at 5 pm, from Kandy at 8 am. Continuing from Kandy it costs Rs 18 to Nuwara Eliya. The bus departs from near the Temple of the Tooth and goes via Hatton, jumping off point for Adam's Peak. Minibuses to Anuradhapura or to Polonnaruwa cost Rs 20.

Getting Around
For destinations close to Kandy buses depart from the Torrington Bus Stand by the market. The Goodshed Bus Stand near the railway station is for 'out station' destinations. CTB buses depart from the Central Bus Stand in front of the market.

For the Botanical Gardens take a Peradeniya bus beside the central market. A Kiribathkumbara or Pilimatalawa bus from the same location will take you to the Lankatilaka Temple. For Katugastota and the elephant bath time take a Katugastota bus from in front of the police station.

The Lakeside Cafe rents out bicycles and motorcycles. A bike costs Rs 9.50 an hour or Rs 39 for a day. Small motorcycles of 50 to 90 cc cost Rs 45 to 60 an hour, Rs 125 to 195 for a day.

KANDY TO THE EAST COAST

Most travellers continuing on from Kandy will go in one of three direction – west to Colombo, north to the ancient cities or south to the rest of the hill country. It is also possible to go east, via Mahiyangana (see Veddah Settlements above) to the Gal Oya National Park, Badulla in the south of hill country, Batticaloa on the east coast or Monaragala on the Wellaraya -Arugam Bay road.

Mahiyangana is the spot where the Buddha is supposed to have preached when he visited Sri Lanka and there's a dagoba to mark the spot. Nearby are the Mahiyangana bends, where the road from Kandy drops steeply down from the hill country to the dry-zone plains. The road winds down through 18 hairpin bends and from the top you have a magnificent view of the Mahaweli development scheme.

The trip up or down the road is one of the most hair raising imaginable, especially on a CTB bus! Don't attempt it if you're of a nervous disposition or if you're familiar with the maintenance standards on CTB buses. On the way up you worry about overheating, on the way down you worry about the brakes. You usually pass at least one jeep or truck which didn't make it and lies in the jungle beneath.

From Mahiyangana you can take a bus to Bibile and from there to Monaragala and then the east coast. Alternatively it is possible to go to Ampara and from there to Batticaloa.

ADAM'S PEAK

Whether it is Adam's Peak – the place where Adam first set foot on the earth after being cast out of heaven; or Sri Pada – the 'sacred footprint'; or simply Samanalakande – the 'butterfly mountain' where butterflies go to die; Adam's Peak is a beautiful and fascinating place. Not all faiths believe the huge 'footprint' on the top of the 2224 metre (7300 feet) high peak to be that of Adam – it is also claimed to be Buddha's, St Thomas the early apostle of India, and even Lord Shiva's.

Whichever legend you care to believe, if any, the fact remains that it has been a pilgrimage centre for over a thousand years. King Parakramabahu and King Nissankamalla of Polonnaruwa provided *ambalamas* or 'resting places' up the mountain to shelter the weary pilgrims.

Today the pilgrimage season commences in December and runs until the start of the south-west monsoon in April. Between May and October the peak is obscured by cloud for much of the time. During the season a steady stream of pilgrims (and the odd tourist) make the weary climb up the countless steps to the top. The walk is lit all the way in season but at other times you can be stumbling up in the dark. Many pilgrims prefer to make the longer, more tiring climb from Ratnapura via the Carney Estate because of the greater merit thus gained.

It is not only the sacred footprint that pilgrims climb to see. As the first rays of dawn light up the holy mountain you're treated to an extremely fine view – the hill country rises to the east while to the west the land slopes away to the sea. Colombo is only 65 km distance and is easily visible on a clear day. It's little wonder that English author John Stills described the peak as 'one of the vastest and most reverenced cathedrals of the human race'.

Interesting as the ascent is and beautiful as the dawn, Adam's Peak saves its piece de resistance for a few minutes after the dawn. The sun casts a perfect shadow of the peak onto the misty clouds down towards the coast. As the sun rises higher this eerie triangular shadow races back towards the peak, eventually disappearing into its base. As you scramble back down the countless stairs to the bottom you can reflect on how much easier the ascent is today than it was a hundred years ago – as described in a Victorian guidebook to Ceylon:

.... others struggle upwards unaided, until, fainting by the way, they are considerately carried with all haste in their swooning condition to the summit and forced into an attitude of worship at the shrine to secure the full benefits of their pilgrimage before death should supervene; others never reach the top at all, but perish from cold and fatigue; and there have been many instances of pilgrims losing their lives by being blown over precipice or falling from giddiness induced by a thoughtless retrospect when surmounting especially dangerous cliffs.

Climbing Adam's Peak

Getting to the base of Adam's Peak is quite simple – there's no need to be there until late afternoon so you've got all day to arrive. Starting point is Hatton, which is on the Colombo-Kandy-Nuwara Eliya railway line. It's also on the Colombo-Nuwara Eliya and Kandy-Nuwara Eliya road and special buses run to Hatton and Dalhousie from Colombo during the pilgrimage season. At that time there are also direct buses from Kandy to Dalhousie, the trip takes about four hours.

In Dalhousie the trail starts from the tea factory. During the pilgrimage season there will be buses direct from Hatton to Dalhousie for about Rs 8. It's about 33 km and takes nearly two hours. Otherwise you will have to take a bus to Maskeliya, about 20 km from Hatton, and another the rest of the way – fairly frequent. It's a rather hair-raising ride; plenty of unguarded sheer drops on tight corners. There is also a direct bus from Nuwara Eliya to Dalhousie, departing at 4 pm and arriving around 8.30 pm.

Dalhousie has a collection of tea shops where you can get something to eat or buy provisions for the expedition ahead. You can get a place to sleep (part of the night) in one of the tea shops; or try the relatively expensive *Wijitha Hotel* – 'Rs 50 for a hole-in-the-wall single'. The bus stops right outside this establishment – the rooms are nothing special but you can cram in as many people as you like and it's only for half the night. Or you can just leave your gear with the police station by the car park.

Apart from the 'usual' route from Dalhousie there are two less used routes from the western side. They are rather longer, much less used and much more difficult – for the last few km they join together. The Dalhousie route involves a climb of about seven km – up steps virtually all the way. It's lit at night by a string of lights which from below look very pretty as they snake up the mountainside. From the Ratnapura side allow about seven hours to make the exhausting ascent through the Carney Estate.

With plenty of rest stops you'll still get to the top in around three hours. 'I spent one hour 45 minutes getting to the top', reported one athlete! A 2 am start will easily get you there before dawn which is usually around 6 to 6.30 am. From the car park the slope is gradual for the first half hour or so. You pass under an entrance archway, then by the Japan-Sri Lanka Friendship Dagoba, construction of which started in 1976. From here the path gets steeper and steeper until it is simply a continuous flight of stairs. There are plenty of teahouses for rest and refreshment all the way to the top.

Since it can get pretty cold and windy on top, and you'll work up quite a sweat on the climb, there's no sense in getting to the top too long before the dawn and have to sit around shivering. Bring plenty of warm clothes including something extra to put on when you get to the summit.

Since the first edition several additional suggestions have been made: one traveller wrote that on a holiday climbing the peak can be much more difficult, 'I climbed it on a full moon holiday – along with 20,000 pilgrims – it took 11 hours'. Another suggestion was that 'while you are waiting for the sun to rise at the top why not write a letter? There is a post box up there and I can vouch that letters sent from there will reach their destination'. 'Why all the emphasis on rushing up in the dark?' was another suggestion. 'The walk up, with stops to wash in the stream, to take tea with the Japanese monks at the beautiful Peace Pagoda, and rest and chat at the chai shops, was as good as the time spent on the top – on Christmas morning'. 'Tremendous view – the best thing I've seen in a year's travelling', was another comment.

NUWARA ELIYA

Situated at 1889 metres (6199 feet) Nuwara Eliya was the favourite hill station of the British who kitted it up like some misplaced British village. The charming old pink brick post office, the English country house-like Hill Club with its hunting pictures, mounted hunting trophies and fish, the 18-hole golf course (said to be one of the finest in Asia) and even the well stocked trout streams, all cry out 'England'. The golf course, wrote one traveller, 'is a real beauty for Asia. I played 11 holes in the pouring rain after being given a caddy (who had a handicap of seven and always played in bare feet), four golf balls and some pretty good clubs for Rs 185. Playing a full round is not too much more'.

Nuwara Eliya also has a fair assortment of 'olde English' style houses, a well kept central park which comes alive with flowers around March to May and August to September, and the pleasant Gregory's Lake, encircled by a variety of walking paths. The trout hatcheries are still maintained and all-in-all a retired tea planter would feel absolutely at home. Come prepared for the evening cool – Nuwara Eliya is much higher than Kandy.

Nuwara Eliya is 'the' place to be in Sri Lanka in April over the Sinhalese new year and accommodation can be hard to find at that time. If you did find a room over that three week period the cost would be through the roof. They hold horse races then too. The name Nuwara Eliya means 'city of light'.

Pidurutalagala

Mt Pedro, as it is also known, is the highest mountain in Sri Lanka at 2524 metres (8281 feet). It rises immediately to the north of the town and since Nuwara Eliya is already at a considerable height, getting to the top is not so much a climb as a stiff walk along well-marked paths. 'A tough scramble up muddy trails', wrote one less-than-convinced climber! It takes less than two hours to walk to the top but you'll probably be pretty tired by the time you get there. The path starts from Keen Rd, close to the Roman Catholic Church, and there are marker stones at 7500 and 8000 feet. Perched on top of the mountain is Sri Lanka's first television transmitter mast.

Hakgala Gardens

The second hill country botanical gardens (after the Peradeniya gardens near Kandy) were originally a cinchona plantation – from which is derived the anti-malarial drug quinine. Later they were used for experiments in acclimatising temperate zone plants to life in the tropics and were run by the same family for three generations right up to the 1940s.

Today they're a delightful small garden, famed for its roses and ferns. The gardens are about 10 km out of Nuwara Eliya (and about 200 metres lower) on the road to Welimada and Bandarawela. The name means 'jaw-rock' and derives from the legend that the Hakgala rock, to the side of which the gardens cling, was carried back from the Himalaya by Hanuman, the monkey god, in his jaw. He had been sent there by Rama to bring back a medicinal herb but forgetting which one it was decided to simply carry back a representative chunk of mountain hoping that the particular herb would be growing on it!

About a km before the gardens you pass the Sita Eliya temple on the left hand side of the road. The temple is said to mark the spot where Sita was held captive by the demon king Rawana and daily prayed for Rama to come and rescue her. On the rock

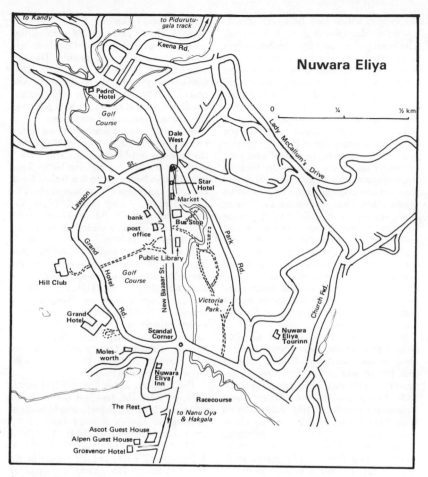

face across the stream you can see a number of circular depressions which are said to be the footprints of Rawana's elephant. The Hakgala Gardens are a couple of rupees bus ride from Nuwara Eliya and there is a Rs 15 admission charge for foreigners (Rs 7.50 for students).

Places to Stay – bottom end

Like Kandy, Nuwara Eliya is plagued by accommodation touts who work overtime in search of rake-offs from the town's plethora of guest houses. Nuwara Eliya is not a great place for cheap accommodation. *Molesworth* is part of the travellers' halt network and close to the Grand Hotel. According to some visitors it's damp, musty and none too special – which doesn't stop it from being the main travellers' locale. There are dorm beds, singles/doubles at Rs 50/75 and a nice lounge and gardens.

There are a number of guest houses in

the vicinity which may be worth investigating if Molesworth does not appeal. The nearby *Nuwara Eliya Inn* has rooms at Rs 125, 150 and up. It gets mixed reviews – 'pretty reasonable' reported one visitor; 'one of the worst places we stayed' said another. *Wattles Inn* on St Andrew's Drive has rooms at Rs 125/150 but also gets distinctly mixed reports.

The *Ascot Guest House*, opposite the race track, has doubles at Rs 125 – they're good value including breakfast and with hot water and extra sheets. On Badulla Rd, *Collingwood* is an amazing old mock-Tudor house originally built by a Scottish planter: 'More like a museum, everything is preserved in its original '30s state including an ancient retainer who served everything in true English style'. Another visitor reported the sitting room bookshelves included copies of *Brideshead Revisited* and Tennyson's poems. Still another commented on the interesting collection of old prints and photos on the walls. There's just one room at Rs 150 including breakfast.

Behind the Fancy Market on Old Bazaar St the *Hemamala Guest House* is pleasant with singles at Rs 50, doubles with hot shower at Rs 125. *Mrs Weeramanthy* on Lebana Rd has rooms for Rs 80 and 'she's a superb cook'. Other guest houses are *Lyndhurst* (tel 0522-347) on Waterfield Drive, and the *Alpen Guest House* by the Grosvenor Hotel. The rooms at the Alpen are good, the staff friendly and doubles are Rs 175; for Rs 20 extra you can have the fire lit in your room.

Mr Cader's *Pink House* has also been recommended – continue past the roundabout to the new town hall and cinema (10 to 15 minutes walk), then turn right up the hill on the track. Ask directions from here, it's hard to find but when you get there rooms cost from just Rs 50.

Note that Nuwara Eliya can get pretty cold at night – impecunious travellers without coats and sweaters can pick up second hand ones from the street stalls.

Places to Stay – top end

Nuwara Eliya's two top end possibilities are both very much in the old English style and located almost side by side. The 114 room *Grand Hotel* (tel 0522-216, 261, 808-10) is right by the golf course and costs Rs 500/650 for room-only singles/doubles. Cultural shows are also put on at the Grand Hotel in the evenings.

It's hard to imagine anything more redolent of the English colonial era than the Grand – until you see the *Hill Club*. I doubt if the *Hill Club* was any better kept in its British heyday than it is today. Even the old magazines look original. The billiard room, dating from 1876, is the oldest part of the building. There are 22 rooms with doubles including breakfast and dinner at Rs 800.

After these two places everything else tends to be a little dull although the Municipal Rest House, now renamed *The Rest* (tel 0522-436), still manages to provide some amusement. Rooms there are Rs 300/400 including breakfast – rather expensive for what it offers. It's a sort of government run, Sri Lankan version of Fawlty Towers and everybody who stays there seems to come up with some amazing tale to tell.

The *Nuwara Eliya Tourinn* (tel 0522-410), on Park Rd, has just seven rooms and costs Rs 400/475 including breakfast. *St Andrews Hotel* (tel 0522-445) has 32 rooms with nightly costs of Rs 475/525.

The *Grosvenor Hotel* (tel 0522-307), at 4 Haddon Hill Rd, has 19 rooms at Rs 150/200. Some of the rooms have open log fires. It's well kept with a fine, old colonial air about the place – a good alternative when you'd like the superb atmosphere of the Grand but can't afford it!

The *Princess Guest House* (tel 0522-462), at 12 Wedderburn Rd, has seven rooms from Rs 250. *Oatlands* (tel 0522-572), on St Andrew's Drive, has five rooms at Rs 200/250 including breakfast. The food is good and it's run by friendly and hospitable people. *Siri Medura* (tel 0522-285), at 60 Badulla Rd, has just two rooms at Rs 180/280 including breakfast. It usually has to be booked through Colombo – phone 84156. There are a number of other guest houses around and *Holiday Cottages* on Upper Lake Drive.

Places to Eat

If you're not eating in your hotel or guest house, Nuwara Eliya has a rather disreputable looking collection of restaurants along the main street. None of them looks terribly inviting and their numbers were reduced by the '83 violence. You could always try the *Star Hotel & Bakery* and the *Dale West* at the end of the road by the roundabout. The Dale West is probably the better of the two. The *New Royal Hotel*, next to the Star Hotel, makes excellent tea and short eats although you are not encourage to linger if it's busy. There's a 'loose beer shop' on Lawson St.

At the other end of the price scale, or at least the Sri Lankan price scale, a meal at the *Hill Club* is an experience not to be missed. Dinner is served at 8 pm and costs Rs 125; lunch is Rs 100. You get a full five-course meal – soup, fish course, main course, dessert, tea or coffee; and the whole process is accomplished with considerable panache. If you have opted for a pre-dinner drink (in either the 'men's bar' or the 'mixed bar') you'll be summoned to the dining room when the meal is ready. At your candlelit table you'll be served by white-uniformed (and white-gloved) waiters. You can retire to the lounge, with its open fire, for your after dinner tea or coffee. All this for about US$5 – although you can soon bump that up if you decide to sample the wine cellar where bottles of European wine run into the high figures. Corkage if you bring your own bottle is Rs 50.

You must be properly dressed – no jeans allowed in this august establishment. Men must wear ties. If, like most travellers, you do not possess such an arcane piece of attire they'll loan you one for a Rs 50 deposit and Rs 5 fee. One

traveller wrote of the embarrassment of having to return his tie, to get back his deposit, before he could pay the bill!

It might be wise to check the menu before deciding on a night out at the Hill Club. Although it's usually as stoutly British as you could ask for it does seem to slip up on occasions. 'The menu I reviewed', wrote an American woman, 'was minestrone soup, egg & sardine pie, chicken with black pepper sauce, coleslaw, french fries, beetroot vinaigrette and strawberry gateau. Yum? Yecch?' Actually after a few months in India that would probably sound pretty good – egg & sardine pie apart. They pull out the stops at Christmas when dinner is accompanied by carol singing, Christmas crackers and paper hats – all very English!

The *Grand Hotel* also has a high class dining area or you can eat rather more cheaply at the *The Rest* and experience their amazing collection of antique waiters. After deciding against meat loaf (meat loaf!) at the Hill Club, a visitor reported the following unbeatable culinary event at The Rest:

The waiters are in great form – on commenting that the price of rum omelette was high our waiter promised to be liberal with the rum. Some 20 minutes later we guessed something was happening when one of the staff turned off and on the dining room lights! Yes; in came the omelette, flambe-style from the kitchen as the room was plunged into darkness. Our waiter had indeed been generous with the rum for the flames rose some two feet above the plate, apprehensively placed on our table. No amount of blowing would extinguish the pyre by which time the omelette was getting black at the edges.

The lights-waiter attempted to illuminate the scene again to regain control, threw all the switches together and fused the dining room, which a few seconds later blew the hotel fuse and (inevitably?) caused something that put all Nuwara Eliya in darkness for the next 20 minutes! By the time candles had been brought and the

omelette extinguished with a soup tureen a charred, smouldering lump remained to the delighted comments of the waiters. Actually this is an experience to replace no end of meat loaf dinners in Nuwara Eliya. Yes, the waiters here are part of the 'attractions not to be missed'.

The Rest does, however, seem to be aspiring to greater culinary heights of late. A last minute report was that the food was 'wonderful value' and the service was just fine. Just beyond the Hakgala Botanical Gardens entrance *Humbugs* is a pleasant small restaurant/snack bar with very fine views out from its hillside location. In season they even have strawberries and cream and in any season they have a most amusing sign out front.

Getting There
From Colombo there are three trains daily to Nanu Oya, the station for Nuwara Eliya; they continue on to Badulla. The break-of-dawn 6.35 am departure stops in Kandy for 15 minutes before continuing. The later morning departures goes straight through while the night departure requires a change of train in Kandy. The second morning departure at 9.30 am has an observation saloon as well as 2nd and 3rd class seats; the night departure (8.15

Hill Country
A   Lawyers' signboards, Kandy
B   Descending from Adam's Peak
C   Rawana Ella Falls – and a CTB bus

pm) has 1st and 2nd class berths and 3rd class sleeperettes as well as 2nd and 3rd class seats.

Fares from Colombo are Rs 104 in 1st class, Rs 66.60 in 2nd, Rs 27.10 in 3rd – plus additional charges for the observation saloon or for berths. From Kandy the trip takes about five to six hours and offers some truly fantastic scenery on the way through the mountains. If you can't get a seat out of Kandy 'grab a seat in the restaurant car and make a cup of tea last', was one suggestion.

Nuwara Eliya does not have a railway station – you have to take a bus (Rs 3) or taxi (about Rs 50) from Nanu Oya, a few km away. You can break the trip at Hatton in order to climb Adam's Peak. The bus between Hatton and Nuwara Eliya passes the Tea Research Institute which makes a very interesting visit.

There are CTB buses and minibuses from Colombo to Nuwara Eliya. A bus to Kandy costs Rs 18. A bus to Badulla is Rs 12.50, slightly less to Bandarawela.

Tea

Sri Lanka is the world's largest exporter of tea and it is tea which is the cornerstone of the Sri Lankan economy. Yet tea only came to Sri Lanka as an emergency substitute for coffee when the extensive coffee plantations were all but destroyed by a devastating disease. The first Sri Lankan tea was grown at the *Loolecondera* estate, a little south-east of Kandy, by one James Taylor in 1867. Today the hill country is virtually one big tea plantation for tea needs a warm climate, altitude and sloping terrain. A perfect description of the Sri Lankan hill country.

Tea grows on a bush; if not cut back it would grow up to 10 metres high and would require some very tall women to pick the leaves! As it is tea bushes are pruned back to about a metre tall

and squads of Tamil tea pluckers move through the rows of tea bushes picking the leaves and buds. These are then 'withered' – demoisturised by blowing temperature controlled air through the leaves either in the old fashioned multi-storey tea factories, where the leaves are spread out on hessian mats, or in modern mechanised troughs. The partially dried leaves are then crushed which starts a fermentation process. The art in tea production comes in knowing when to stop the fermentation by 'firing' the tea to produce the final, brown/black leaf. Tea plantation and factory tours are readily available all over Sri Lanka.

There are a very large number of types and varieties of teas which are graded both by size (from cheap 'dust' through fannings and broken grades to 'leaf' tea) and by quality (with names like flowery, pekoe or souchong). Tea is further categorised into low-grown, mid-grown or high-grown. The low-grown teas (under 600 metres) grow strongly and are high in 'body' but low in 'flavour'. The high-grown teas (over 1200 metres) grow more slowly and are renowned for their subtle flavour. Mid-grown tea is something between the two. Regular commercial teas are usually made by blending various types – a bit of this for flavour, a bit of that for body.

Unfortunately, as in India, the Sri Lankans may grow some very fine tea but they're not always very adept at making a good pot of it. If you've got a taste for fine teas you're best advised to take some home with you.

WORLD'S END

The Horton Plains are situated south of Nuwara Eliya, west of Haputale and Bandarawela. They are on a high, windy plateau standing at around 2000 metres (7000 feet). A number of rivers cross this sparsely populated grassland and there are many excellent walks – the few roads are generally suitable for jeeps only.

Farr's Inn, which used to be a rest

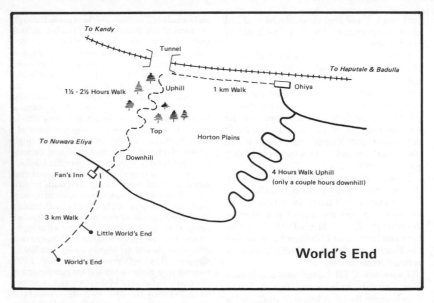

To Kandy

Tunnel

To Haputale & Badulla

1½ - 2½ Hours Walk   Uphill   1 km Walk   Ohiya

To Nuwara Eliya   Top   Horton Plains

Downhill

Fan's Inn   4 Hours Walk Uphill
(only a couple hours downhill)

3 km Walk

Little World's End

World's End

World's End

house, is a delightful old English-style guest house and a convenient landmark on the plains. From here it is about a five km walk (only the first part of it is passable by jeep) to World's End. Here the Horton Plains come suddenly to an end and drop straight down 300 metres then slope off to the coastal plain, 1500 metres below. It's one of the most stunning sights in Sri Lanka but, unfortunately, the view is often obscured by mist. Dawn or the very early morning usually offers the best chance of catching a glimpse of this scenic wonder.

From Haputale you can reach the Horton Plains by taking a train two stations back to Ohiya. From there you walk along the tracks to the tunnel and then branch off. Farr's Inn can also be reached via the Diyagama Estate in Agrapatna. Two of Sri Lanka's highest mountains, Kirigalpotta at 2387 metres (7832 feet) and Totapolakanda at 2361 metres (7746 feet) rise on the western edge of the plains.

Places to Stay on the Horton Plains
There are two places you can stay on the Horton Plains. *Anderson Lodge* (tel 071-4146) costs Rs 100 and will accommodate five people – you can have the use of the cook but must provide the food.

Farr's Inn (contact phone 23501) is close to Ohiya and has nine rooms with all-inclusive prices of Rs 300/500 (Rs 150/200 room only) for singles/doubles. Food is expensive.

Getting There
On Saturdays and Sundays there is a bus from Ohiya to Farr's Inn on the Horton Plains at 9 am and 2 pm for Rs 8. The bus departure connects with the arrival of the train from Haputale. The return bus to Ohiya is at 3 pm; winding down such a nightmare zig-zag road that you'll probably wish you'd walked. 'World's End was an anti-climax after the bus ride', wrote one heart-in-mouth bus rider. If you're going to Farr's Inn on weekdays, and you're not up to walking, the only option is Ohiya's single and outrageously expensive taxi.

BANDARAWELA

Coming from Nuwara Eliya it's a steady descent through Welimada (where you may have to change buses) to Bandarawela at 1230 metres (4036 feet). From here you can either head south and leave the hill country via Haputale to the south coast or head north and leave the hills via Badulla to the east coast.

Bandarawela is not of great interest in itself but it does make an excellent base for exploring other places in the area or for making walks. About five km out of Bandarawela on the road to Badulla, pause to see the interesting Dowa Temple on the right hand side of the road. The little temple is pleasantly situated close to a stream and on the rock face below the road there is a beautiful four-metre high standing Buddha image cut in low relief into the rock. The temple is very easy to miss so ask the bus conductor to tell you when to get off. The turnoff for Ella is eight km out from Bandarawela.

Places to Stay – bottom end

Close to the centre of town, but up a rise overlooking it, the *Rest House* is well signposted and just a few paces beyond the big Orient Hotel. Singles/doubles including breakfast are Rs 150/275.

Right next to the Orient, at 8 Mt Pleasant, is the *Chinese Union Hotel* (tel Bandarawela 502) with six rooms from Rs 60 plus a restaurant. Closer to the town Senanayake Mawatha branches off and runs up by the very clean and pleasant *YWCA Holiday Home* where there are three rooms plus an annexe available for visitors – couples only.

Just out of town towards Welimada the *Ventnor Guest House* (tel Bandarawela 511) is at 23 Welimada Rd and has singles/doubles at just Rs 30/40, all with attached bathroom.

Smack in the middle of town you could try *Justin Fernando's*, next door to the post office and across the road from the bus station. It's very cheap and has a reasonable looking restaurant downstairs.

Or try the *Riverside Inn* (tel Bandarawela 448), at 114 Ellatota Rd on the way to Haputale, with singles/doubles at Rs 100/150. The *Himalie Guest House* is a fair distance out of town on the Badulla road.

Places to Stay – top end

The two top of the top end hotels here are very close to the centre. The *Bandarawela Hotel* (tel Bandarawela 501) is on Welimada Rd, the entrance runs up to it from beside the post office. There are 36 rooms and nightly costs for room only singles are Rs 250-275, for doubles Rs 275-300.

The similarly sized, but a little more modern, *Orient Hotel* (tel Bandarawela 407) is at 10 Dharmapala Mawatha, the road that runs up to the rest house, but still close to the centre of town. There are 36 rooms with room-only charges of Rs 270/300.

Other upper price category places are not so central – the *Ideal Resort* (tel Bandarawela 476) is about a km and a bit beyond the town on the Welimada road. It's an old tea plantation bungalow – a pleasantly spacious and old fashioned place with just six rooms. They are available with and without breakfast and other meals with singles from Rs 100 to 195, doubles Rs 125 to 305. The *Alpine Inn* (tel Bandarawela 569) is also small (just five rooms) and priced from Rs 200/250. Or there is the *Rovim Tourist Hotel* at Bindunuwewa and the *Holiday Cottages* on Golf Links Rd.

Getting There

From Nuwara Eliya buses cost about Rs 12. You can take a Badulla bus and change at Welimada. Welimada has a *Rest House*, on the north-east side of town. There are regular buses from Bandarawela to Haputale, Badulla and Ella.

ELLA

Sri Lanka is liberally endowed with

beautiful views but Ella has one of the best. To fully appreciate it walk up through the town to the rest house, up their path and into the garden in front of it. Suddenly the world simply drops away at your feet. In front of you there is a narrow gap in the mountains and you look down from Ella's 1100 metre altitude to the coastal plain nearly a thousand metres below.

The road down through the spectacular Ella Gap to Wellawaya, 27 km to the south, was only completed in 1969. Coming uphill from Wellawaya can be quite a struggle for a rickety CTB bus. The railway line from Haputale passes through Ella on the way to its terminus at Badulla. About 10 km out of Ella at Demodara it performs a complete loop around a hillside and tunnels under itself at a level 30 metres lower. There's a model of this spectacular piece of colonial-era railway engineering in the National Museum in Colombo.

Rawana Ella Falls

These spectacular falls are situated about five km down the gap from Ella towards Wellawaya. The water comes leaping down the mountainside in what is claimed to be the wildest looking fall in Sri Lanka. Naturally they are connected with the Ramayana saga; the demon king Rawana was said to have held Sita captive in a cave, which you can visit, in the cliff facing the rest house.

Places to Stay

A great many of Sri Lanka's rest houses are blessed with attractive settings but the *Ella Rest House* tops the lot. If you come from the Badulla or Bandarawela side and walk up the path and across the front lawn, the view of Ella Gap that unfolds before you is simply stunning. The small (just six rooms) rest house costs Rs 250 and meals are also available. It's a pleasant place.

There are a number of other places right around the centre of the small village.

Actually overlooking the Rest House, the *Rock View Rest House* has singles at Rs 125 to 150, doubles at Rs 175. Next door is the simple *Ella Rest Inn* with rooms from Rs 25 to 75.

Just round the corner, the *Ella Gap Tourist Inn* has rooms from Rs 75 to 150 or rooms with attached bath for Rs 200. It's a friendly, well run place with a wide choice of extremely good food. Although it doesn't have the superb location of the Rest House it does have a pleasant patio and all in all it's a pretty good place.

Going down hill towards the railway station you come to *Lizzie's Villa Rest House* on the right and the *SK Tourist Rest House* on the left – rooms at these places are down to around Rs 50. At Lizzies you have to 'bargain a bit – she's nice, but a businesswoman'. Her food is very good.

Unfortunately the *Sunnyside Lodge*, a very popular place, was burnt out in the '83 violence and it's uncertain if it will reopen.

BADULLA

Standing at about 680 metres (2200 feet) Badulla marks the south-eastern extremity of the hill country and is the gateway to the east coast of Sri Lanka. The railway line from Colombo, Kandy and Nuwara Eliya terminates here and if you come by bus you will have to change buses here so either way those heading down to the coast will have to pause in Badulla. It's a pleasant little town, capital of the Uva Province and neatly ringed by mountains.

The Church of St Mark in Badulla was built in memory of the British administrator Major T W Rogers who has been described as a 'sportsman'. Whether that is a correct label to apply to a man whose chief purpose in life seemed to be to wipe out the elephant population of Sri Lanka single-handed, I'm not sure. What is more certain is that some protector of elephants finally decided that enough was enough and Rogers was struck dead by a bolt of lightning while sitting on the verandah of the Haputale rest house!

Dunhinda Falls

About six km out of Badulla are the 60 metre high Dunhinda waterfalls – said to be the most 'awe inspiring' in Sri Lanka. There's a good observation spot at the end of the path. A bus 314 – there are two or three an hour – will take you close to the falls. From the bus stop it's about a km along a clearly defined, sometimes rocky, path. The falls are well worth a visit and a fine spot for a picnic. You can also see a lower falls on the walk to the main one.

Namunukula

You can climb this 1850 metre peak by taking a Spring Valley bus (number 308) from Badulla. Spring Valley is in the centre of tea estates and is an interesting place to walk around with many fine views.

Places to Stay – bottom end

Smack in the centre of town the *Budulla Rest House* has rooms at Rs 60/100 for singles/doubles. Centrally located, five minutes walk from the railway and bus stations to the east of the centre, the *Castle Hotel* (tel 055-2334) is at 134 Lower St and has doubles at Rs 60. Eastern and western food is available. Lower St was virtually wiped out by the '83 riots, the Castle Hotel was one of the few survivors.

A little further down the street is the very simple *Uva Hotel* with rooms at Rs 60 to 100. The *Riverside Holiday Inn* (tel 055-2090) is at 27 Lower King St, 300 metres from the bus stand and has doubles all the way from Rs 30 to 150. The *Myura Tourinn* is 100 metres past the bus stand on the top road away from the clocktower. Doubles are Rs 60 to 100 and the food here is good.

Mrs Mala Jayakody's guest house at 7 Race Course Rd has also been recommended; rooms cost Rs 20 to 50. *Richard & Astrid Fernandez* have a small guest house at 26 Old Bede's Rd, just out of town. Ask directions at the YMCA, where Richard works. Rooms are cheap and the food is plentiful – 'enough leftovers to feed your pet elephant'.

Places to Stay – top end

The *Dunhinda Falls Inn* (tel 055-2406), at 35/11 Bandaranaike Mawatha not too far from the falls, is pleasant, modern, good value and has good food in its *Sugimal Restaurant*. There are 22 rooms with singles at Rs 100 to 150, doubles Rs 150 to 350.

Getting There

Buses run every half hour or so from Nuwara Eliya to Badulla (Rs 12.50); change at Welimada for Bandarawela. It's about two (perhaps more) hours in either case.

From Badulla to the east coast there are just a few buses each day – sometimes direct but more often the trip involves a change at Monaragala (Peacock Rock) where you meet the Wellawaya-Pottuvil (Arugam Bay) road. The first half hour down from Badulla is very scenic. There are a number of places to stay in Monaragala, see the relevant section below.

Badulla is the end of the railway line from Colombo – about a nine-hour trip. The three daily Colombo-Nanu Oya trains all continue to Badulla. Between Haputale and Ella it's a particularly lovely journey.

HAPUTALE

The little village of Haputale is perched right at the southern edge of the hill country. One of its most spectacular views, which makes its position very clear, is seen coming in from Bandarawela. The road rises up to the ridge which Haputale is built along, crosses the railway line, dips down the main street – then suddenly and unexpectedly simply sails off into space! Actually what happens is that the road makes a sharp right turn at the edge of town and runs along the ridge before dropping down out of the hills, but at first glance it looks like the main street simply disappears into thin air. On a clear day you can see from this ridge all the way to the south coast and at night the Hambantota lighthouse may be visible.

Haputale is a pleasant little town with some good accommodation including one of the best cheapies in Sri Lanka. It also has an excellent market but most important it makes a very good base for exploring other places around the area or simply taking pleasant walks in the cool mountain air.

Idalgashinna (only eight km from Haputale and also on the railway line), the Tangamalai nature reserve and the scattered traces of the Portuguese Katugodella Fort (a reminder of one of their attempts to capture the hill country) are all within easy reach of Haputale. It also makes a good base for visits to World's End. If you're staying at Highcliffe there's a book here with a number of interesting walks described. A couple of places to try:

Diyaluma Falls
Heading down from Haputale towards Wellawaya you pass one of Sri Lanka's highest waterfalls, just five km beyond the town of Koslanda. They're probably easier to visit from Wellawaya than Haputale. If you're heading towards Colombo from Haputale it's only a short sidetrip back from the Beragalla road junction to reach the 170 metre high Diyaluma Falls. The falls leap over a cliff face and fall in one clear drop to a pool below – very picturesque and clearly visible from the road.

If you're feeling energetic you can climb up to the beautiful rock pools and a series of mini-falls at the top of the main fall. Walk about a km from the bus stop to a sharp fork, doubling back uphill. From there you follow the tracks to a small rubber factory, about 20 minutes walk. Strike off left uphill from here, the track is very indistinct although there are some white arrows on the rocks. At the top you can hear and then see the falls or small boys will guide you to the pools, for a small

fee! There are other routes to the top (about 45 minutes' climb), but either way it's a pretty hard climb. Once you're there it's a delightful and secluded spot for a swim in the pools above the second set of waterfalls.

You could make an interesting day trip circuit from Haputale by going down to the Diyaluma Falls, another bus from there to Wellawaya, then up to the Rawana Ella Falls, on to Ella and the gap and finally back through Bandarawela to Haputale.

Adisham
This is a Benedictine monastery about an hour's walk from Haputale, you can bus part way. It's in an old British planter's house, a replica of the planter's Yorkshire home. They take guests here for Rs 125 all inclusive but note that although the monks make 'unbelievable good jam' they also have 'terrible food' and the father 'doesn't like hippies'. You should call or write in advance for reservations if you intend to stay. There's lots of stonework around here – stone walls, stone steps, stone terracing – all done by hand.

Places to Stay
Haputale has one of Sri Lanka's most pleasant and popular budget priced place to stay. *Highcliffe* (tel Plessey 296) is in the centre of town, close to where the railway line crosses the main road, it looks directly across the railway line to the rest house. Singles/doubles are Rs 15/30 (double with bath Rs 40) and food is also low priced and very good value. Rice and curry plus fruit for dessert costs from just Rs 15. It's an old fashioned and easy going place with lots of information about the locality, they have numerous suggestions for walks and other activities in the area.

Should Highcliffe be full there are a number of places you can fall back on although the '83 devastation hit Haputale particularly hard. The *Amerasinghe Guest House* is still operating but the owner's shop in town was burnt down and without him to tell you the way finding it may be difficult. 'It's worth the long walk' reported a recent visitor. Next door to Highcliffe is the *Friendly Place Guest House* which is indeed very friendly and has very good food. The *Bawa Inn* is another low priced Haputale possibility with large rooms with French doors onto the verandah from where you can look down to the south coast. All for Rs 50, view included. *Deepthi*, on the Welimada road, has excellent Sinhalese food although the rooms are a bit musty.

Another pleasant guest house is Mrs Daniel's *Hyacinth Cottage* on Temple Rd. To find it walk back along the railway line for about 100 metres, past a sign saying 153 then up a small path on the left and the house is 50 metres up the road on the right. Once again food is delicious and cheap here and Mrs Daniel 'is a terrific scrabble player'. Another visitor humourously added that she 'cheats a little by inventing ridiculous Lankan-English words'!

Haputale now has two rest houses. The old *Rest House* is right across the railway tracks from Highcliffe. It's a bit bleak and bare and singles/doubles are Rs 87.50/175. The new *Rest House* is a km or two out of town on the Bandarawela side and costs Rs 100/200. The *Monamaya Holiday Guest House* is about a km out of Haputale along the ridge and overlooking the town. It's a nicely 'olde English' looking place with just four rooms.

Getting There

Haputale is on the railway line between Colombo and Badulla. Buses from Haputale cost Rs 3 to Bandarawela, Rs 6 to Badulla or Rs 28 for a CTB bus to Colombo. It takes about six hours by bus to Colombo or Kandy.

RATNAPURA

The gem centre of Sri Lanka, Ratnapura (the name means 'City of Gems') is situated 100 km (63 miles) from Colombo. It's on an alternate route to the hill country, you skirt round the southern edge of the hill country and then ascend into the hills through Haputale.

The scenery around Ratnapura is really magnificent and this is reputed to be the best place for views of Adam's Peak. Here you view it from below while from the other side you're looking at it from more or less the same level. Ratnapura is also the starting point for the 'classical' (read 'hard') route up Adam's Peak via Gilimale and Carney Estate. Less arduous walks can be found much closer to town, even right from the rest house.

A trip to the Gem Museum is worth making while in Ratnapura although it's mainly just gem polishing you see here. There's an interesting collection of gemstones from Sri Lanka and all over the world. You can also inspect a wide range of gems for sale but here, as elsewhere in Ratnapura, gem merchants sell only the stones. There are no jewellery shops, no stones available in settings as there are in Kandy or elsewhere and some travellers have reported that prices were not competitive with Colombo. The Gem Museum also has a very fine art gallery of mostly silver objects designed by the owner. The art objects are 'top class, he uses traditional elements in a very creative manner'. To get to the museum take a bus from the railway station to Getangama, it's only a few stops. Admission to the gem museum is free.

There's another gem museum on the Badulla road out of town – the Gem Bank Gemmological Museum is at 6 Ehelapola Mawatha, Batugedera

Ratnapura also has a small museum on the Wellawaya and Badulla side of town, opposite the CTB bus depot. The museum has a collection of pre-historic fossil skeletons of elephants, hippopotamuses and rhinoceroses – all found in caves or gem pits in the area. The museum is open from 9 am to 5 pm except on Fridays and Saturdays and admission is Rs 1.50.

Places to Stay – bottom end

The Ratnapura bus station is just off the centre of town, on the rise that culminates in the rest house. Half way up the hill you will find *Travellers' Rest* at 66 Inner Circular Rd (or Rest House Rd). It's simple and very basic with rooms from just Rs 30. Right beside it at number 60 is the similar standard *Star Light Tourist Rest*.

A third possibility for shoestringers is the *Travellers' Halt* at 30 Outer Circular Rd. It's about 15 minute brisk walk from the bus station (which is the old, and now disused, railway station). Walk away from the town, when you pass the Ratnapura convent number 30 is about 100 metres beyond it. There are some slightly hidden signs along the way, follow the signs for Polhengoda village. Dorm beds are Rs 10, doubles from Rs 40. In Polhengoda the *Hotel Kalawathie* 'is a beautiful hotel, like a museum and surrounded by herb gardens'.

Places to Stay – top end

Right at the top of the hill road from the bus station, beautifully situated overlooking the town, Ratnapura's *Rest House* (tel 045-2299) has once again grabbed the best site in town. From up here you can overlook the town and surrounding countryside, well above the noise and confusion down below. There are 11 rooms as well as accommodation for a whole flock of swallows who nest under the porch – a sign warns you not to park your car there! There's a spacious verandah, a small grassy garden in the back and airy rooms upstairs. Singles/doubles with bath are Rs 110/210. Breakfast costs Rs 25 to 45, lunch or dinner Rs 60 to 75. There are also some more basic rooms downstairs.

A little distance out of town on the Colombo side at Kahangama, the *Ratnaloka Tour Inn* (tel 045-2455) has 53 rooms and is centrally air-conditioned, swimming pool, all mod cons. Singles/doubles are Rs 375/425, room only.

Places to Eat

In the town the *Ratnaloka Hotel* (no relation to the Ratnaloka Tour Inn) is a good place for a tasty and very inexpensive curry and rice – go upstairs. Or, around the corner from the central square, there is the cool, clean and rather more expensive *Nilani Tourist Restaurant* – it's well signposted. The *Rest House* has good food with the usual graciously old fashioned service. The *Gem Museum*, out of town, has a pleasant, but rather pricey, restaurant. The *Gem Bank* also has a restaurant.

Getting There

Although Ratnapura has the remains of a railway station, the railway line from Colombo no longer runs all the way there. So it's back to the buses, which cost Rs 10.50 for a CTB bus, Rs 12 for a minibus for this approximately two to three hour trip. From Ratnapura there is a direct, but roundabout, bus to Matara and Tangalla at 8.45 am and 2 pm.

Gems

Ratnapura is the gem centre of Sri Lanka, every second person you meet on the street is likely to whisper that he has the bargain of your lifetime wrapped up in his pocket. If you're no expert on gemstones the bargain is 100% likely to be on his side of the line, not yours.

Gems are still found by an ancient and traditional mining method. Gem miners look for seams of *illama*, a gravel bearing strata likely to hold gemstones. *Illama* is usually found in lowland areas – along valley bottoms, riverbeds, and other, usually very damp, places. On the Colombo-Ratnapura road you'll see countless gem mining operations going on in paddy fields beside the road – but there are far, far more off in the hills and fields all around. Gem mining is a co-operative effort, you can't just set out to dig them all by yourself. You need someone to dig out the *illama*, someone to work the pump to keep water out of the pit or tunnel, someone to wash the muddy gravel and an expert to search through the pebbles for the stone that may make all their fortunes. If a stone is found the profit is divided up between all the members of the co-op from the man who supplies the finance to the one up to his neck in mud and water, clad only in a tiny loin cloth known as an *amudes*. The mines are rarely very deep but they can be vertical or horizontal depending on which way the *illama* runs.

It's a peculiarity of Sri Lankan gemming that a variety of different stones are almost always found in the same pit. There are many different types and varieties of gems and their value depends on a number of factors including the gem's rarity, hardness and beauty. Gems are still cut and polished by hand although modern methods are also coming into use. Some stones are cut and faceted *(en cabochon)* while others are simply polished. The division between precious and semi-precious stones is a purely arbitrary one – there is no clear definition of what makes one stone a precious stone and another only semi-precious. Popular stones include:

Corundrums This group includes sapphires and rubies, both precious stones and second only to the diamond in hardness. Rubies range from pink to red, the latter being most valuable. Sapphires can be yellow, orange, pink, white and, most valuable, blue. You can often find corundrums which contain 'silk', minute inclusions which give the stone a star effect, particularly with a single light source.

Chrysoberyl Cat's-eye and Alexandrite are the best known in this group. Cat's-eyes, with their cat-like ray known as *chatoyancy*, vary from green through a honey colour to brown; look for translucence and the clarity and glow of the single ray. Alexandrite is valued for its colour change under natural and artificial light.

Beryl The best known stone in this group, the emerald, is not found in Sri Lanka. The aquamarine, which is found here, is quite reasonably priced since it is not so hard or lustrous as other stones.

Zircon The appearance of a zircon can approach that of a diamond although it is a comparatively soft stone. They come in a variety of colours from yellow through orange to brown and green.

Quartz This stone can vary all the way from transparent to opaque and is usually quite low priced. Quartz can also vary widely in colour from purple amethyst to smoky quartz right through to brown stones so dark they look almost black.

Feldspar The moonstone is almost Sri Lanka's special gem – usually a smooth, grey colour they can also be found with a slight shade of blue although this colouring is rather more rare.

Other Spinels are fairly common but they are also quite hard and rather attractive. They come in a variety of colours and can be transparent or opaque. Topaz is a hard, precious stone and can be very highly polished when it develops a characteristic 'slippery' feel. Garnets are a sort of poor man's ruby; light brown garnets are often used in rings in Sri Lanka.

RATNAPURA TO HAPUTALE

There is beautiful scenery in abundance from Ratnapura to Haputale, the southern 'gateway' to the hill country. Along this route you'll soon realise just how abruptly the hills rise from the surrounding plain. At Belihul Oya there's another of those exquisitely situated rest houses. Here it perches beside the stream that rushes down from the Horton Plains. There's a natural bathing pool in the stream, behind the rest house, while out front you can sit on the verandah, sipping afternoon tea, admiring the huge tree and watching the occasional bus cross the stone bridge.

You can reach World's End, Farr Inn and the Bambara Kanda Falls – at 240 metres (790 feet) the highest in Sri Lanka – from here but since most roads are only barely passable you'll have to plan on quite a bit of strenuous hiking.

Places to Stay – Belihul Oya & Haldummulla

Accommodation in the *Rest House* at Belihul Oya costs Rs 150/200 for singles/doubles. Further on at Haldummulla, only about 10 km before Haputale, shoestring travellers may like to investigate the *Dew Drop Inn*, picturesquely situated and with dorm beds as well as singles and doubles. It's a good base for tea plantation visits.

WELLAWAYA

The small town of Wellawaya is just a crossroads town apart from the nearby Buduruvagala images. In Wellawaya you have really left the hill country and descended back down to the plains. From Wellawaya roads run north, south, east and west. The north road ascends past the Rawana Ella Falls and through the spectacular Ella Gap to Ella. The south road runs directly down to the coast at Hambantota. The east road runs through Monaragala to Arugam Bay on the east coast. The west road goes through Ratnapura to Colombo with a branch off up to Haputale in the hill country.

Buduruvagala

About five km south of Wellawaya, on the road to the coast at Hambantota, a small track branches off the road westward to the huge rock-cut Buddha figure of Buduruvagala. A small signpost points the way but although the unsurfaced road is fairly good almost all the four km to the site there are a number of badly deteriorated stretches so unless you have a jeep or a motorcycle you will have to walk it. The half-hour stroll is well worthwhile – it's one of the quietest, most peaceful and secluded historic sites in the country. At the end of the track you cross a small footbridge and suddenly a sheer rock face rises before you with a 15 metre (51 foot) standing Buddha figure flanked by six smaller figures.

The figures are thought to date from around the 10th century AD and are of the Mahayana Buddhist school which enjoyed a brief heyday in Sri Lanka. The gigantic standing Buddha still bears traces of its original stuccoed robe and a long streak of orange paint suggests it was once brightly painted. The central of the three to the Buddha's right is thought to be his Bodhisattva (disciple) *Avalokitesvara*.

To the left of this white-painted figure is a female figure in the 'thrice bent' posture which is thought to be his consort *Tara*. The three figures on the Buddha's left appear, to my inexpert eye, to be of a rather different style. One of them is holding up the hour-glass shaped Tibetan thunderbolt symbol known as a *dorje* – an unusual example of the Tantric side of Buddhism in Sri Lanka. One of them is said to be Maitreya, the future Buddha, while one is Vishnu. Several of the figures are holding up their right hands with two fingers bent down to the palm – a beckoning gesture. It is worth obeying for the effort of getting to this uncommercial and unfrequented spot is amply repaid.

The walk used to be somewhat shorter but construction of an irrigation tank flooded the old road. For a time you had to take a boat across the tank to the site but now a new road skirting the lake has been constructed. As you walk to the site notice the scattered pillars and the mound of an old dagoba to the right. The pillars are said to be the remains of an old palace. If you take the short detour to the tank and look down the water channel out of the tank you may be able to make out a stone faintly carved with a triple-headed cobra.

Buduruvagala means Buddha (Budu) images (ruva) of stone (gala).

Places to Stay

There are several places to stay in Wellawaya. The *Old Rest House* is temporarily out of commission while it is being renovated. It's just a short walk from the central crossroads in the middle of town on the Old Ella Rd. If you continued up the Old Ella Rd a couple of hundred metres it merges with the New Ella Rd and runs north to Ella. Just beyond that junction is the shiny new *Wellawaya Inn Rest House* with doubles at Rs 150.

Between these two rest houses, almost next to the old one, is the *Wellawaya Rest Inn*, which has doubles at Rs 40, good food and a very energetic manager who goes all out to look after his guests. The *City Hotel*, right in front of the bus stop if you can find it, can tell you about other rock temples near Wellawaya.

Getting There

Coming down from Haputale towards the

coast there is a direct bus at 8.50 am or you can go to Wellawaya and change. Buses from Ella also run down to Hambantota via Wellawaya. You're virtually back down at sea level when you get to Buduruvagala and it is much warmer.

MONARAGALA
The small town, known as 'Peacock Rock', is another junction point on the road to the east coast. Here the roads from Badulla and Wellawaya meet. If you get stuck here there are a number of places to stay.

If you travel south of Monaragala, about 25 km via Okkampitiya, you reach Maligawila with a series of ruins of the Rununa kingdom including a fallen 7th century Buddha image 10 metres high.

Places to Stay
The pleasant *Wellassa Inn Rest House* is Rs 220 a double including breakfast. There are several other places to stay in this small town. The *de Silva Guest House* is just Rs 60 a night, it's opposite the Rest House. A bit further back towards

Wellawaya the *YMCA* is very good, the friendly owner asks for a small donation.

There are several small curry and rice places down towards the bus stand.

OTHER PLACES
There is also a small hill country *Rest House* at Pussellawa (tel 08-78397) on the Kandy-Nuwara Eliya road – rooms are Rs 125-175. At Kitulgala there's another *Rest House* (tel Kitulgala 28) on the Colombo-Avissawella-Hatton road with rooms at Rs 175/225. Believe it or not *Bridge on the River Kwai* was filmed here!

In Dickoya, near Hatton, the *Upper Glencairn Bungalow* (tel 0512-348) has five rooms at Rs 230/280. Other places to stay in Dickoya include the *Ottery Tourist Bungalow* (tel 0512-521) on the Ottery Estate with rooms from Rs 125 and the small *Cosy Inn* (tel 0512-573) on the New Newton Estate with rooms at Rs 225/285. Koslanda, between Haputale and Wellawaya and near the Diyaluma Falls also has a 'great *Rest House* with a perfect view'.

The Ancient Cities

The ancient city region of Sri Lanka lies to the north of the hill country, in one of the driest parts of the island. The golden age of Sinhalese civilisation reached its peak over a thousand years ago but suffered continual harassment from invading south Indian forces. Despite these problems the Sinhalese contrived to build two great cities and leave many other magnificent reminders of the strength of their Buddhist culture – only to abandon them all. For a thousand years the jungle did its best to reclaim them but major archaeological excavations over the past century have restored them to some of their past glory.

Admission Charges

There are now admission charges at four of the ancient city sites. At Polonnaruwa, Anuradhapura and Sigiriya the charge (to foreigners) is Rs 75. At Dambulla it is Rs 50. You can get a Cultural Triangle pass for Rs 225 which admits you to all four sites although I suspect that cost may increase since it was the same price when there was no admission charge to Dambulla. The pass is available in Colombo or at any of the sites. It only allows entry to each site on one day. Not all the ancient city areas in Anuradhapura are included in the area where fees are charged – and in any case local children there are doing a thriving trade showing people how to visit the widely dispersed sites without passing the entry points!

Architecture & Ruins

Sri Lanka's ancient cities have a real lost city story line. After the abandonment of first Anuradhapura and then Polonnaruwa, in the face of repeated invasions from south India, they gradually reverted to the jungle. At times efforts were made to restore them or at least slow the decline but generally it was a downhill slide. Parakramabahu I, the great king of Polonnaruwa, still tried to maintain a foothold

in Anuradhapura, even building the Brazen Palace from bits and pieces purloined from other buildings. A king of Kotte and one from Kandy made feeble attempts at minor restoration as late as the 18th century, but overall the ancient cities were little more than a legend when the British arrived.

At this time the great archaeological awakening was taking place in Europe but it was not until the late 1880s that the Sri Lankan ruins were effectively excavated. The systematic study of the ancient cities began in 1890 with the first Government Archaeologist, H C P Bell, whose truly inexhaustible energy even lives on today. The discovery of some new ruin will still be initially labelled a *bal kalla* or 'Bell Fragment'.

The ruins display a number of set forms. First there are dagobas – in other countries these might be stupas, pagodas or chedis but everywhere the basic form is the same; a solid hemisphere rising to a point or spire. The Sinhalese variation on this simple pattern is that the 'relic chamber' is sometimes raised up above the hemisphere, rather than being buried in its centre. This chamber contains more than just a relic of the Buddha, it is also supposed to represent a model of the Buddhist cosmos. You can see the contents of an excavated relic chamber in the Anuradhapura Museum. The solidity of a dagoba sometimes comes as a shock to westerners accustomed to our hollow churches, designed to hold a congregation. A dagoba is a focus not an enclosure – meditation and worship take place out in the open. You should always walk around a dagoba in a clockwise direction.

Other, more uniquely Sinhalese, architectural concepts include the *vatadage* or 'circular relic house'. Today you can see *vatadages* in Anuradhapura, Polonnaruwa and, perhaps the finest, at Medirigiriya. They consist of a small central dagoba, flanked by Buddha images and encircled by rows of columns. Long ago these columns held up a wooden roof but in all the ancient cities all traces of the wooden architecture have long disappeared and you must get your imagination into top gear to picture how things really were. Only important religious buildings were built of stone – everything else from the king's palace to the monk's monastery was made, at least partially, of wood so the picture we get today from the ancient cities is a very incomplete one. You can see a complete model of the Thuparama *Vatadage* in the Anuradhapura Museum.

Another peculiarly Sinhalese style is the *gedige* – a hollow temple with extremely thick walls topped by a 'corbelled' roof. Often the walls are so thick that a stairway to an upper level can be built right into the wall. There are a number of *gediges* in Anuradhapura and Polonnaruwa but in almost all cases the roof has long ago collapsed.

The most interesting Sinhalese designs are found not in entire buildings but in the little artistic touches that embellish them. Moon-stones, no relation to the semi-precious stone, are one of the recurring elements that you can study at both cities. They're essentially semi-circular stones at the base of stairways or the entrance doors to buildings – like a rock doormat. The design of moonstones follows a set pattern representing the Buddhist view of life with its pain of birth, disease, death and old age. The outermost band is a ring of fire symbolising the state of the world. The next band of animals – elephants, horses, lions or bulls – symbolises the vitality of the world despite its problems and pains. The band of geese symbolise those who leave home in search of the meaning of life and finally, in the central half-lotus, those who continue the search find enlightenment.

Guardstones are another design element one sees frequently – they generally flank entrances or doorways with sculptures of cobra kings holding auspicious objects or similar themes. Other interesting figures may also be included in the guardstones, including the ever-present dwarves who add a touch of humour to so many ancient buildings. Another element of Sinhalese art and architecture which it is impossible to miss is the extraordinary quality of rock-cut figures. It has been said in Burma that the Burmese are unable to see a hill without plonking a pagoda on top of it. Well the Sinhalese seemed, at one time, to be unable to see a rock without cutting a Buddha into it. Some of the best figures include the Gal Vihara in Polonnaruwa, the gigantic Aukana image and the impressive Buduruvagala group in the south of the island.

ANURADHAPURA

For over a thousand years Sinhalese kings, with occasional south Indian interlopers, ruled from the great city of Anuradhapura. Today it is the most extensive and important of the Sri Lankan ancient cities but the very length of its history, and equally the length of time since its downfall, make it a more difficult experience to assimilate and appreciate than younger, shorter lived Polonnaruwa. Which is not to say the effort is not amply repaid!

Anuradhapura first became a capital in 380 BC under Pandukabhaya but it was under Devanampiya Tissa (260-210 BC) that it first rose to great importance, for it was during his reign that Buddhism reached Sri Lanka and rapidly spread across the country. Soon Anuradhapura became a great and glittering city only for it to fall before a south Indian invasion – a fate that was repeatedly to befall Sri Lanka for over a thousand years. Elara, the last Chola king of this invasion, was a responsible and just man, or so the legends insist, but his reign was a brief one. From a refuge on the south coast Dutugemunu led his army to recapture Anuradhapura for the Sinhalese. The 'Dutu' part of his name, incidentally, is from 'Duttha' meaning 'undutiful' for his father, fearing for his son's safety, forbade him to attempt to recapture Anuradhapura, but his son disobeyed him – sending his father a woman's ornament to indicate what he thought of his courage.

Dutugemunu, who ruled from 161 to 137 BC, immediately set a vast building programme into operation which includes some of the most impressive monuments in Anuradhapura today. Other important kings who followed him included Valagambahu, who lost his throne to another Tamil invasion but later regained it, and Mahasena (276-303 AD) who built the colossal Jetavanarama dagoba and is thought of as the last of the 'great' kings of Anuradhapura. He also held the record for tank construction, building 16 of them in

all and a major canal. Although Anuradhapura was to survive for more than another 500 years before finally being replaced by Polonnaruwa, this was its acme. In the centuries that followed it was again and again harassed by invasions from south India and the very importance of the city – with cleared land and great roads – made these invasions much easier.

Anuradhapura is spread out and does not have concentrations of related structures like its younger sister Polonnaruwa. Nevertheless there is one important starting point for exploring the ancient city and that is the sacred Bo-tree and the cluster of buildings around it.

Like Polonnaruwa and Sigiriya there is a Rs 75 entry charge to the sacred areas for foreigners. Enterprising young kids do a good business showing people around by routes that avoid the entry charge! It's only the northern part, which is more enclosed, where the charge applies.

Around the Sacred Bo-Tree

The sacred Bo-tree makes a convenient centre for Anuradhapura in both a spiritual and physical sense. The huge tree is grown from a sapling brought from Bodh Gaya in India by the Princess Sangamitta, brother of Mahinda, who introduced the Buddha's teachings to Sri Lanka, so it has a spiritual connection to the very basis of the religion of Sri Lanka. It also serves as a reminder of the force that inspired the creation of all the great buildings at Anuradhapura and it is within easy walking distance of many of the most interesting monuments.

Sri Maha Bodhi The sacred Bo-tree is the oldest historically authenticated tree in the world for it has been tended by an uninterrupted succession of guardians for over 2000 years, even during the periods of Indian occupation. The steps leading up to the tree platform are very old but the golden railing around it is quite modern.

Brazen Palace So called because it once had a bronze (brazen) roof the ruins of the Brazen Palace stand close to the Bo-tree. The remains of 1600 columns are all that is left of this huge palace – said to have had nine storeys and accommodation for a thousand monks and attendants.

It was originally built by Dutugemunu over two thousand years ago but down through the ages was rebuilt and restored many times, each time a little less grandiosely. The current rather nondescript jumble of pillars is all that remains from the last rebuild – that of Parakramabahu around the 12th century AD.

Anuradhapura Museum Follow the road which runs between the Bo-tree and the Brazen Palace and you'll soon find yourself at Anuradhapura's excellent museum. Amongst the many interesting exhibits is a restored relic chamber, as found during the excavation of the Kantaka Cetiya Dagoba in nearby Mihintale. There is also a large scale model of the Thuparama Vatadage, as it would have been with its wooden roof.

Many fine carvings and sculptures can also be seen, plus a few amusing little items like the carved squatting plates from the Western Monasteries. The monks here had not only forsaken the world but also the luxurious monasteries favoured by their more worldly brothers.

Ancient cities
A Elephant bas-relief at Isurunumiya, Anuradhapura
B Potgul Vihara statue, Polonnaruwa
C Wall painting, Sigiriya

To show their contempt for these luxury loving effetes they produced beautifully carved stone, squat-style toilets – with their brother monks' monasteries represented on the bottom! Their urinals illustrated the god of wealth, showering handfuls of coins down the hole. The museum is open from 8 am to 4 pm except on Tuesdays.

Ruvanvelisaya Dagoba Continuing north of the museum or the Brazen Palace you soon come to this fine dagoba, guarded by a wall of hundreds of elephants standing shoulder to shoulder. Beside the western entrance to the dagoba platform there are still a few of the original stone elephants left standing, the others are a modern replacement.

Dutugemunu was responsible for the Ruvanvelisaya and it is said to be the best of his constructions but he did not live to see its completion. As he lay on his death bed, his brother organised a false bamboo and cloth finish to the dagoba so that Dutugemunu's final sight could be of his 'completed' masterpiece. Today, after suffering much damage from invading Indian forces, the white dagoba rises to a height of 55 metres (180 feet), considerably less than in its original state, nor is its form the same as the earlier 'bubble' shape.

A limestone statue standing to the south of the great dagoba is popularly thought to be of its constructor Dutugemunu. On the eastern stairway you can see a stone inscription left by the Polonnaruwa king Nissanka Malla – who also spent much energy erecting stone slabs in his own city to inform the world of his greatness. This one merely announces that he visited Anuradhapura and restored a few dagobas. Close to the northern porch there is a huge octagonal limestone pillar rising to a height of over six metres.

The land around the dagoba is rather like a pleasant green park, dotted with patches of ruins, the remains of ponds and pools, or collection of columns and pillars, all picturesquely leaning in different directions. If you continued walking north you would soon come to the oldest dagoba in Anuradhapura.

Thuparama Dagoba Constructed by Devanampiya Tissa this is the oldest dagoba in Anuradhapura, if not Sri Lanka, and is said to contain the right collar-bone of the Buddha. The dagoba was originally in the classical 'heap of paddy' shape (shaped like a heap of paddy rice) but was restored in 1840 to a more conventional bell-shape.

It is only a small dagoba, standing just 19 metres (63 feet) high, and at some later point in its life was converted into a vatadage or circular relic house. The circles of pillars of diminishing height around the dagoba would have supported the conical roof. Although the Thuparama is an attractive ruin, with a beautiful woodland setting, it suffers from a bad case of the honky-tonks – festooned with coloured lights, banners and flags, all of which detract from its natural simplicity.

Northern Ruins
There is quite a long stretch of road running north from the Thuparama to the next clump of ruins. Coming back you can take an alternative route to visit the Jetavanarama Dagoba.

Royal Palace The Sangamitta Mawatha,

Ancient cities
A Anuradhapura
B Sigiriya

the road running north from the Thuparama to the Abhayagiri, runs through the old Royal Palace site. This palace actually dates from after the fall of Anuradhapura as the Sinhalese capital. It was built by Vijayabahu I around the 11th century AD and is indicative of the attempts made to retain at least a foothold in the old capital.

Close to it is a deep and ancient well and the Mahapali, a monk's refectory notable for its immense trough, nearly three metres long and two wide, for the lay followers to fill with rice for the monks. You can also find a tooth-relic temple and a gedige in the Royal Palace area; the gedige is in very poor repair, particularly compared to some of the Polonnaruwa gediges.

Abhayagiri Dagoba During the restoration of Anuradhapura this huge dagoba somehow became confused with the equally huge Jetavanarama dagoba – which still causes confusion today because some books and maps say this is the Abhayagiri, others that it is the Jetavanarama.

The name means 'fearless Giri' and refers to a Jain monk whose hermitage was once at this spot. When Valagambahu fled from the city, before a Tamil invasion, he was taunted by the monk and so, when he regained the throne, 14 years later, foolish Giri was promptly executed and this great dagoba built over his hermitage in the 1st century BC.

After a later restoration by Parakramabahu the dagoba may have stood over 100 metres high but today it is only 75 metres (245 feet). The dagoba has some interesting bas-reliefs including an energetic elephant pulling up a tree near the western stairway. A large slab with a Buddha footprint can be seen on the northern side of the dagoba and the eastern and western steps have unusual moonstones made of concentric stone slabs.

Mahasen's Palace If you wander off to the north-west of the Abhayagiri you soon come to the ruins of this palace which is notable for having the finest carved moonstone in Sri Lanka – photographers will be disappointed that the railing around it makes an unshadowed picture almost impossible.

Ratnaprasada Follow the loop road a little further and you will find the finest guardstones in Anuradhapura. The design of guardstones went through a number of phases and these, of the 8th century AD, were the final refinement of guardstone design, illustrating a cobra-king. You can see examples of much earlier guardstone design at the Mirisavatiya dagoba.

Towards the end of Anuradhapura the Ratnaprasada was the scene of a major conflict between the forces of the current king and the Buddhist monks who lived here. Court officials at odds with the king took refuge here but the king, ignoring the principle of sanctuary, sent his supporters in to capture and execute them. The monks, disgusted at this invasion of a sacred place, immediately departed en masse. The general population, equally disgusted, then besieged the Ratnaprasada, captured and executed the king's supporters and the king was then forced to apologise to the departed monks in order to get them back to the city and restore peace.

Samadhi Buddha Statue Returning from your guardstone and moonstone investigations you can continue east from the Abhayagiri to this 4th century AD seated statue. It is said to be one of the finest Buddha statues in Sri Lanka and this is a site visiting dignitaries and heads of state are inevitably brought to admire. There may originally have been four statues here, flanking the enclosure which at one time surrounded a Bo-tree.

Kuttam Pokuna The 'twin ponds' are a little further along this road, on the other

side. These huge, swimming pool-like ponds were probably used by monks from the monastery attached to the Abhayagiri. They are the finest ponds in Anuradhapura and although referred to as 'twins' the southern pond, 28 metres in length, is much smaller than the 40 metre long northern pond. Water entered the smaller pond through a *makara's* (dragon-demon's) mouth and then flowed to the larger pond through an underground pipe. Notice the five-headed cobra figure close to the *makara*.

Dalada Maligawa Just beyond the twin ponds the road reaches a junction and a right turn will take you back towards the Bo-tree and Brazen Palace area. On your right you soon reach this building that may have been the original Temple of the Tooth – now located in Kandy. The tooth originally came to Sri Lanka in 313 AD.

Jetavanarama The huge, grass-covered dome of the Jetavanarama rises to the right a little further along. Built in the 3rd century AD by Mahasena the original height of this huge dagoba may have been over 100 metres but today it is only about 70 metres – very similar to the height of the Abhayagiri with which it has been confused.

An early British guidebook to Ceylon calculated that there were sufficient bricks in the dagoba (it is constructed solidly of bricks) to make a three metre-high wall stretching all the way from London to Edinburgh. The dagoba stands on a platform of remarkably uneven flagstones which were a much later addition. Behind the dagoba stand the ruins of its associated monastery – one building has door jambs still standing over eight metres high with another three metres underground. At one time massive doors opened to reveal a large Buddha image.

Buddhist Railing A little south of the Jetavanarama, and on the other side of the road, there is a stone railing built in imitation of a log wall. It encloses a site 42 metres by 34 metres but the building within has long disappeared.

Along the Banks of the Tissawewa

Three very interesting sites can be visited in a stroll along the banks of the Tissawewa tank. This is a pleasant visit to make on foot and brings you back to the Brazen Palace and Bo-tree area after starting at the Isurumuniya.

Isurumuniya This rock temple dates from the reign of Devanampiya Tissa and is one of the most interesting in the city – not for the temple itself, which is now rather smaller than it was originally and has also had some rather less tasteful later additions, but for its very fine carvings. The rock face is fronted by a square pool, fed from the Tissawewa, and it is around this pool that you can see the sculptures. The best known is the 'lovers', which is of the Gupta school and was probably brought here from elsewhere at a later date – since it is carved into a separate slab. It dates from around the 5th century AD and a popular legend relates that it is of Prince Saliya, son of Dutugemunu, who

forsook his right to the throne by marrying a commoner.

A bas relief to the south of the image house shows a palace scene – said to be of Dutugemunu with Saliya and Asokamala, the two lovers, flanking him and a third figure, possibly a servant, behind them. Another sculpture shows elephants playfully splashing water from the pool and above them is the fine 'man and horse' sculpture showing a man and the head of a horse. South of the pond the image house has a reclining Buddha cut from the rock. The view from the top of the temple is superb at sunset – looking out over the tank.

Pleasure Garden If you walk behind the Isurumuniya and follow the tank bund, you soon come to the extensive pleasure gardens. This royal park, known as the 'Park of the Goldfish', covers 14 hectares (35 acres) with pavilions and two ponds skilfully designed to fit around the huge boulders that stand in the park. The ponds have adjacent changing rooms, fine reliefs of elephants on the sides of the ponds, and it was here that Prince Saliya was said to have met Asokamala. From atop the rocks there was once a platform intended for looking out over the tank.

Mirisavatiya Dagoba Continuing around the tank bund you pass behind the rest house and then turn off the bund track to this huge dagoba. There are various legends associated with this dagoba, which was the first to be built by Dutugemunu after he defeated Elara and captured the city. One is that he was bathing in the tank and had left his sceptre, containing a relic of the Buddha, implanted in the ground. When he returned he found it was impossible to pull his sceptre out and taking this as an auspicious sign had a huge dagoba built.

Notice the plain guardstones around the dagoba, quite unlike later carved ones. North-east of the dagoba was the monk's refectory complete with the huge stone troughs, in which the faithful placed boiled rice, as found in other locations around the city.

The Tanks

Apart from the numerous ponds, wells and small tanks – many of which have been filled in to reduce the risk of malarial mosquitoes – Anuradhapura has three great tanks. Nuwarawewa covers about 1200 hectares (3000 acres) and is the largest of the three. It was built around 20 BC and is well away from the old city, the new town of Anuradhapura stands on its banks.

The 160 hectare (400 acres) Tissawewa is the southern tank in the old city – the Isurumuniya Temple stands on its bank and the Tissawewa Rest House backs on to it. The northern tank is the 120 hectare (300 acre) Bassawak Kulama – the Tamil word for tank, wewa in Sinhala, is kulam. This is the oldest tank, probably dating from around the 4th century BC.

Other

The remains of two stone bridges can be seen not too far from the Twin Ponds. They once crossed the Malvatu Oya and the Yoda Ela and were so substantial that it is conjectured they were used for taking elephants across. On your way to the bridges you can inspect the remains of the Vijayarama shrine with its 12 viharas.

Just north of the Archaeological Museum is a smaller Folk Museum – it's open from 9 am to 5 pm except on Fridays and Saturdays, admission is Rs 10.

Slightly south-east of the Ruvanvelisaya you can see yet another monk's refectory – keeping so many monks fed and happy was a full-time job for the lay followers. This whole area around the Ruvanvelisaya, Sri Maha Bodhi and Brazen Palace was once probably part of the Maha Vihara – the 'Great Temple'. Close to the Ratnaprasada, in the north of the city, is the Lankarama, a 1st century BC vatadage.

South of the Isurumuniya there are the extensive remains of the Vessagiriya cave

monastery complex which dates from much the same time as the Isurumuniya. Situated off to the north-west of the Bassawak Kulama are the ruins of the Western Monasteries. The monks here had totally forsaken the luxurious life their brother monks often lived – their contempt was evidenced in the squatting plates seen in the Anuradhapura Museum. Here they dressed in scraps of clothing taken from corpses and lived only on rice.

Places to Stay

Nothing, apart from one of the two rest houses, is very convenient in Anuradhapura. The town is divided into an old (the sacred) area and a new area – with an expanse of fields and the river separating them. Only the Tissawewa Rest House is in the old town-sacred area. All the other places are in the new town and generally not very close to the centre.

Places to Stay – bottom end

Most of the popular centres for shoestring travellers in Anuradhapura are away from the centre of town. Pick of the bunch is probably the *Shanthi Guest House* (tel 025-2515) at 891 Mailagas Junction, about two km from the new town centre. To get there take a Wijepura bus to the Mailagas Junction which is right beside it. Or you can walk from the New Bus Depot but it's a long, sweaty walk if you're carrying much gear. Because Anuradhapura is also besieged by accommodation touts they will pick you up or pay for a taxi if you phone from the bus station and check there is room available. There are a whole series of rooms ranging from Rs 50 for the simplest economy rooms in a separate building through to Rs 100 for doubles, Rs 150 with bath or Rs 250 for deluxe doubles. The food is good, it's comfortable and clean and they have bicycles for rent. The owner's lovely old 1931 Austin 7 is still going strong although it has been supplanted by a Mini Moke!

On the other side of town, at the

junction where the Jaffna road joins the Mihintale road, is the *Travellers' Halt* (tel 025-290) at 15 Jaffna Junction, another in the island wide network and probably the best known since it's often a first stop for travellers arriving from the Indian ferry. Rooms are Rs 25/50 and there's a dormitory. They'll give you a discount if you arrive without touts in tow.

King's Dale is about a hundred metres along the Mihintale road from the junction and well back from the road. If you're coming in from Trincomalee by bus get down outside it or at the junction if you're going to the Travellers' Halt – don't go all the way into town. Singles/doubles with bath are Rs 30/50 at King's Dale. Dinner is good here, it costs about Rs 25 to 30 and you should order a couple of hours ahead.

The *Tourist Holiday Home* is a recently opened place close to the post office. Rooms cost Rs 75/100 downstairs, Rs 100/125 upstairs. It's conveniently located and good value – rooms all have mosquito net, fan and attached bathroom. The food here is pretty good too. Right across the road from it is the *Paramount Hotel* which is really an emergencies-only, grubby dive. Singles/doubles are just Rs 50/100.

Other places include the *Dilkushi Holiday Home* on the Kandy road which costs Rs 150/250 including breakfast. Two rooms share a common bathroom. According to reports it's superbly mosquito proofed and has 'unbelievably' good and filling food. Near the bus stop at 63 Freeman Mawatha the *Hotel Monara* (tel 025-2110) has 10 rooms with singles/doubles at Rs 100/150. The *Dew Drop Guest House* is on Jayanthi Mawatha, nothing special. The *Sevana Tourist Rest* at 43 Harichandra Mawatha, with good rooms at Rs 125 to 150 and excellent food, has been recommended. *Number 5*, about a hundred metres beyond the Tissawewa Rest House, is a rather anonymous, rock bottom place to stay.

There are *Railway Retiring Rooms* at Rs 110 for a double with bath – choose a room on the road side rather than the railway side.

Places to Stay – top end

Anuradhapura has two very pleasant rest houses, a group of hotels all close together and a couple of up-market guest houses. The *Tissawewa Rest House* (tel 025-2299) is really quite delightful and has the considerable advantage of being right in there with the ruins. This does have the minor drawback, for some people, that since it is in the 'sacred area' they can't provide alcohol – although you can bring your own with you. It's one of those elderly places with class that the Sri Lankans seem to be able to do so well. A big spacious verandah looks out on gardens, with lots of monkeys, in the front and it backs on to the Tissawewa Tank. There are 25 enormously spacious rooms with room only costs of Rs 300/400 for singles/doubles. Breakfast costs Rs 40, dinner Rs 70. Highly recommended but it can often be booked right out.

The *Nuwarawewa Rest House* (tel 025-2565) is the second rest house and is fairly convenient for the New Town area. It backs on to the Nuwarawewa Tank and while it is not as 'olde worlde' as the Tissawewa Rest House it is still very pleasant in its own way. In what seems to be rest house fashion there is an open air verandah dining area. There are 60 rooms, 35 of them with air-con, and costs are Rs 300/330, Rs 70 more with air-con. The rest house also has a swimming pool and an unpleasantly large mosquito population. Food here can be very good. At Mihintale, about 14 km out of Anuradhapura, there is another, smaller, rest house.

The clump of hotels also sits on the edge of the tank but rather further around and less conveniently situated for New Town. The 50 room *Miridiya Hotel* (tel 025-2112 & 2519) is the top establishment in town with 50 air-con rooms at Rs 400. It's on Rowing Club Rd as is the 100 room *Rajarata Hotel* (tel 025-2578) where rooms cost Rs 335/420 including breakfast. The 26 room *Ashok Hotel* (tel 025-2735) is also on Rowing Club Rd and costs Rs 150/ 200; some economy rooms are available for Rs 125.

Places to Eat

The *Paramount Hotel* has a reasonable, if sometimes terribly slow, restaurant but there's not much else by the way of eating places apart from the places to stay. When you're visiting the ruins, you can save money by buying soft drinks from the numerous shops along the roads, not from vendors at the sites. Just east of the Isurumuniya, however, the *Madhura Cool Hut & Coffee Centre* is a nice place for refreshments and does quite good simple food like eggs on toast.

Getting There

Anuradhapura is on the railway route between Colombo and Talaimannar or Jaffna. There are two trains a day running through the city for Talaimannar and four or five for Jaffna, plus one that terminates or starts in Anuradhapura. The trip takes four to five hours Colombo-Anuradhapura or Anuradhapura-Jaffna, three to four hours Anuradhapura-Talaimannar. Fares from Anuradhapura (add the usual sleeper, berth, etc supplements) include:

	1st	2nd	3rd
Colombo	Rs 102.50	Rs 65.60	Rs 26.70
Jaffna	Rs 95.50	Rs 61.20	Rs 24.90
Trincomalee	Rs 112.30	Rs 72.00	Rs 29.30
Talaimannar	Rs 65.00	Rs 41.60	Rs 15.90
Kalkudah	Rs 125.00	Rs 80.10	Rs 32.50

There is also a three times weekly Inter-City Express service running Colombo-Anuradhapura-Jaffna. It takes 3¼ hours Colombo-Anuradhapura at a fare of Rs 51 – there is only class in these new, high speed trains. Anuradhapura-Jaffna takes three hours at a fare of Rs 48.

By road there are plenty of buses

Colombo-Anuradhapura each day, the trip takes about 6½ hours. CTB buses cost Rs 23, minibuses Rs 28. There are also about a dozen buses making the five hour trip to Kandy (Rs 18 CTB, Rs 23 by minibus). Three or four go on the six hour trip to Jaffna (Rs 21, Rs 25). Other services include Trincomalee (Rs 16.50, Rs 20) and Polonnaruwa (Rs 15, Rs 20). A bus to Dambulla costs about Rs 8. Minibuses go from the New Town centre, CTB Colombo buses go from the station there. Other CTB buses go from the new bus station.

Getting Around

As in Polonnaruwa the city is too spread out to investigate comfortably on foot. A quick taxi tour would cost about Rs 100 but a bicycle (Rs 15 to 20 a half day, Rs 25 to 30 a day) is the nicest way to explore the ruins in a leisurely fashion although concentrated groups are pleasant to walk around. Prices depend on where you hire them, the rest houses and several guest houses can provide them. You can also hire motorcycles for Rs 150 a day.

It's a fairly short bus ride costing a couple of rupees out to Mihintale. A taxi there and back with two hours to climb the stairs would cost about Rs 100. As an Anuradhapura taxi driver disarmingly explained it, the price is actually lower for tourists than Sinhalese – 'because tourists just rush up and down, Sinhalese spend ages'.

MIHINTALE

Situated 11 km north-east of Anuradhapura on the road to Trincomalee, Mihintale is of enormous spiritual significance to the Sinhalese because this is where Buddhism originated in Sri Lanka. In the year 247 BC, King Devanampiya Tissa of Anuradhapura was deer hunting around the hill at Mihintale and met Mahinda, son of the great Indian Buddhist-Emperor Ashoka and was converted to Buddhism. Each year a great festival is held at Mihintale on the full moon night of Poson (usually

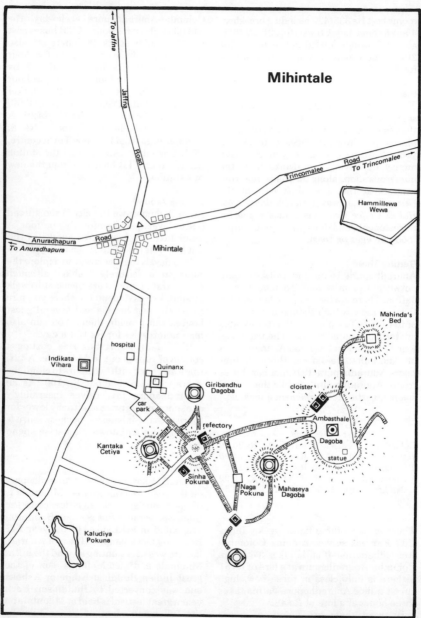

Mihintale

June). Exploring Mihintale involves quite a climb so you are wise to visit it early in the morning or late in the afternoon to avoid the midday heat.

The Stairway
A ruined 'hospital' and the remains of a *quincunx* of buildings, laid out like the five dots on a dice, flank the roadway before you reach the base of the steps. In a series of flights, 1840 ancient granite slab steps lead majestically up the hillside. The first flight is the widest and shallowest, higher up the steps are narrower and steeper.

Kantaka Cetiya
At the first landing a smaller flight of steps leads off to the right, to this partially ruined dagoba. Standing 12 metres high and measuring 130 metres around its base it was built sometime before 60 BC. It is particularly notable for its altar-piece panels with their excellent sculptures of dwarves, geese and other figures. The dagoba, which at one time was probably over 30 metres high, was only discovered in the mid-1930s and you can see a reconstruction of its interior design in the museum in Anuradhapura.

Monk's Refectory
At the top of the next flight of steps you reach the monk's refectory where there are huge stone troughs, which it was the lay-followers' responsibility to keep filled. There are also two 10th century AD stone slabs inscribed with the rules and regulations of the monastery. They were erected during the reign of King Mahinda IV. Looking back from here you get an excellent view of Anuradhapura.

Ambasthale Dagoba
The final, narrow and steep, stairway leads to the place where Mahinda and the king met. The dagoba was built over the spot where Mahinda stood and nearby stands a statue of the king at the position where he stood. The name Ambasthale means 'mango tree' and refers to a riddle about mango trees which Mahinda used to test the king's intelligence.

Maha Seya Dagoba
A path to the right leads to a higher dagoba which is thought to contain relics of Mahinda. Again there is an excellent view of Anuradhapura from the dagoba.

Mahinda's Bed
Above the Ambasthale Dagoba is the huge stone slab said to be the 'bed' on which Mahinda waited for his meeting with the king.

Naga Pokuna
Half way down the top, steep flight of steps a path leads off to the left and cuts around the side of the hill which the Maha Seya Dagoba tops. Here you will find the Naga Pokuna or 'snake pool' – so called because of the five-headed cobra which is carved in low relief on the rock face of the pool. Its tail is said to reach right down to the bottom of the pool. You do not need to retrace your path to the steps, if you continue on you will eventually loop back to the second landing.

Sinha Pokuna
Just below the monk's refectory on the second landing is a small pool surmounted by a rampant lion said to be one of the best pieces of animal carving in the country. There are also some fine friezes carved around this pool. Do not go back down the main steps, continue on beyond the lion pool and follow the gently sloping track down to the road.

Kaludiya Pokuna
If you turn left on the main road and walked a little southward you will soon come to the turn-off to the Kaludiya Pokuna or 'dark-water pool'. This artificial pool was carefully constructed to look like a real one and features a rock-carved bath-house and the ruins of a small monastery. It's a peaceful, quiet and beautiful little escape. Back towards the village of

Mihintale you could search for the hermit caves in the 'royal cave hill' or divert into the ruins of the Indikatu Vihara.

Tanks

A casual glance at the map of Sri Lanka would immediately indicate that the island is dotted with lakes, even in the dry northern area. It's a false impression for lake-like though they may be, most of them are in fact artificial 'tanks'. Many of them are around two thousand years old and virtually all of them are over a thousand years in age. Even today they would be quite considerable engineering projects – for their time they are simply fantastic.

The tanks were constructed by the great kings of ancient Ceylon to provide irrigation water for the growing of rice; particularly in the dry northern region. They are in many ways a more lasting reminder of their power and ability than the great cities they also built; for the cities reverted back to the jungle whereas the tanks have become part of the landscape.

Useful though they may have been, and indeed still are, one suspects that tank building was not purely an altruistic activity for the great kings. Like many other dry-land rulers the Sinhalese kings seem to have taken a considerable interest in water and its enjoyment – as the many pools and ponds at Anuradhapura and Polonnaruwa will testify. Two of the greatest tank builders were Mahasena (276-303 AD) and Dhatusena (459-477 AD) who is better known for his death at the hands of his son Kasyapa, the architect of Sigiriya.

POLONNARUWA

When Anuradhapura became too exposed to attack from south India the reluctant decision was made to shift south. In actual fact the Indian Chola dynasty had already established a city at Polonnaruwa but from the time Vijayabahu I (1111-1132) defeated the invaders Anuradhapura was abandoned in favour of the new, more remote, centre. It was Parakramabahu I (1153-1186) who raised Polonnaruwa to its heights, erecting huge buildings, planning beautiful parks and, as a crowning achievement, building a 2400 hectare (5940 acres) tank – so large that it was named the Parakrama Samudra – the 'Sea of Parakrama'. The present lake

incorporates three older tanks so it may not be the actual tank he created.

Parakramabahu I was followed by Nissanka Malla (1187-1196) who succeeded in virtually bankrupting the kingdom in his attempts to match his predecessors' achievements. By the early 1200s Polonnaruwa was beginning to prove as susceptible to Indian invasion as Anuradhapura and despite two further centuries of efforts to stand strong, eventually it too was abandoned and the Sinhalese capital shifted to the very south of the island.

Polonnaruwa stands 104 km (65 miles) south-east of Anuradhapura and 213 km (133 miles) north-east of Colombo. Although it is now nearly a thousand years old it is still much younger than Anuradhapura and its monuments are generally in much better repair. Furthermore they are arranged in a more compact area and their development is easier to follow. All-in-all, if you're something less than a professional archaeologist you'll probably find Polonnaruwa the easier of the ancient sites to appreciate. Like Anuradhapura there is a new satellite town built well away from the ancient ruins, but Polonnaruwa also has a fair size town right in amongst the ruins.

The ruins at Polonnaruwa can be conveniently divided into five groups: (1) a small group near the rest house on the banks of the tank; (2) the royal palace group a little to the east of the rest house; (3) a very compact group just a short distance north of the royal palace group – usually known as the quadrangle; (4) a rather spread out group further north – the northern group; (5) a small group far to the south towards the new town – the southern group. There are also a few scattered ruins outside these groups. As at Anuradhapura and Sigiriya there is a Rs 75 entry charge for non-Sri Lankans.

Rest House Group

The rest house is delightfully situated on a small promontory jutting out into the

Topawewa tank. It's a delightful place for a refreshing post-sightseeing lemonade. The small archaeological museum is slightly to the east of the rest house, above the canal. It's not of great interest. Concentrated a few steps to the north of the rest house are the ruins of Nissanka Malla's royal palace – they are not in anywhere near the same state of preservation as the Parakramabahu palace group.

The royal baths are nearest to the rest house. Furthest north are the King's Council Chamber where the king's throne in the shape of a stone lion once stood – it is now in the Colombo Museum. Inscribed into each column in the chamber is the name of the minister whose seat was once beside it. The mound nearby becomes an island when the waters of the tank are high – on it are the ruins of a small summer house used by the king.

The Royal Palace Group

Across the main road from the rest house and museum, to the north of the moat, this group of buildings dates from the reign of Parakramabahu I. There are three main things to see in this group:

The Royal Palace Parakramabahu's palace was a magnificent structure. It measured 31 by 13 metres (102 by 42 feet) and was said to have had seven stories. The three-metre thick walls certainly have the holes to receive the floor beams for two higher floors but if there were a further four levels they must have been constructed of wood. The roof in this main hall, which had 50 rooms in all, was supported by 30 columns.

Audience Hall The pavilion used as an audience hall by Parakramabahu is particularly notable for the frieze of elephants around its base – every elephant is in a different position.

Bathing Pool In the south-east corner of the palace grounds the Kumara Pokuna,

or Prince's Bathing Pool, still has one of its crocodile-mouth spouts remaining.

Quadrangle

Only a short stroll north of the Royal Palace ruins, the area known as the Quadrangle is literally that – a compact group of fascinating ruins, in a raised up area, bounded by a wall. It's the most concentrated collection of buildings you'll find in the Sri Lankan ancient cities.

Vatadage Standing right by the quadrangle entrance the Vatadage is a typical 'circular relic house'; there are similar structures at Medirigiriya and Anuradhapura (the Thuparama). The outermost terrace of the Vatadage is 18 metres (58 feet) in diameter and the second terrace has four entrances flanked by particularly fine guardstones and with a moonstone at the northern entrance which is said to be the finest in Polonnaruwa, although not of the same standard as some of the best at Anuradhapura. The four entrances lead to the central dagoba with its four seated Buddhas. The stone screen is thought to be a later addition to the Vatadage, probably made by Nissanka Malla.

Thuparama Situated at the southern end of the quadrangle the Thuparama is a *gedige*, an architectural style which reached its perfection at Polonnaruwa. This is one of the best. It's the smallest gedige in Polonnaruwa but the only one with the roof still intact. The building shows strong Hindu design influence and is thought to date from the reign of Parakramabahu I. A stairway, built into the extremely thick walls, leads to the roof. There are several Buddha images in the inner chamber.

Gal-Potha The stone-book, standing immediately east of the Hatadage, is a colossal stone representation of a palm-leaf *ola*-book. It measures nearly nine metres long by 1½ metres wide and from 40 to 66 cm thick. The inscription on it,

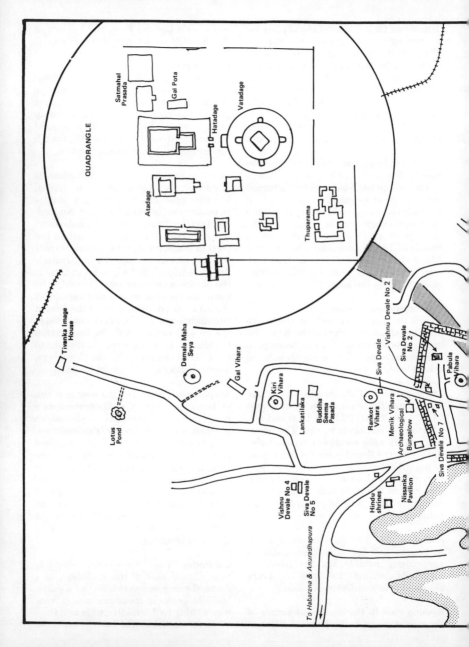

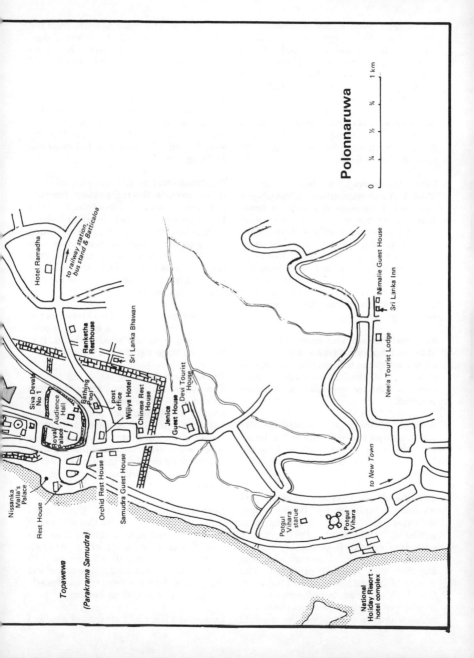

Polonnaruwa

Topawewa

(Parakrama Samudra)

Nissanka Malla's Palace

Rest House

Orchid Rest House

Samudra Guest House

Royal Palace Audience Hall

Siva Devale No 1

Bathing Pool

post office

Wijiva Hotel

Chinese Rest House

Hotel Ramadha

to railway station, bus stand & Batticaloa

Ranketha Resthouse

Sri Lanka Bhawan

Devi Tourist House

Jenica Guest House

Potgul Vihara statue

Potgul Vihara

National Holiday Resort - hotel complex

to New Town

Neela Tourist Lodge

Nimalie Guest House

Sri Lanka Inn

0   ¼   ½   ¾   1 km

the longest such stone inscription (of which they are many!) in Sri Lanka, indicates that it was a Nissanka Malla production. Much of it extols his virtues as a king but it also includes the footnote that the slab, weighing 25 tonnes, was dragged from Mihintale, nearly 100 km away!

Hatadage Also erected by Nissanka Malla this tooth-relic chamber is said to have been built in one day – or 60? – or contained 60 relics?

Latha-Mandapaya The busy Nissanka Malla was also responsible for this unique structure. It consists of a latticed stone fence, a curious imitation of a wooden fence with posts and railings, surrounding a very small dagoba surrounded by stone pillars. The pillars are shaped like lotus stalks topped by unopened buds. Nissanka Malla is said to have sat within this enclosure to listen to chanted Buddhist texts. It stands outside the quadrangle enclosure.

Satmahal Prasada This curious building, about which very little is known, has a very clear Cambodian influence in its design. It consists of six diminishing storeys (there used to be seven) like a stepped pyramid.

Atadage This tooth-relic temple is the only surviving structure in Polonnaruwa dating from the reign of Vijayabahu I. Like the Hatadage it once had an upper wooden storey.

Siva Devale No I Southernmost of the quadrangle buildings this Hindu temple indicates the Indian influence that persisted throughout Polonnaruwa's period as capital. It is notable for the superb quality of its stonework which fits together with unusual precision. The domed brick roof has collapsed but when this building was being excavated a number of excellent bronzes were discovered and these are now in the museum

in Colombo. The building dates from the 13th century, one of the latest Polonnaruwa structures, and actually stands just outside the raised quadrangle platform.

Close to the Quadrangle
Continuing along the road north from the quadrangle a gravel road branches off to the right, just before you reach the city wall. It leads to the oldest Polonnaruwa building:

Siva Devale No 2 Similar in style to No 1, at the quadrangle, this is the oldest structure in Polonnaruwa and dates from the brief Chola period when the invading Indians established the city. Unlike so many buildings in the ancient cities it was built entirely of stone so the structure today is seen much as it was when first built, one does not have to imagine the now missing wooden components.

Parakramabahu Vihara Also known as the Pabula Vihara this is a typical dagoba from the period of Parakramabahu. It is the third largest stupa in Polonnaruwa.

The Northern Group
The northern structures are much more spread out – while you could easily walk around the royal palace and quadrangle buildings you will need a bicycle or other transport to comfortably explore these ruins, which are all north of the city wall. They include the Gal Vihara, probably the most famous Buddha images in Sri Lanka.

Rankot Vihara After the three great dagobas at Anuradhapura this is the next biggest in Sri Lanka. Built by Nissanka Malla, in clear imitation of the Anuradhapura style, it stands 55 metres (180 feet) high. It is situated to the left of the road, about half way from the quadrangle to the Alahana Parivena buildings.

Lankatilaka Built by Parakramabahu, and

later restored by Vijayabahu IV, this huge *gedige* has walls still standing 17 metres (55 feet) high although the roof has collapsed. The cathedral-like aisle leads to a huge, but now headless, standing Buddha image. The outer walls are decorated with bas reliefs showing typical Polonnaruwa structures in their original state. The group of buildings around here are part of the Alahana Parivena group – the name means crematory college since the temples and monasteries stood in the royal cremation grounds established by Parakramabahu.

Kiri Vihara This is the best-preserved unrestored dagoba in Sri Lanka and is credited to Subhadra, Parakramabahu's queen. It was originally known as the Rupavati Cetiya but the present name means milk-white since when the overgrown jungle from 700 years of neglect was cleared the original lime plaster was found to be still in perfect condition.

There is also a fine *mandapaya* (raised platform with decorative pillars) and the monastery abbot's convocation hall in this same Alahana Parivena group, but south of the Lankatilaka.

Gal Vihara Across the road from the Kiri Vihara you come to a group of Buddha images which probably mark the high point of Sinhalese rock carving. They are part of Parakramabahu's northern monastery. The Gal Vihara consists of four separate images, all cut from one long slab of granite. At one time each was enshrined within a separate enclosure – you can clearly see the sockets cut into the rock behind the standing image, into which wooden beams would have been inserted.

The standing Buddha is seven metres tall and is said to be the finest of the series. It stands with the arms in an unusual position and this, plus the sorrowful expression on the face, led to the theory that it was an image of the Buddha's disciple Ananda, grieving for his master's departure for nirvana since the reclining image is next to it. The fact that it had its own separate enclosure, and the later discovery of other images with the same arm position, has discounted this theory and it is now accepted that all the images are of the Buddha.

The reclining image of the Buddha entering nirvana is 14 metres long and to

· POLONNARUWA ·

my mind the beautiful grain of the stone of the image's face is the most impressive part of the Gal Vihara group. Notice also the subtle depression in the pillow under the head and the sun-wheel symbol on the pillow end. The other two images are both of the seated Buddha, one is smaller and of inferior craftsmanship within a small cavity in the rock. The other is, like the standing and reclining images, out in the open.

From the Gal Vihara you can cut back around the hill to rejoin the northern road further along on foot. With wheels you have to follow the road along and turn right to reach the final spread out series of ruins.

Demala Maha Seya A typical Parakramabahu truncated dagoba, now largely overgrown, it stands to the right of the road. You pass by the base of this huge structure if you walk from the Gal Vihara.

Lotus Pond Further north, a track to the left leads to the unusual Lotus Bath – nearly eight metres in diameter, the bath is in the shape of an eight-petalled lotus blossom. You descend into the empty pool by stepping down the five concentric rings of petals.

Tivanka Image House The northern road ends at this image house – the name means 'thrice bent' and refers to the fact that the Buddha image within is in a three-curved position normally reserved for female statues as opposed to the more upright male form. The building is notable for the energetic dwarves who cavort around the outside and for the fine frescoes within. Some of these date from Parakramabahu III's later attempt to restore Polonnaruwa but others are far earlier.

Southern Group
The small southern group is close to the compound of new 'top end' hotels. By bicycle it's a pleasant ride along the bund of the Topawewa tank over the ancient spillway.

Potgul Vihara Also known as the library dagoba this unusual structure is a thick walled, hollow, stupa-like building which may have been used to store books. It's effectively a circular *gedige* and four smaller solid dagobas arranged around this central dome form the popular Sinhalese *quincunx* arrangement.

Statue There are various other lesser ruins in the southern group but most interesting is the statue at the northern end. Standing nearly four metres high it's an unusually lifelike representation, in contrast to the normally idealised or stylised Buddha figures. Exactly whom it represents is a subject of some controversy. Some say that the object he is holding is a book and thus the statue is of the Indian religious teacher Agastaya. The more popular theory is that it is a rope representing the 'yoke of kingship' and the bearded stately figure is of Parakramabahu I.

Places to Stay – bottom end
There are a couple of pleasant places out in New Town, not so bad if you have a *good* bicycle, plus a few others around the Old Town bazaar. The *Nimalia Guest House* is at No 2 Channel, New Town and has

A   Gal Vihara, Polonnaruwa
B   Wewurukannala Vihara seated Buddha image near Dondra
C   Tissamaharama Dagoba

doubles at Rs 150. The food here is very good, but it's a long way from the centre. To get there take an 847 bus from the railway station or the Old Town bus halt. At the junction beyond the New Town statue a sign directs you – it's about a km walk.

Right next door is the *Sri Lankan Inns* (tel 027-2403) with 17 rooms, all with attached bath, at Rs 150/200 for singles/ doubles. On you way to these two places from New Town you'll pass the *Neela Tourist Lodge* which has just a couple of rooms at Rs 150/175.

In the Old Town area there is the *Chinese Rest House* with rooms starting from Rs 50 and going up to Rs 125 and 150 with attached bathrooms. The food here gets mixed reports.

Right in the centre of Old Town the *Orchid Rest House* has rooms from Rs 50 to 150, some of the more expensive ones with attached bathroom. Next door the simple *Samudra Hotel* has rooms from Rs 30 to 75 and has had several recommendations. Generally the food here seems to be pretty good. The *Wijaya Hotel* costs Rs 40 a double – big, clean rooms but poor food. Near the old town post office the *Free Tourist Resort* has clean singles from Rs 75 and good food.

About a half km down the road towards New Town, signs point off to the left to two other rock bottom places. The rather basic and grubby *Jenica Guest House* has dorm beds at Rs 10 and rooms from Rs 25 to Rs 75. Just a bit further down this small road is the *Devi Tourist Home* with very similar prices and a helpful and knowledgeable owner.

On the road out of town (Batticaloa Rd) towards the railway station is the new

Ranketha Guest House (tel 027-2080) with rooms at Rs 150 to 200. Meals are also available – it's clean, well kept – if a little sterile – and has good food. There are two other places on this side of town. The *Sri Lanka Bhawan* is off the road just before the Ranketha Guest House. It's got good toilets and showers, new fans and mosquito nets and brand new bicycles. At Rs 150 a double this recently opened and friendly place is good value. The *Hotel Ramadha* is a little further along towards the bus and railway stations.

There is not much choice of places to eat apart from the hotels and guest houses. The Rest House and the Ranketha Guest House are probably your best bets.

Places to Stay – top end
At the top end you've got a choice of the extremely conveniently and attractively situated rest house or a complex of three tourist hotels. The *Polonnaruwa Rest House* (tel 027-2299) is on a promontory right by the tank. It's small (just 10 rooms) with room-only costs of Rs 275 per night plus breakfast available at Rs 40, lunch or dinner at Rs 55. Not one of the best rest houses but not bad.

The three-hotel complex, known as the National Holiday Resort, is located slightly beyond the Potgul Vihara ruins. Here you'll find three very similar standard hotels – the 34 room *Amaliyan Niwas* (tel 027-2405) with doubles at Rs 250, the 30 room *Araliya Hotel* (tel 027-2421) with doubles at Rs 350 and the 40 room *Hotel Seruwa* (tel 027-2411) with rooms at Rs 350. Bed and breakfast or all-inclusive rates are also available. All the rooms are air-conditioned. The complex

A Buduruvagala Buddha images
B Seated Buddha image, Gal Vihara, Polonnaruwa
C Reclining Buddha image, Aluvihara

overlooks the tank and there is a swimming pool which non-residents can use for Rs 15.

At Giritale, overlooking the Giritale Tank, about 12 km from Polonnaruwa, there is another modern hotel complex consisting of the 54 room *Royal Lotus Hotel* (tel 027-6316) with rooms at Rs 450 and the 44 room *Giritale Hotel* (tel 027-6311) with rooms at Rs 320. Also in Giritale, but on the Polonnaruwa road, is the small 15 room *Hotel Hemalee* (tel 027-6257) with rooms at Rs 250. There's also the *Wood Side Inn*.

Getting There
Polonnaruwa is on the Colombo-Batticaloa rail line, shortly after the junction where the line to Trincomalee splits off. There are three trains daily in either direction, the train from Colombo splitting into a Trinco and Batti train at the junction. From Colombo the day train takes about six hours but the night train takes seven or eight. Fares are Rs 130 in 1st class, Rs 85.20 in 2nd, Rs 33.80 in 3rd.

Batti is only about 1½ hours from Polonnaruwa, you go via Kalkudah. The railway station and the bus station are both several km from the Old Town on the Batticaloa road.

To and from Colombo there are a number of buses a day, via Dambulla the trip takes about six hours. There are also buses to and from Anuradhapura (Rs 16 CTB, Rs 25 minibus), Batticaloa (Rs 20 minibus) and to Kandy (Rs 28 minibus); the latter goes via Dambulla (Rs 15).

Getting Around
Bicycles are the ideal transport for Polonnaruwa's not too widely scattered monuments. A number of guest houses or bicycle shops in the old town centre hire out bikes – the going rate is about Rs 3 an hour, Rs 20 per day. Some of the bikes are the usual Sri Lankan old nails; caveat emptor, etc! A bike hire place which has been recommended is H S Weerasinghe's (Uncle Weera's) opposite the public

library. At the National Resort complex the Hotel Seruwa hires out good bikes for Rs 35 a day.

Arriving in Polonnaruwa by rail you can take an 847 bus from the station to the Old Town and on to the New Town if you wish. A car can be hired for three hours for around Rs 75, long enough to have a quick look around the ruins. Solo women should exercise a little caution if wandering around the more remote ruins.

MEDIRIGIRIYA
The Mandalagiri Vihara, a vatadage virtually identical in design and measurement to that of Polonnaruwa, is about 40 km from Polonnaruwa and takes a little effort to get to. You may feel it worthwhile for whereas the Polonnaruwa vatadage is crowded amongst many other structures the vatadage here stands by itself. Furthermore it tops a low hill and this adds to the eerie, lost-city feel of the remote ruin.

An earlier structure may have been built around the 2nd century AD but the one that stands there today was constructed in the 8th century. A granite flight of steps leads up the hill to the vatadage which has concentric circles of pillars around the central dagoba. The circles have 16, 20 and 32 pillars respectively. Four large, seated-Buddhas, one of which is still in good condition, face the four cardinal directions. The vatadage is noted for its ornamented stone screens. Look for the medicine bath in the shape of the bottom half of a coffin. People added herbs to the water and lay down in it if they were sick.

Getting There
Without your own transport, getting to Medirigiriya can be a little time consuming and, as usual on Sri Lankan buses, tiring. Medirigiriya is about 24 km north of Minneriya, which is on the route between Polonnaruwa and Anuradhapura or Dambulla. To get there by bus involves at least one change – you can bus to Giritale

or Minneriya then catch another bus from there to Medirigiriya.

The surprise comes at Medirigiriya because the vatadage is not actually there – it's three km away along a road where buses rarely run. We walked all the way there and three quarters of the way back before a bus came by, fortunately we were able to stow our bags in a tea boutique first. From Minneriya on to Dambulla the bus fare is about Rs 6.

DAMBULLA

The great rock caves of Dambulla are situated 100 to 150 metres above the road and the village of Dambulla. The first part of the climb up to the cave temple is along a vast, sloping rock face. From the caves you have a superb view over the surrounding countryside, Sigiriya is clearly visible to the north-east, only 19 km away. The cave's history is thought to date back to around the 1st century BC when King Valagam Bahu was driven out of Anuradhapura and took refuge here. When he regained his throne he had the caves converted into a magnificent rock temple. Later kings made further improvements including King Nissanka Malla who had the temple interior gilded, earning it the name of 'Ran Giri' – the Golden Rock.

There are five separate caves, the largest of which is over 50 metres long and about six metres high. In this cave there is a 15 metre-long reclining Buddha. The second cave has many large images of Hindu gods and all the caves are full of Buddha images in a variety of positions and are decorated in glowing colours with frescoes showing scenes from the Buddha's life and events in Sinhalese history. The frescoes are comparatively modern and not of particular significance. As dusk draws in hundreds of swallows swoop and dart around the cave entrance.

The temple closes at 7 pm and it is also closed between 11 am and 2 pm. In common with the policy of charging foreign visitors for anything they can be

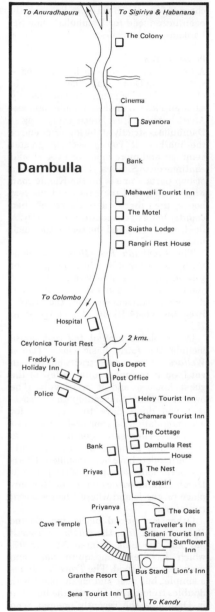

charged for a Rs 50 entry fee has recently been introduced for Dambulla – non-Sri Lankans only of course.

Places to Stay

A lot of basic to very-basic lodges have sprung up in Dambulla in the past couple of years. They're generally conveniently situated, close to the cave-temple entrance. Apart from the Rest House everything at Dambulla is strictly at the low price end of the market. If you're seeking greater comforts and more mod-cons you should continue on to Sigiriya. Dambulla consists of two parts – one is on the Kandy road where you'll find the caves and the rest house, then there's about a km of open country before you reach the junction with the Colombo Rd and the rest of the small town.

The *Dambulla Rest House* (tel 066-8299) has rooms at Rs 220, a very pleasant garden and a cool, breezy verandah where you can sit and sip an evening drink. And it's very convenient for the caves. Breakfast costs Rs 40, dinner Rs 65 to 75.

Other places around the rest house include the fairly basic *Oasis Tourist Welfare Centre* – no electricity but you can get food here (unlike quite a few of the guest houses) and it is friendly. The owner, Wimal Sikuradhipathy, insists that you don't have to even pay for accommodation on your first night – just for food. There are four doubles, two singles and a dormitory and recently modern toilets have been installed. This is one of the longest running of the places at Dambulla and, wrote one visitor, 'the only place on the island where I had a *decent* cup of tea'!

Other low priced places include the *Heley Tourist Inn*, the *Chamara Tourist Inn* and the pink painted *Number 97*, which has fans, mosquito nets and prepares good food. The *Travellers Inn* is a simple, but neat and clean, place with doubles from Rs 50. Close to the bus stop in Dambulla the recently opened *Sena*

Tourist Inn is similarly priced (singles from Rs 20) and has good food.

Take the turn off towards the police station and directly below the rock (about 400 metres off the main road) *Freddy's Holiday Inn* is a fine little place with rooms from Rs 50 to 150, with bath and fan. Next door is the *Ceylonica Tourist Rest* with equivalent cheap rooms.

Continue up the road to the junction and the *Rangiri Rest House* is plain and spartan with doubles from Rs 50. It's pretty reasonable value and centrally located. A bit further down is the rather grubby, and rather expensive for what you get, *Motel*. Then the cheap *Wahaveli Restaurant* and still further down the road, behind the cinema, is the *Sayanora Lodge*. It is reasonably clean and well kept and does have running water, mosquito nets and fans but it's a long way from the cave entrance. Rooms cost from Rs 100.

Right up at the end of this stretch, at the Mirigoniyama Junction, *The Colony* has cabana-style rooms from Rs 60 and a restaurant. It's almost a mid-point between Dambulla and Sigiriya.

Getting There

Dambulla is 72 km north of Kandy on the main road from there to Anuradhapura, Polonnaruwa and Trincomalee. The road from Colombo intersects the Kandy road about a km north of Dambulla village which actually consists of two parts – the village proper around the bottom of the cave hill and another part around the Colombo-Kandy road junction. Because it's on so many major routes, plenty of long distance buses pass through Dambulla with the usual Sri Lankan inconsistent frequency but the nearest railway station is at Habarana, 22 km to the north.

SIGIRIYA

The rock fortress of Sigiriya is one of Sri Lanka's major attractions – it takes a little effort to get there but the experience is well worthwhile. In 473 AD King Dhatusena was overthrown by a palace revolt led by his son Kasyapa. The king, so one of the many legends goes, was walled up alive by his ungrateful son.

Kasyapa was the son of Dhatusena and a palace consort while his half-brother Moggallana, who fled to India swearing revenge, was the son of the king and his true queen. Fearing an invasion by his half-brother, Kasyapa decided to build an impregnable fortress on the huge rock of Sigiriya. When the long expected invasion finally came, 18 years later in 491, Kasyapa did not simply skulk within his stronghold but rode out at the head of his army on an elephant. In attempting to outflank his half-brother Kasyapa took a wrong turn, became bogged in a swamp, his troops deserted him and, finding himself alone, he took his own life.

Sigiriya later became a monastic refuge but eventually fell into disrepair and was only rediscovered by archaeologists during the British era. Describing it as merely a fortress does Sigiriya no justice. Atop the 200 metre high rock (377 metres above sea level) Kasyapa built a 5th century penthouse – a rock-top pleasure garden. It is hard to imagine Sigiriya at the height of its glory but at one time it must have been something akin to a European chateau, plonked on top of Australia's Ayers Rock!

The base of the rock, which rises sheer and mysterious from the surrounding jungle, is ringed by a moat and rampart. To the west of the rock an extensive garden was laid out, you can clearly trace its pattern from the top of the rock. A switchback series of steps leads to the western flank of the rock and then ascends it steeply.

As at Anuradhapura and Polonnaruwa there is a Rs 75 admission charge to foreign visitors. It closes at 5 pm. An early ascent for the sunrise is worthwhile.

Frescoes – the Sigiriya Damsels

About half way up the rock a modern spiral stairway leads up from the main route to a long, sheltered gallery in the sheer rock face. Painted in this niche are a series of beautiful women – similar in style to the rock paintings at Ajanta in India. These 5th century pin-ups are the only non-religious paintings to be seen in Sri Lanka. Although there may have been as many as 500 portraits at one time only 22 remain today – several were badly damaged by a vandal in 1967. Protected from the sun in the sheltered gallery they remain in remarkably good condition, their colours still glowing. They're at their best in the late afternoon light.

Mirror Wall with Graffiti

Beyond the fresco gallery the pathway clings to the sheer side of the rock and is protected on the outside by a three metre high wall. This wall was coated with a mirror smooth glaze on which visitors of over a thousand years ago felt impelled to note their impressions of the women in the gallery above. The graffiti were principally inscribed between the 7th and 11th century and 685 of them have been deciphered and published in a two volume edition – Sigiri Graffiti (Dr S Paranavitana, Oxford University Press, 1956). They are of great interest to scholars for their evidence of the development of the Sinhalese language and script. A typical graffiti reads:

> The ladies who wear golden chains on their breasts beckon me. As I have seen the resplendent ladies, heaven appears to me as not good.

or, by a female graffitist:

> A deer-eyed young woman of the mountain side arouses anger in my mind. In her hand she had taken a string of pearls and in her looks she has assumed rivalry with us.

Lion Platform

At the northern end of the rock the narrow pathway emerges onto a large flat platform from which the rock derives its name of Sigiriya – the lion rock. In 1898 H

C P Bell, the British archaeologist who was responsible for an enormous amount of archaeological discovery in Ceylon, was excavating on this platform and discovered two enormous lion paws. At one time a gigantic brickwork lion sat at this end of the rock and the final ascent to the top commenced with a stairway which led between the lions paws and into its mouth!

Today this once sheltered stairway has totally disappeared apart from the first steps and the paws. To reach the top means clambering across a series of grooves cut into the rock face. Fortunately there is a stout metal hand rail but those who suffer from vertigo are strongly advised not to look down. Still, sari-clad Sri Lankan women manage it, even on windy days, so it can't be that bad. Beware, however, of the Sigiriya wasps which sometimes appear here.

The Summit

The top of the rock covers 1.6 hectares (four acres) and at one time must have been completely covered with buildings, only the foundations of which remain today. The design of this rock-top palace, and the magnificent views it enjoys even today, makes one think that Sigiriya must have been much more palace than fortress. There is a pond, scooped out of the solid rock and measuring 27 metres by 21 metres. It looks for all the world like a modern swimming pool although it may have been used merely for water storage.

The king's stone throne, also cut from the solid rock, faces towards the rising sun. You can sit here and gaze across the surrounding jungle, as no doubt Kasyapa did 1500 years ago, and watch for an invading army, complete with elephants.

Other

At the base of the rock there is a small archaeological museum and nearby there are the ruins of associated monasteries and dagobas. If you would like to know a lot more about Sigiriya including the many points of interest on the route up the rock, I suggest you try and find a copy of R H de Silva's booklet *Sigiriya*, published by the Department of Archaeology in Colombo, 1976.

Places to Stay

Once again the *Rest House* (tel 066-8234) has an all but unbeatable location, directly opposite the side entrance to the rock. There are 17 rooms, a couple of which are air-conditioned. Nightly cost is Rs 225 to 275 per room and meals are available at Rs 40 for breakfast, from Rs 60 for lunch or dinner. This is one of the nicest rest houses and is a popular meal or snack stop for tour bus groups – they make good sandwiches and from their spacious verandah you can sit and study the rock.

Shoestringers at Sigiriya often head for the *Nilmini Lodge* where basic (even primitive) doubles cost Rs 30 to 50. Basic though it is, backpackers find it a friendly and convenient place to stay. It's the first place you come to, on the right hand side of the road by the ruin's entrance. Lionel, the owner, is a helpful local and his wife prepares excellent food. Beyond the rock is the *Ajantha Guest House* with good food and rooms from Rs 50 and also the *Susantha Guest House*. There's also the cheap *Sigiri Guest House*.

Further on beyond the rock is the *Apsara Holiday Resort* and campsite. You can camp here for Rs 20 or there are cabins and cabanas for Rs 150. Meals are available here but it's a little off-the-beaten-track, about a km beyond the rock.

There are a couple of upper bracket hotels a little beyond the rock. The *Sigiriya Village* (tel 066-8216) and the *Sigiriya Hotel* (tel 066-8311) are side by side, both have swimming pools which non-residents can use for Rs 25. The 100 room Sigiriya Village has rooms for Rs 500. The Sigiriya Hotel has 50 rooms with singles/doubles at Rs 400/450.

Getting There

Sigiriya is about 10 km (six miles) off the main road between Dambulla and Habarana. The turn off is at Inamaluwa and recently buses to Sigiriya seem to have become a little more frequent. There are buses about every hour from Dambulla in the morning (around Rs 2.50), less frequently in the afternoon.

There is also a bus direct to Sigiriya from Kandy each day at 8 am. If you can't get a direct bus you can always get off a bus that goes by the Inamaluwa junction and hope something else comes along. Note that the main paved road does not continue beyond Sigiriya although there is a smaller dirt road that eventually meets the Habarana-Polonnaruwa road quite close to Habarana.

HABARANA

This small village is a central location for all the ancient city sites and a new hotel complex has been built there principally for package tourists, although many better-heeled independent visitors also use it. There are a couple of cheaper accommodation alternatives and Habarana is also the nearest railway station to Dambulla and Sigiriya.

Places to Stay

The 110 room *Habarana Village* (tel 066-8316) has rooms at Rs 500, a fine open-air dining area and bar, a swimming pool and extensive grounds. The whole complex is done with considerable good taste, the white-painted rooms are functional but comfortable.

Sharing the same compound the *Habarana Lodge* (tel 066-8321) has 150 rooms from Rs 600. Breakfast costs Rs 40, lunch or dinner Rs 80. The rooms here are rather more luxurious and also have air-con, those at the Village are fan-cooled.

Habarana also has a *Rest House* (tel Habarana 4) with rooms at Rs 175/200. It's just to the north of the new hotel complex, while just to the south and just beyond Habarana is the *Habarana Inn*. This very pleasant little place has singles/doubles at Rs 175/250 including breakfast.

AUKANA

The magnificent 12 metre-high (39 feet) standing Buddha of Aukana is believed to have been sculptured during the reign of Dhatusena in the 5th century AD. The Kalawewa Tank, one of the many gigantic tanks he constructed, is only a couple of km from the statue and the road to Aukana from Kekirawa runs along the tank bund for several km. Aukana means 'sun-eating' and dawn is the best time to see it – when the sun's first rays light up the huge, but finely carved, statue's features.

Unfortunately, after many years of standing out in the open, an ugly (even if it is authentic) brick shelter has recently been constructed over the image. Note that although the image is cut out of the rockface, and still narrowly joined to it at the back, the lotus plinth on which it stands is a separate piece.

The Aukana Buddha is well known and frequently visited despite its relative isolation. Few people realise that 11 km to the west there is another image, also standing 12 metres high although of inferior workmanship. The Sasseruwa image was not completed and is now virtually forgotten in its jungle setting. A legend relates that the two images were carved at the same time in a competition between a master and his pupil. A bell would be rung to signal the completion of the first image – carving them took several years but it was the finer Aukana image, the work of the master, which was finished first and the Sasseruwa image was abandoned by the pupil.

Getting There

It's easier than it used to be to get to Aukana's remote jungle site as there is now a direct bus from Dambulla at 10 am which goes via Kekirawa and leaves Aukana for the return trip at 1.15 pm. Alternatively Aukana is fairly close to the

Colombo-Gal Oya railway line. There is an Aukana railway halt only a short walk from the Buddha statue but it's unlikely that express trains will halt there – apart from the special rail-tour cars that is.

Kalawewa station is, however, only about four km away and trains do halt there. You could get an early morning look at the Buddha then catch a train heading up or down the line. By road Kekirawa is the jumping off point on the main Dambulla-Anuradhapura road. Buses run through there with reasonable frequency and from there to Aukana with somewhat less regularity. Hiring a car from the Kekirawa taxi sharks will set you back about Rs 100 for a Kekirawa-Aukana-Kalawewa or back to Kekirawa circuit.

YAPAHUWA

This rock fortress, rising 100 metres from the surrounding plain, is similar in concept to the much better known Sigiriya. It is onl four km from Maho, the railway junction where the Colombo-Trincomalee line splits from the Colombo-Jaffna line, but a long way from anywhere else.

Yapahuwa, the 'excellent mountain', was originally constructed in the early 1200s as a fortress against the invading Kalingas of south India. For a very brief period between 1272 and 1284 it was the Sinhalese capital under Bhuvanekabahu I and it is believed that it was from Yapahuwa at that time that invading Indians carried away the sacred tooth-relic (now in Kandy), only for it to be recovered in 1288 by Parakramabahu I. A building to the east of the main fortifications is possibly the tooth-temple.

Some of the buildings on the rock top are of much more recent construction, but Yapahuwa's magnificently carved ornamental staircase is its best point. The porch on the stairway had very fine pierced-stone windows, one of which is now in the museum in Colombo.

PANDUVASNAVARA

About midway between Chilaw on the west coast (north of Negombo) and Kurunegala, the ruins at Panduvasnavara are free to visit but somewhat difficult to find. There is a very picturesque village next to the ruins and a very pleasant tank. Panduvasnavara has a small museum but the main attraction is the unusually good condition of what is left. The Royal Palace area is very interesting with a fine moat surrounding it. One of the most interesting items in the palace is the site of an external flame which was fueled by the excreta of the palace residents! The city was the capital of a region around the 12th century but was only excavated after WW II. Almost no one visits this interesting site.

ALUVIHARA

The rock monastery of Aluvihara is beside the Kandy-Dambulla road, just beyond the town of Matale – about 29 km from Kandy and 45 km before Dambulla. The monastery caves are situated in rocks which have fallen in a jumble from the mountain sides high above the valley. It's an extremely picturesque setting – in fact it has even been described as 'theatrical'. Some of the caves have fine frescoes, there is a 10 metre long reclining Buddha image and one cave is dedicated to the Indian Pali scholar Buddhagosa, who is supposed to have spent several years here. It is said that the doctrines of the Buddha were first recorded here, in the Pali script, around the first century BC.

In one of the monastic caves there is a horror chamber reminiscent of the Tiger Balm Gardens in Singapore. Colourful statues of devils and sinners show the various forms of punishment handed out in the afterlife. One writer 'particularly liked the punishment of a sexual sinner who had his skull cut open and was having his brains ladled out by two demons while he wept bitterly'.

There are a number of other points of interest along the Kandy-Dambulla road.

At Akurana there is a fancily painted mosque, the Moslem influence in this area is as a result of early Arab involvement in the spice trade. There are many spice gardens just north of Aluvihara. They include a government run spice garden where you can take a free guided tour and get a free sample of spice tea. Lots of spices can be bought at good prices.

Places to Stay

At Matale there is a *Rest House* (beautifully situated as usual). The *Tourist Guest House* (tel 0662-2259) at 145 Moicey Crescent has doubles at Rs 150.

East Coast Beaches

Compared to the beach strip stretching south of Colombo on the west coast, the east coast is relatively undeveloped. The only real beach resort developments are at Nilaveli, north of Trincomalee, and at Passekudah, a little north of Batticaloa. There are, however, many other places to stay at Uppuveli, immediately north of Trincomalee, and at Arugam Bay, at the southern end of the east coast road. The east coast's big attraction is that it is at its best when the monsoon is making things unpleasant on the west coast. Apart from beaches there are also two important wildlife sanctuaries and the interesting towns of Trincomalee and Batticaloa.

TRINCOMALEE

The major east coast port of Trincomalee (or 'Trinco') has the most convoluted post-European history of any place in Sri Lanka. The Dutch (or rather the Danes because the Dutch-sponsored visit actually used Danish ships!) first turned up here in 1617, but their visit was a brief one. At that time Portugal was the dominant European power in Ceylon but they did not arrive in Trinco until 1624 when they built a small fort. The Dutch took it from them in 1639 but promptly handed it over to the King of Kandy with whom they had a treaty. In 1655, treaties conveniently forgotten, they took it back, but in 1672 they abandoned it to the French who promptly handed it back to the Dutch. Finally it was the British's turn and they took it from the Dutch in 1782 but promptly lost it to the French who turned round and gave it back to the Dutch a year later!

Much of this back-and-forth trading was a result of wars and political events in Europe of course. In 1795 the British were back again and the Dutch, months away from the latest news in Europe, were totally uncertain whether to welcome them as allies in their struggles with the French or fend them off as enemies of themselves and their friends, the French. After a bombardment lasting four days the British kicked the Dutch out and Trincomalee was once again the first British possession in Sri Lanka.

Much of the interest in Trinco was due to its immense harbour, hailed by Lord Nelson in 1770 (at that time still a lowly midshipman) as 'the finest harbour in the world'. It was bombed by the Japanese during WW II but remained a British naval base for some years after the war and Sri Lanka's independence. The Mahaweli Ganga, Sri Lanka's largest river, which starts near Adam's Peak and flows through Kandy, reaches the sea at Trinco's Koddiyar Bay. It's an interesting town with a number of places of interest and some worthwhile excursions to investigate.

Fort Frederick

Originally constructed by the Portuguese the fort, which stands on the spit of land pointing out into the sea, is still used by the military today. Parts of it are off limits but you are quite free to enter it and follow the road through the fort to Swami Rock, at the seaward end of the spit. Close to the gate there is a stone slab, inscribed with the double-fish emblem of the south Indian Pandyan empire and with an inscription said to predict the 'coming of the Franks'. You've got to search to find it as it is built into the fort entrance arch on the right hand side, obscured by the black and white traffic guides.

As you follow the road through the fort, about a hundred metres from the gate a large building with a verandah stands on your right. This is Wellesley Lodge (although nobody in Trinco seems to know it!) where the Duke of Wellington, the 'Iron Duke' of Waterloo fame, recovered

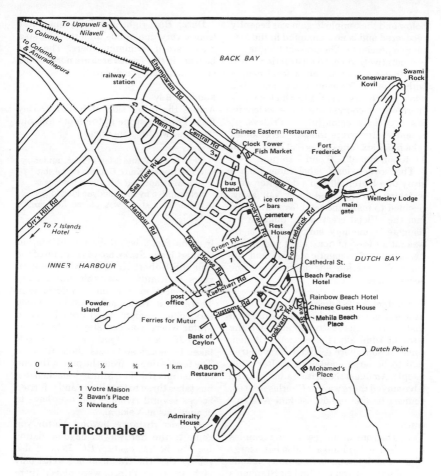

Trincomalee

To Uppuveli & Nilaveli
to Colombo
to Colombo & Anuradhapura
railway station
Ehamparam Rd
BACK BAY
Koneswaram Kovil
Swami Rock
Main St
Central Rd
Chinese Eastern Restaurant
Clock Tower
Fish Market
Fort Frederick
3
Sea View Rd
bus stand
Konesar Rd
Inner Harbour Rd
ice cream bars
cemetery
main gate
Wellesley Lodge
Orr's Hill Rd
To 7 Islands Hotel
Power House Rd
Green Rd.
Rest House
Fort Frederick Rd
Cathedral St.
DUTCH BAY
INNER HARBOUR
1
Beach Paradise Hotel
Kachcheri Rd
Customs Rd
post office
Powder Island
Rainbow Beach Hotel
Chinese Guest House
Mehila Beach Place
Dockyard Rd
Ferries for Mutur
2
Bank of Ceylon
Dutch Point
0   ¼   ½   ¾   1 km
ABCD Restaurant
Mohamed's Place
1 Votre Maison
2 Bavan's Place
3 Newlands
Admiralty House

from an illness in 1799 after taking on Tippu Sultan in India. The boat he should have taken went down with all hands in the Gulf of Aden so his poor health was fortunate for him but not so for Napoleon.

Swami Rock

At the end of the road through the fort you come to Swami Rock, also known as 'lover's leap'. Since a Hindu temple occupies the end of the spit you must leave your shoes at the gate house. When the

Portuguese arrived here in 1624 there was an important Hindu temple perched atop the rock so with typical religious zeal they levered it over the edge. Little wonder that E F C Ludowyk wrote of the Portuguese:

They laid forcible hands on everything. There was nothing they touched that they did not destroy.

Skin divers have found traces of the temple under the waters over 100 metres below and the temple lingam was recently recovered and is now mounted in the new temple precincts. The present temple is a comparatively recent construction since the British would not allow local people within the fort for many years. There is a *pooja* here every evening to which visitors (barefoot of course) are quite welcome; it's especially colourful on Fridays. A recent visitor wrote that the ceremonies take place six times a day – at 6.45, 9 and 11.45 am and at 5, 6 and 7.15 pm.

The 'lover's leap' label came from a story of a Dutch official's daughter who, watching her faithless lover sail away, decided to make the fatal leap. In actual fact the official erected the pillar in his daughter's memory simply because he was rather fond of her – eight years after her supposed romantic demise and the column's erection she married for the second time.

Fort Ostenberg & Admiralty House

You will need special permission if you wish to visit this restricted area. On the lawns of Admiralty House, another British construction, there is a huge Banyan tree said to be large enough to shelter 1000 people. Amongst the British admirals who have stayed there was Sir Charles Austen, younger brother of novelist Jane Austen.

Other

Trinco has one of the few Vishnu temples to be seen in Sri Lanka. It also has a large Chinese population, another rarity outside of Colombo. If you can find St Stephen's Cemetery (we weren't sure if we could or couldn't) then you might also be able to find the grave of P B Molesworth, the first manager of Sri Lanka's railway systems who, in his spare time, dabbled in astronomy and while living in Trinco discovered the famous Red Spot on Jupiter – didn't know that did you? A traveller wrote that the cemetery is on Dockyard Rd, when you come from the bus stop it's just beyond the ice cream bars.

Dutch Bay, right in Trinco, can suffer from a very dangerous undertow so take great care if swimming there. The best beaches in the Trinco area are north of the city, particularly at Nilaveli.

Koddiyar Bay

Across the other side of Koddiyar Bay from Trinco a stone at the foot of an old tree near Mutur announces:

This is the White Man's Tree, under which Robert Knox, Captain of the ship *Ann* was captured AD 1660. Knox was held captive by the Kandyan king for 19 years. This stone was placed here in 1893.

In actual fact is was Robert Knox's father (Robert Knox Snr) who was captain of the *Ann* and Robert Knox Jnr who spent 19 years in Kandy – see the introductory Books section for more information. There is a reasonably regular launch service (up to eight daily) from Trinco to Mutur where you can stay in the *Mutur Guest House* – the food there is good. It takes 1½ hours and costs about Rs 8.50. The ferries depart from the pier at the end of Customs Rd. The Mutur-Valachchenai bus takes three to four hours and is ferried across several rivers – you may have to change bus at Vakarai.

A short distance beyond Mutur you come to the Seruwawila dagoba, dating back to the 3rd century BC. Legend also relates that the Kanniyai hot wells, only eight km from Trinco, were placed there by Vishnu to distract the demon king Rawana, who named them after his mother, thinking that she had died. There's no place to soak here but you can slosh with buckets of hot water. Frequent buses and minibuses run there but it's wise to go early in the morning or in the evening as many people at once deplete the wells faster than they refill.

The lighthouse at the southern point of Koddiyar Bay, Foul Point, affords a fine view over the bay. Getting round to this side of the bay involves either a boat trip or a long series of ferry crossings by land. There are a number of pleasant islands in the bay, particularly Sober Island which is popular locally for picnic excursions, and a number of good beaches.

Only about eight km offshore from Trincomalee the wreck of the British aircraft carrier *Hermes* lies in 50 metres of water, sunk by Japanese bombers in WW II. Diving on the wreck is strictly for experts.

Places to Stay – bottom end

Trinco has a lot of cheap places but few in the middle or upper range. Almost next door to the rest house on Dockyard Rd is the *Beach Paradise* where reasonably clean, if rather spartan and drab, doubles cost from Rs 50. The engagingly named, if very unspecial, *Guest 'Ome* (it used to be the Tourist 'Ome) is a little back off the main road here.

If you carry on another hundred or so metres, keeping close to the waterfront on Dyke St, you come to a string of popular cheap places. They include the *Rainbow Beach Hotel* (tel 026-2365) at 322 Dyke St, a more expensive place (by Dyke St standards) with rooms from Rs 100 to 250, they all have attached bathrooms. There's an open air dining area looking out on to the beach and the food here is very good. Across the road, and with the same owners, is the *Kitsinn Tourist Inn* (tel 026-2568) at 255 with doubles at Rs 150.

At 312 the *Chinese Rest House* (tel 026-2455) has a variety of rooms – fairly spartan doubles cost from Rs 60. Almost next door, and also backing on to the beach, is the rather dingy *Travellers' Halt* at 300 Dyke St. There are dorm beds or rooms from Rs 50. Then there's the *Mehila Beach Place*, a travellers' halt place with dorm beds and rooms, at 224. Finally at 210/1 Dyke St you come to *Dyke Corner* with rooms from Rs 80.

Votre Maison at 45 Green Rd (behind the Nelson Cinema) is signposted from both ends of the road. It's a spartan, basic, sort of place but popular with shoestring travellers. There are dorm beds for Rs 10, singles from Rs 25, doubles from Rs 50 to 60. They do good food, especially seafood, and delicious curd too. The owner can recommend a beach hut south of Dutch Point which travellers might care to investigate.

More cheapies can be found scattered around town. *Bavan's Pension*, close to the Dyke St places, is another simple place with rooms at Rs 35. They have bicycles to rent and it has been recommended by several people. Also down at this end of town *Mohamed's Place*, opposite the general hospital, has rooms from Rs 30. There's a good little beach nearby.

Back in the centre, close to the bus stand, *Newlands* (tel 026-2668) at 87 Rajavarothayam Rd has rooms from Rs 40 to 75, from Rs 100 to 150 with bathroom. The manager and owner are pleasant people and food, particularly the seafood, at this well run and clean place is particularly good. Several travellers have written to speak highly of Newlands.

The beach places at Uppuveli are no great distance from town – it would be no hardship staying out there and getting into town when necessary.

Places to Stay – top end

Trinco's top end accommodation is mainly out at the beaches to the north. If you want to stay in or close to the town your choice apart from the bottom end places is limited.

The *Rest House* now costs around Rs 200 room-only and the food is good. The *7 Islands Hotel* (tel 026-2373) is on Orr's Hill Rd and used to be a British officer's club in the days when this was a big naval base. It's a pleasant place but most of the peninsula on which it is located is a fenced-off naval base and there is nothing by the way of beaches or attractions around here. There are 25 rooms with singles/doubles at Rs 375/450. The meals here are good.

Places to Eat

There is not a great choice of food places although the *Beach Paradise Hotel* has surprisingly good food in their restaurant including boiled crab which is a real taste treat and an economical one too. There are several Chinese restaurants along Ehamparam Rd; the *Chinese Eastern Restaurant* by the clocktower is cheap and OK.

You can get Chinese food at the *ABCD Chinese Restaurant* or the *Sunlaing Restaurant*. A couple of other places are good for a snack – ice cream and milk shakes in a duo of snack bars on Dockyard Rd towards the bus station (the *Flora Fountain* is the better of the two); good curd and honey at the *Sirasara* store just down from the ABCD. And plenty of local boutiques for a cheap rice and curry, near the bus station. On the Dockyard Rd side of the junction with Dyke St, near the ABCD, *Miranda's* sells cheap, cold beer.

Getting There

There are several daily trains to Trinco from Colombo via Polonnaruwa, taking about nine hours if you travel overnight or six to seven hours if you take the early morning departure. Fares from Colombo are Rs 148.50 in 1st class, Rs 95.10 in 2nd, Rs 48.70 in 3rd. To get a sleeper on the night train to Colombo you need to reserve at least three days in advance. If you cannot get a sleeper it's worth boarding on 3rd and asking the conductor if he has any vacant berths – for a little baksheesh he may well find one!

Buses run frequently from Trinco to Anuradhapura, fare is Rs 16.50 by CTB, Rs 20 by minibus. There is a direct public bus to Polonnaruwa at 6 am, but if that is too early you can get a minibus at noon to the Habarana crossroads and change there for a public bus. There are direct buses between Trinco and Jaffna – the trip takes six hours and costs about Rs 35. A direct Colombo-Trinco bus is Rs 40.

Getting Around

The short bus ride up the coast to Nilaveli costs just a few rupees. To get to Kuchchaveli, further up the coast beyond Nilaveli, get a Podawakathu bus from Trinco. An amusing sight in Trinco is petrol being delivered to the stations by ox and cart! You can rent bicycles to get around Trinco. It's easy to ride the eight km out to Kanniyai and you can walk along the beach to Uppuveli.

UPPUVELI

This beach area is immediately north of Trincomalee and there are places to stay along the beach, just three to six km from town. It's not as nice a beach as further north at Nilaveli but it's not bad and it's certainly convenient.

Places to Stay – bottom end

The *Pragash Guest House* at French Gardens, about five km north of Trinco, has rooms with fan and bath for Rs 100 to 200. It's very close to the beach. At the 3rd milepost in Uppuveli the *Shangri La Tourist Beach Inn* is a really nice place with eight rooms, all with fan, bath and mosquito net, and with excellent food, particularly seafood.

The *Golden Sands Tourist Inn* has rooms at Rs 250, good food and a pleasant beach location nearby. The *TF Tourist Beach House* at 686 Ehamparam Rd has also been recommended. You can buy fish at the local market and the helpful owner will fix up a barbecue for you to cook it on. *Sandpiper*, at 16 Murugapuri Avenue, is another Uppuveli guest house which has been recommended – 'homely, good food and a friendly atmosphere'.

Places to Stay – top end

About six km north of the city at Uppuveli the 75 room *Hotel Club Oceanic* (tel 026-2307, 2611) has room-only rates of Rs 750. It's not a very exciting looking place although it has a swimming pool and other resort-style goodies.

Getting There
An 867 or 900 bus from Trinco will take you to Uppuveli.

NILAVELI
The beautiful beach of Nilaveli stretches for quite a distance north of Trincomalee. The village itself is found around the 9th milepost but the places to stay are concentrated around the 11th milepost (the more expensive ones) and the 13th milepost (the cheaper ones). Nilaveli has three more expensive places, a handful of high-medium price places, and a few cheaper ones.

A stay at Nilaveli is really just a pleasant spell of suntan collecting. You can hire a boat for a trip out and back to Pigeon Island for around Rs 100. The big hotels also have boats for getting out there. The island used to be used for gunnery practice by the British Navy but today is put to better use for skin diving and snorkelling. Please don't souvenir the coral here. The big hotels also offer a variety of water sport activities. Beware of the currents near the lagoon mouth, in fact all along the beach.

Places to Stay – bottom end
There has been quite a spate of building along the beautiful stretch of beach at Nilaveli although, as before, the rooms tend to be either expensive or cheap, there is little in the middle range. If you travelled right down to the end of Nilaveli and crossed the lagoon bridge, about a hundred metres on your right you come to the two real cheapies – *Trails End* and *Travellers' Halt*. They're both basic and spartan places – no glass in the windows, water from the well, that sort of thing. If you can face that then they are pleasant and relaxed places to drop out for a while. Double rooms are Rs 40. When you cross the bridge you move from Nilaveli to Kumburupiddy although the village of

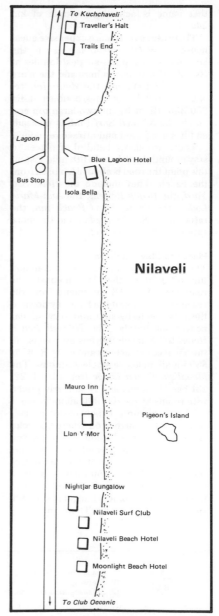

that name is actually a couple of km inland.

There are several more expensive guest houses. The *Isola Bella* is close to the lagoon mouth and has singles/doubles at Rs 150/175. Between here and the more expensive hotel group the *Mauro Inn* (tel Nilaveli 802) has singles/doubles at Rs 250/350. Right by the two large top end hotels the *Nilaveli Surf Club* is pleasant and has good food and attractive rooms.

There are also a handful of places to stay around the 9th and 10th milepost, at this point the road is about a km back from the beach. They include the *Hotel Sea Yard*, the *Beach Retreat*, the *Ann-Marie Lodge*, the *Sunny Sand Beach Inn*, the rather basic *Sea Breeze Inn* and the more expensive *Shahira Hotel*.

Places to Stay – top end

The two premier places share a common turn-off at about the 11th milepost. The road runs about 1½ km inland from the sea at this point so it is a long way down to these two side-by-side and very similar beachfront hotels. The *Nilaveli Beach Hotel* (tell Nilaveli 95) has 80 rooms, all the usual conveniences and costs Rs 675/850 for all inclusive singles/doubles. The *Moonlight Beach Lodge* (tel Nilaveli 22, 23) has 70 rooms and is similarly priced with rooms at Rs 700/900 all inclusive.

The third more expensive place is a couple of km further on where the road crosses the large lagoon mouth as you leave Nilaveli. Here you'll find the *Blue Lagoon Hotel* (tel Nilaveli 26) just before the bridge. There are 50 rooms – some of them basic economy rooms but most of them are two-roomed bungalows – each sharing a verandah. There are big,

mosquito-netted beds (Nilaveli has powerful mosquitoes) and each comfortable room has its own bathroom. The economy rooms cost Rs 50 or 100, the bungalows are Rs 260. Meals cost Rs 30 for breakfast, Rs 55 for lunch and Rs 65 for dinner and the food is very good indeed – big, filling, appetising meals. The Blue Lagoon Hotel has the best of both worlds, the beach right in front of it and the calm waters of the lagoon to one side. It's a pleasant, relaxing place to stay.

There are a number of small food stalls and snack bars near the bridge on the main road where you can get delicious vegetable and egg rotis, curd, baked goodies and fruit.

KUCHCHAVELI

You can continue a further 15 km up the coast to Kuchchaveli where there are some other accommodation possibilities. The coast road continues further north from here and intrepid travellers could, with several ferry crossings over coastal lagoon mouths, make their way through Pulmoddai to Mullaitivu, near the Chundikkulam bird sanctuary, almost at the Jaffna peninsula.

In Kuchchaveli you can see the foundations of an ancient temple close to the roadside. A small archaeological museum houses an exhibit of statuary, bas reliefs and other items found here.

Places to Stay

The Shanty, at the 21st milepost, is another rock bottom accommodation possibility with very basic rooms at Rs 25/40. A little further north, beyond the 23rd milepost, the *Pirates Roost* has cabanas by the beach. Between Nilaveli and Kuch-

---

A Lotus Pond, Polonnaruwa
B Steps up to Mulkurigala, near Tangalla
C Jetavanarama Dagoba, Anuradhapura

chaveli you pass the *Red Rock Beach Inn* and *Paynters Reef Beach Cabins*.

KALKUDAH-PASSEKUDAH

The major tourist development on the east coast is at Passekudah Beach, about 30 km north of Batticaloa or 65 km south of Trincomalee. Due to the ferry crossings involved in travelling down the coast the usual route from Trinco is to loop inland towards Polonnaruwa – but see below for more details. The main railway station for Kalkudah and Passekudah is at nearby Valachchenai and the beach at Passekudah is less than a km off the road from the junction at Kalkudah.

There's a fine beach at Kalkudah too, but it's not like the wide, reef-protected bay you find at Passekudah. The Kalkudah headland juts out to separate Kalkudah beach from the golden sweep of Passekudah where the reef turns the bay into a calm, blue, shallow swimming area.

This region was badly hit by the late-'78 cyclone and although the resort was rapidly rebuilt it will be a long time before the tree cover completely regenerates. The intention here is to have a high class development to attract the big-spending European package tourists but there are also plenty of cheaper places to stay, particularly back from the beach. This package orientation has another benefit for the independent traveller – since the 'season' officially starts on the first of April the resort is virtually deserted prior to that date; even though the monsoon can be finished much earlier and the weather may be just fine.

Places to Stay – bottom end

There's a neat division here; the cheap places are in Kalkudah while the expensive ones are at Passekudah. There is quite a selection of cheapies although most are not so conveniently situated for the beach as the de-luxe hotels. Prices at Kalkudah are very variable with demand and season. In the November to March off-season, when visitors are few, the prices plummet and many places simply close up.

In some of the cheaper places you should beware of theft while you're on the beach – one letter warned that 'small boys systematically go through the luggage; threatening to go to the police has some effect'.

Valachchenai Road Starting from the rest house junction and moving along the main road to Valachchenai places to stay include the *Mala Guest House*, with new rooms at Rs 100 and 125 with attached shower. The *Kalkudah Holiday Resort* is a more expensive place with rooms with attached bathroom at Rs 250 to 300. There are a great number of other guest houses and lodges along the Valachchenai road including the *Shamila*, the *Nanthang Tea Room*, the *Kalkudah Guest House*, the *Yoga Centre*, the *Green Wood Guest House*, *Kalkudah Holiday Homes* and the *Sunnyland Pensione*. The Yoga Centre is recommended by enthusiasts – there are morning and afternoon sessions and you can go for a week's course or just for individual sessions.

A dirt road leads off the main road and eventually reaches the *Sun Rise Bay Bungalow* on the riverside – rooms with toilet and shower for Rs 150 for those who want to get away from it all.

Maldives
A   Coral and lime house, Felidhu
B   Maldives fisherman aboard his dhoni
C   Typical coral atoll, Felidhu

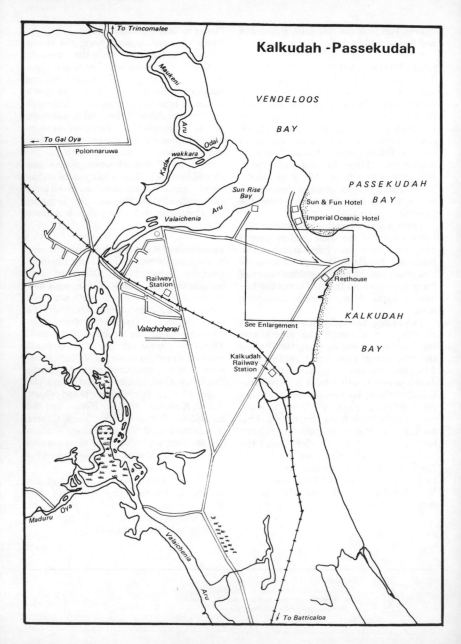

To Trincomalee

Kalkudah -Passekudah

Maukeni

Aru

Odai

VENDELOOS

BAY

To Gal Oya

Polonnaruwa

Kada wakkara

Aru

PASSEKUDAH

BAY

Sun Rise Bay

Sun & Fun Hotel

Imperial Oceanic Hotel

Valaichenia

Railway Station

Resthouse

KALKUDAH

Valachchenai

See Enlargement

BAY

Kalkudah Railway Station

Maduru Oya

Valaichenia Aru

To Batticaloa

Batticaloa Road Starting from the rest house junction once again, but now following the road towards Batticaloa, you come to another collection of places including *Sandyland*, one of the longest established places at Kalkudah. The cabanas here are good value at Rs 150 to 200 in season. Further along, the *Blue Land Tour Inn* is another pleasant place with rooms as low as Rs 50 and up to Rs 150 with attached bathroom. The atmosphere here is relaxed and the food very good.

The *Seaview Guesthouse* has rooms at Rs 75 to 100. Behind the post office *Mahadevi's Cabanas* is basic (no electricity and water from the well) but friendly, cheap and the food is not only good 'but it's the two-chili tourist variety as opposed to the 20-chili Tamil type'! The *Siloam Guest House* has rooms from Rs 100 to 150 in season – all with fan and attached bathroom. They serve an interesting variety of genuine Sri Lankan food as well as western food. There are numerous other places along the Batticaloa road or there's the *Leguana Club*, down towards the beach.

A paved road leads off the Batticaloa road towards the beach, where you'll find the *Fishing Village – Madawala's Place* with rooms in the Rs 100 to 150 bracket again. In the afternoon you can see the fishermen bring in the catch on the beach here.

Rest House Junction There are also several places around the rest house junction – like the *Ashok Land* and *Hotel Flamboyant* with rooms at Rs 150 to 200. The Flamboyant has a shady courtyard/dining area and the friendly people who run it produce good food.

A couple of medium price places have recently appeared on the Passekudah road – the *Santhiago Inn* and *Trinity Lodge*.

Places to Stay – top end
All the Passekudah hotels were badly damaged by the cyclone – situated right on the beach they bore the full brunt of the storm. They were all soon back in operation and today there is no indication of the event. The rest house on the Kalkudah corner, however, has never been reopened.

On the Passekudah beach there are three upper-bracket places, all fronting on to the magnificent sweep of sand. At the Kalkudah end of the beach the smaller, 24 room *Sun Tan Beach Hotel* (tel 065-7321) is somewhat cheaper than the two large hotels which stand side by side at the centre of the beach. Rooms here are Rs 500.

The two larger hotels are similar in design and feel. The *Imperial Oceanic* (tel 065-7206, 7207) has 66 rooms costing Rs 750 a night. The 60 room *Sun & Fun* (tel 065-7280, 7296) also costs Rs 750 and is similarly open and airy, making maximum use of white paint and tiled floors.

Places to Eat
There are a number of good places to eat in Kalkudah including the popular *Goat in the Gutter*, near the rest house junction, which does good breakfasts, snacks and ice cream. On the beach near the rest house *Vitha's* ('a lovely place with friendly people') has good food.

Along the road towards Batticaloa, just along from the junction, there is a string of restaurants including *Gopaluta's Hut*, another of Kalkudah's more popular eating places. The *Seaview Restaurant* in this stretch is also good although the service can be excruciatingly slow.

Getting There
The direct route down the coast from Trinco to Kalkudah did not use to be so widely used because of the numerous ferry crossings involved. You used to have to loop inland to the ancient city area, then back to the coast, irrespective of whether you travelled by road or rail. The coastal route is now rather more straightforward and definitely much more interesting,

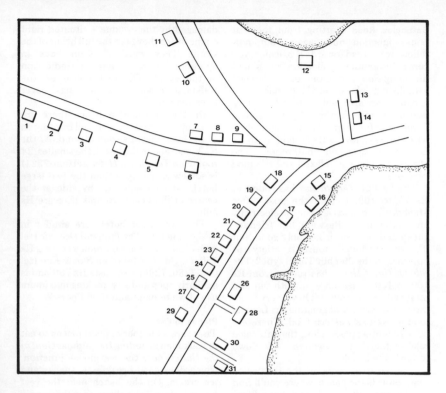

1 Yoga Centre
2 Aquarius Inn
3 Pearl Inn
4 Eden Land Guest House
5 Kalkudah Holiday Resort
6 Meezan Tulip Hotel
7 Kalkudah Cottages
8 Goat in the Gutter
9 Mala Guest House
10 Trinity Lodge
11 Santhiago Inn
12 Sun Tan Hotel
13 Ashok Land
14 Hotel Flamingo
15 Rest House (closed)
16 Mahadevi's Cabanas

17 Post Office
18 Loke's Restaurant
19 Pattah's Restaurant
20 Shantha's Restaurant
21 Sheraton Restaurant
22 Bom Bom Ristorante
23 Gopaluta's Hut
24 Seaview Guest House
25 Medway Inn
26 Sandyland Hotel
27 Blue Land Tourinn
28 Leguana Club
29 Siloam Guest House
30 Surf Beach Guest House
31 Madawala's Place

although it still involves a number of ferry crossings. Starting from Trinco there's the 1½ hour ferry trip to Mutur which costs about Rs 8.50. You can take a bicycle for Rs 5.

From there to Valachchenai, the bus and train halt for Kalkudah, takes three to four hours, usually with a bus change at Vakarai, about 25 to 30 km north of Passekudah. Close to Vakarai you can see elephant herds and also deer, bears, crocodiles and even leopard – the land is natural jungle, there is no sanctuary here. You can still dogleg there via Polonnaruwa but the coastal route is much more interesting.

The road runs along the coast from Kalkudah all the way through Batticaloa to Pottuvil and Arugam Bay. If you're going to pause in Kalkudah you'll find it initially a rather confusing place. Buses terminate in Valachchenai, about three or four km from Kalkudah. So heading south you then have to take another bus on to Batticaloa, or even the few km to Kalkudah. Some of the cheaper hotels are found along the Valachchenai-Kalkudah road, so if you're heading north from Batticaloa don't hop off the bus at Kalkudah, unless you're planning to stay at one of the expensive Passekudah hotels. The cheapies are generally a km or so after the Kalkudah corner.

If you arrive in Valachchenai by train you'll find yourself a couple of km from the bus station so that much further away from Kalkudah. There is, however, a small Kalkudah Railway Station so it's worth continuing on to there, or getting off there if you're coming north from Batticaloa. In season there will probably be people from the hotels waiting to meet potential customers off the train in any case.

There are three trains a day on the Colombo-Polonnaruwa-Batticaloa route – coming from Colombo the trains divide at Gal Oya for Batti or Trinco; in the other direction the Batti and Trinco trains join here. There are numerous bus services to and from Valachchenai.

Getting Around
You can rent bicycles (Rs 4 an hour) from various places, also motorbikes and mopeds.

A cyclone devastated the Batticaloa area on 23 November 1978. The winds started building up in the afternoon and soon after 6 pm trees started to fall, the wind grew steadily worse until at 9 to 9.30 pm the eye of the storm passed over. An hour or so later the eye had passed and the winds started again with equal ferocity but in the opposite direction and continued until 4 am after which it tapered off.

A Batticaloa resident told me how his family sheltered under a central arch in their house – protecting their heads from flying tiles with umbrellas and pillows after the roof flew off. His 84 year old grandfather said it was the worst storm in his life. In Kalkudah his brother sheltered with 60 to 80 local residents under the concrete roofed verandah of an estate house after all the neighbouring houses had been flattened. Electricity was not restored to Batticaloa until February 1979 and rebuilding was a long, slow process. Millions of trees were uprooted, depriving thousands of people of their livelihoods – particularly toddy tappers.

BATTICALOA
Situated mid-way down the east coast road Batticaloa (Batti to its friends) was the first Dutch foothold on the island in 1602. The east coast has many lagoons and Batti is virtually surrounded by one of the largest. You must cross bridges and causeways to enter or leave the town.

The town has an interesting little Dutch fort but Batti is most famous for its 'singing fish'. Between April and September a distinct, deep note can be heard from the depths of the lagoon. It is strongest on full moon nights and out in mid-lagoon a pole thrust into the lagoon bottom will permit you to hear it even more clearly if you then hold the pole to your ear. Nobody is sure what causes the noise but theories range from shoals of catfish to bottom-lying shellfish. The 'song' is described as the type of noise produced by rubbing a moistened finger around the rim of a wineglass.

Places to Stay

There is not a lot to see or do in Batti and most travellers simply pass straight through on their way between Passekudah-Kalkudah and Arugam Bay. On Trincomalee Rd, between the railway station and the riverside bus halt, the *Orient Hotel* has 12 rooms and doubles cost from Rs 60 to 100.

The *Rest House* is situated right beside the old Dutch Fort on the Arugam Bay (bus stand) side of the river and has rooms for Rs 150. It was virtually demolished by the cyclone and had to be rebuilt from scratch but the rooms are nothing special. The smaller *Jothi's Tour Inn* is on the other side of the river, directly across from the bus halt. Rooms are available for around Rs 50 but it's very basic, as is the *Wijayaweena Hotel*. Close to Jothi's the *Subaraj Guest House* is behind the Subaraj Cinema. Rooms here cost from Rs 50 and it's reasonably clean.

The *Sunshine Inn* at 118 Bar Rd is a good place to stay with clean rooms, fan, mosquito nets, a beautiful garden and a pleasant verandah. Singles cost Rs 25, doubles Rs 50 to 100. To find it turn left out of the railway station, cross the railway tracks and turn left again, away from the town centre. It's about 150 metres along on the right.

The *Beach House*, a guest house by the lighthouse at the end of Bar Rd, is a friendly, quiet and pleasant place to stay right by the beach. A double with fan is just Rs 50 to 75 and the food here is also very good. Next door is *East Winds*, which is similarly priced and has also been recommended as a friendly place. You can get there by taking a Bar Rd bus number 884 to the end of the line ('and maybe the bus', added one visitor, 'the road is bad'). It's only about five km from town and once there these place are easy to find.

There are eight *Railway Retiring Rooms* (tel 065-2271) at Batticaloa Station. They cost Rs 110. There are one or two places to stay along the coast from Batticaloa to Arugam Bay.

Places to Eat

There's not a lot of choice of food in Batti. The *Orient Hotel's* restaurant downstairs does short eats or you could try the *Rasheediya Hotel*, opposite the petrol station.

Getting There

There are three trains daily between Colombo and Batticaloa and the trip takes 7½ to nine hours. As far as Gal Oya this is the same train service as for Trincomalee but there the trains split and the Batticaloa train goes via Polonnaruwa. Batticaloa is the end of the line. Fares are Rs 175 in 1st, Rs 112 in 2nd, Rs 45.50 in 3rd.

Buses run north and south of Batticaloa, It's only a couple of hours to Polonnaruwa. Direct from Kandy takes about 4½ hours but it's a very scenic trip.

ARUGAM BAY & POTTUVIL

The coastal road runs a little further south from Arugam Bay but effectively this is the end of the east coast road. From Pottuvil you can head inland to Badulla and the hill country or skirt round the Yala park to rejoin the coast at Hambantota.

Pottuvil is the junction town but it's a dreary little place and Arugam Bay, 2½ km to the south, is the place to stay. There's a wide, sweeping beach with crashing surf that can be dangerous for the unwary swimmer although it's probably the best surfing beach in Sri Lanka. The small fishing village, just south of the lagoon mouth, has become the focus for one of those Asian travellers' centres which just seem to spring up out of nowhere.

The lagoon at Arugam Bay has a large population of waterbirds at certain times of year. This is a good base for visits to the Lahugala wildlife sanctuary with its large seasonal elephant population. About five km south along the beach see 'crocodile rock'. Further south at Panama there is also the Kumana Bird Sanctuary.

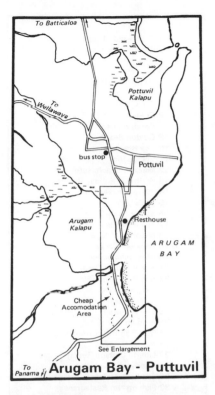

Arugam Bay - Puttuvil

Places to Stay

There is no accommodation in Pottuvil, you have to head two or three km south to Arugam Bay to find places to stay. There are local buses running from Pottuvil to Arugam Bay and on to Panama. The bay itself is backed by a huge, shallow lagoon which is separated from the sea by a narrow strip of sand. Whereas a few years ago accommodation here consisted of just a handful of places on the Pottuvil side of the lagoon there are now also many places on the south side.

North of the Lagoon Bridge Starting on the Pottuvil side of the lagoon, first of all there's the *Cuckoo's Nest Rest House* with basic cabana style accommodation at Rs 15 and rooms with bath at Rs 150. Right next door is the very comfortable *Arugam Bay Rest House* which has doubles at Rs 150. It's pleasantly situated and the food, though it can be rather variable, may include wild boar as a taste treat – they are said to be far too numerous in the Arugam Bay area. Breakfast costs Rs 30, dinner is Rs 60. Another hundred metres down towards the lagoon mouth is *Sea Sands* (tel 067-7372), right by the beach with rooms in the Rs 125 to 200 range.

Still on the Pottuvil side of the lagoon mouth, but on the lagoon side of the road rather than the sea side, is *Crystal Isle*, by the bridge. Here rooms cost Rs 100 or Rs 150 with attached bathroom. Meals are also available. A bit further back towards Pottuvil is the friendly *Crosswinds Tourist Inn*, where rooms are also Rs 150. Good meals here.

South of the Lagoon Bridge Cross the bridge over the lagoon mouth to the Arugam Bay fishing village and you'll come to a whole series of accommodation possibilities – many of them very cheap. A couple of years ago you could rent rooms off the fishermen and many of the places to stay are still of that nature – basic little *kachan* (palm leaf) cabanas with prices down to less than Rs 50 a night. An example is the *Golden Beach Hotel*, at the northern end, with spartan cabanas, good food and rock bottom prices.

Just a selection of other places include the beachfront *Meezan Beach Hotel* where reasonable doubles with bath are Rs 150. Also on the beachfront the *Mermaid Village* has rooms at Rs 75. On the lagoon side of the road the attractive *Hideaway* has rooms upstairs at Rs 150 or a series of very pleasant little cottages with bathroom and verandah for Rs 200. On the same side is *Sooriya's Beach Hut*, basic little cabanas but a number of travellers have spoken very highly of this place. It's run by brothers and is very well kept.

Continuing along the road you'll find the *Jez Look Holiday Cottages*, related to the popular Jez Look in Matara on the

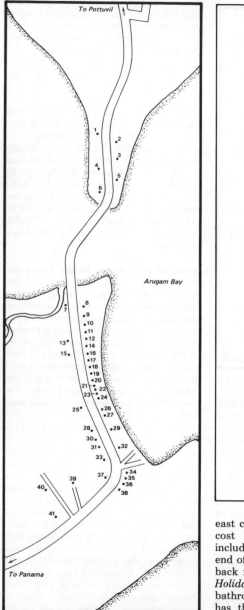

1 Crosswinds Tourist Inn
2 Cuckoo's Nest Rest House
3 Rest House
4 Blue Max
5 Sea Sands Hotel
6 Crystal Isle Hotel
7 Cabana Park
8 Golden Sands & Ocean
   Rendezvous
9 Golden Beach
10 Sea Breeze
11 Village Inn
12 Meezan Beach Hotel
13 Welltreat Holiday Resort
14 Wave Breaker Inn
15 Sudu Veli
16 Sun & Swim Tourist Inn
17 Silver Sands
18 Mermaid Village
19 Paradise Sands
20 Blue Oceanic Inn
21 Seeni's Palm Garden
22 Sun Rise Beach Hotel
23 Banana Island
24 Surfers Rest Cabins
25 The Hideaway
26 Arugam Bay Hilton (!)
27 Star Fish Guest House
28 Namal Gardens
29 Liberty Cottage Resort
30 Sooriya's Beach Hut
31 Jez Look Holiday Cottage
32 Fishing Net Restaurant
33 Mauna Beach Resort
34 Arugam Bay Tourist Hotel
35 Arugam Bay Restaurant
36 Rupa's Restaurant
37 Kudill Resort
38 Hotel Moon Shadow
39 Suduveli Inn
40 Palm Groove Holiday Inn
41 Bamburi Beach

east coast. The comfortable rooms here cost Rs 150/225 for singles/doubles including all meals. Right up at the north end of the village, and rather a long way back from the beach, the *Palm Groove Holiday Inn* has pleasant rooms, each with bathroom and verandah, at Rs 200. It also has that superbly groovy name and a signboard on the roadside which is a real work of art!

Places to Eat

Sooriya's is said to have very good vegetarian food and the *Beach Hut* has good food including muesli with curd. Or try *Golden Sands* or the rather fly-ridden *Rupa's Restaurant*.

Getting There

The road hugs the coast from Batticaloa south to Pottuvil (just before Arugam Bay) where it turns inland to Badulla and the hill country. At times it actually runs on causeways along narrow sand spits separating the sea from the vast lagoons that are found all along this coast. There are a number of small villages, a fair size town (Akkaraipattu) and some wide open stretches of beach along the 107 km (67 mile) trip.

If you want to stop there are on-the-beach rest houses at Kalmunai and a little south of Akkaraipattu. The trip takes about four hours. There are also regular bus services from Wellawaya or Badulla via Monaragala to Pottuvil.

Getting Around

There is now fairly regular transport between Pottuvil and Arugam Bay. You can rent bicycles in Arugam Bay for Rs 4 an hour or Rs 30 per day.

LAHUGALA SANCTUARY

Only 15 km inland from Pottuvil, Lahugala is renowned for its superb variety of birdlife and its equally crowded elephant herds. The lush green pastures watered by the Mahawewa and Kitulana tanks attract elephants at any time of year but around August, when the dry season drought has dried out surrounding areas, the elephants start to move in, eventually forming the largest concentrations to be seen anywhere in Sri Lanka. With the October rains most of them drift back to their regular haunts but throughout the year you can see herds of elephants here,

even from the main road as your bus passes by.

Lahugala also has the ruined Magul Maha Vihara, one of the most evocatively 'lost in the jungle' ruins in Sri Lanka. There's a vatadage, a dagoba and numerous guardstones and moonstones. It's located about four km back towards Pottuvil and a km south of the ruins you can see the remains of a circular structure which may have been an elephant stable.

Getting There

To get there from Pottuvil take a Monaragala bus and ask to be dropped off at Lahugala Park, it takes about 45 minutes. The best time is around 3 to 5 pm during the dry season. Continuing on from Pottuvil and Lahugala the next town of any size is Monaragala, see the Hill Country section for details.

Jaffna & the North

The north of Sri Lanka is the least visited region of the entire country. It's a contrast to the rest of the country both in the general landscape, the people and their religion. Although the south Indian Tamils can be found all over Sri Lanka, this is the region where they predominate. For the visitor the north means basically just two areas: the Jaffna peninsula at the extreme northern tip and the island of Mannar, which is the ferry arrival and departure point for India.

JAFFNA

The Jaffna peninsula is a considerable contrast to the rest of Sri Lanka both in its climate and landscape and in its people and culture. Whereas the south of the island is lush and green the Jaffna region is dry and sometimes barren. Where the Sinhalese of the south are Buddhists and easy-going, sometimes almost to an extreme, the Tamils of the north are Hindus and industrious. The population of the peninsula is about 750,000.

The peninsula is actually almost an island, only the narrow causeway known as Elephant Pass – for once elephants did wade across the shallow lagoon here – connects Jaffna with the rest of Sri Lanka. Jaffna is low lying, much of it covered by shallow lagoons, and has a number of interesting islands offshore. In all it is 2560 square km (999 square miles).

Jaffna has always been greatly affected by its proximity to India and Indian culture still has a strong influence on the region. 'It is interesting to see how property conscious the people are', wrote one visitor. 'There are fences everywhere but I must admit they do a lot with the land; surprisingly more flowers here than in the south'. If you're interested in Sri Lanka for its history and current situation then a visit to the north will give you an insight into the Tamil side of Sri Lanka.

History

Jaffna was the last Portuguese stronghold on the island and they only lost it to the Dutch after a long and bitter struggle in 1658. As elsewhere on the island the Portuguese had made themselves less than popular with the local population and a disgruntled local leader brought the Dutch forces by an overland route to the town of Jaffna. The Portuguese, expecting an assault from the sea, were taken by surprise and 4000 of them squeezed into their fort, designed to hold only 200. Despite lack of space and provisions they held out against the Dutch siege for over three months – until one in every three was dead and every cat and dog had been eaten. Even on surrender they insisted that they should depart with banners flying, muskets loaded and with a field piece. But, reported a Dutch observer, they were so weakened by their long ordeal that: 'the enemy found themselves unequal to dragging the desired gun'.

Jaffna Fort

The fort, built in 1680 by the Dutch, is perfectly preserved and is probably the best example in Asia of the typical Dutch fortification pattern of that period – a grass covered mound, surrounded by the moat, from which the fort rises. It was a grander and more heavily armed fort than that of their headquarters in Batavia (Jakarta), Indonesia. The star-shaped fort occupies a total of 22 hectares (55 acres) and was built over the earlier Portuguese fort. The outerworks were constructed over a century after the innerworks, just three years before it was quietly handed over to the British in 1795.

Jaffna Fort is not a walled city like Galle in the south, it was built purely and simply as a fort and most of the buildings within are much as the Dutch left them. They include the now deserted and little used

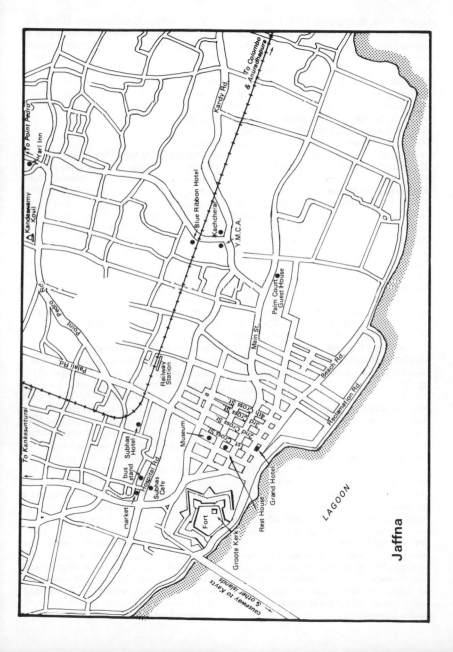

To Point Pedro

Yarl Inn

Kandaswamy Kovil

Point Pedro Rd.

Palali Rd.

To Kankesunturai

Kandy Rd.

To Colombo & Anuradhapura

Blue Ribbon Hotel

Kachcheral

Y.M.C.A.

Palm Court Guest House

Main St.

Beach Rd.

Reclamation Rd.

Railway Station

Subhas Hotel

bus stand

Hospital Rd.

Subhas Cafe

market

Museum

3rd Cross St.

2nd Cross St.

1st Cross St.

Rest House

Grand Hotel

Fort

Groote Kerk

Causeway to Kayts & other Islands

LAGOON

Jaffna

Groote Kerk, dating from 1706. Inside the floor is paved with tombstones, some as old as 1606. The church is open Monday to Friday.

Close to the church, but up on the outer fort wall, is a small house dating from the British period in which Leonard Woolf, Virginia Woolf's husband, lived for some time. It features in his autobiography *Growing*. Also within the fort the King's House, one time residence of the Dutch commander, is an excellent example of Dutch architecture of the period.

Archaeological Museum
Jaffna has an interesting little museum (itself a fine old Dutch building) on Main St, no distance at all from the rest house. Amongst the exhibits are some from the archaeological excavations currently taking place at Kantarodai, about 16 km out of Jaffna. Here 'a miniature Anuradhapura, buried in the Tamil country' has been rediscovered, fascinating evidence of a Sinhalese-Buddhist culture predating the Tamil-Hindu period. There are also interesting exhibits connected with Jaffna Tamil life and culture. Main St is also interesting for the amazing number of undertakers who seem to operate from it!

Hindu Kovils (temples)
Jaffna has many kovils but most of them are of comparatively recent construction. The destructive Portuguese tore all the earlier ones down and while the Dutch were more tolerant they certainly did not encourage their reconstruction so most of them date from the British era. The architecture is generally typical of the south Indian Dravidian style and each temple will have its gigantic wooden festival cars – the 'juggernauts' from which the word is derived. The most spectacular car festival is held from the Kandaswamy Kovil in Nallur during July or August of each year. Evening *pooja* services are held each day and visitors are generally welcome.

The original Kandaswamy Kovil has been variously described as dating from the 15th, 10th or even an earlier century. Its modern successor is topped by a typically Dravidian gopuram – the tall 'spire', alive with a technicoloured Disneyland of Hindu characters. Other important kovils are generally outside the city limits.

Other
Jaffna has an active little market – with plenty of the mangoes for which the peninsula is famous, in season. Also plenty of palmyrah caneware including surprisingly cheap straw hats. The shady Honduras mahogany trees, which dot many parts of Jaffna, were introduced by Percy Acland, a British administrator who was nicknamed the 'Rajah of the North'. He also designed the Jaffna kachcheri which is, unfortunately, now falling apart. There is much more to the Jaffna peninsula than just the town of Jaffna – other attractions are covered under 'Around the Peninsula' and 'Islands'.

Places to Stay – bottom end
It must be a faded memory now but a framed picture shows the manager of the *Grand Hotel* receiving an award for the best hotel in Jaffna in 1969. These days the rooms start from around Rs 40 – they are clean, plain, flimsily walled and wide open to the mosquitoes, of which Jaffna has plenty. If you order so much as a cup of tea here, first ascertain the price or be prepared to dispute the bill when you come to depart. The Grand is within walking distance of the train or bus station or less than Rs 10 by taxi.

Other very cheap hotels include the *Paradaise Hotel* in the middle of town – with a good, inexpensive restaurant downstairs. You can get a reasonable double with fan for Rs 25 although overall it's a pretty scruffy place. It's near the Windsor Cinema, which you'll probably find easier to find.

Five minutes walk from the bus station

the *Kumaran Tourist Inn* at 67 Stanley Rd is also cheap but not very special. The *Blue Ribbon Hotel*, similarly priced to the Grand, is near the *YMCA*. The Y is quite a modern establishment with rooms with fan for Rs 25, but is open to men only. Jaffna also has a *Rest House* which is very centrally located but certainly doesn't rate against some of Sri Lanka's excellent rest houses.

Only five minutes from the bus stand, the recently opened *Hotel Gananams* is said to be good value – clean, reasonably friendly and centrally located. At 4 Brodie Lane, near the 317 km post on the main road, the *Brodie Guest House* has singles for Rs 75. 'One of my most expensive places but definitely worth it', wrote one northern visitor. Mr and Mrs Brodie are full of information on Hindu legends and the Tamil lifestyle, plus Mrs Brodie's food is excellent.

Jaffna Station has five *Railway Retiring Rooms* (tel 021-636) at Rs 110 for regular rooms, Rs 163 for family rooms.

Places to Stay – top end

The relatively new *Hotel Ashok* (tel 021-24246, 224336) at 3 Clock Tower Rd has 32 rooms, all air-con, at Rs 500. The *Subhas Tourist Hotel* (tel 021-23228) at 15 Victoria Rd has 45 rooms, a balcony restaurant and is close to the railway station. There are rooms with and without air con; room-only singles cost Rs 250 to 400, doubles Rs 300 to 450. Tariffs including breakfast or all meals are also available.

The pleasantly relaxed *Palm Court* (tel 021-22628) is not quite so central at 202 Main St. There are just 10 rooms and costs are Rs 125/200 for singles/doubles. There is also the *Yarl Inn Guest House* (tel 021-27674) at 241 Point Pedro Rd, a little beyond the Kandaswamy Kovil; *Pearl Villa* (tel 021-22276) at Kadduvan Myliddy South; and up at Point Pedro there is *Rarora*, near the lighthouse.

Places to Eat

Jaffna has a few places to try for a meal apart from the hotels. Right by the bus station there's the *Subhas Cafe*, a three-part complex with ice cream and refreshments in one air-conditioned section, meals in another. The food here is quite good and the ice cream is excellent – it qualifies as Jaffna's taste treat.

Ricoh, only a couple of doors away, is another ice cream specialist and also has a good selection of Indian sweets in the front window. In the modern bazaar complex there are a number of food counters with appetising-looking short eats.

The *Vegetarian Restaurant* on Hospital Rd, close to the bus station, does good meals for Rs 5. At 124 R R Nalliah Rd (1st Cross St) the *Yarl Chinese Restaurant* is pricey (say Rs 100 for a meal for two), but good – try the crab claws in ginger sauce for Rs 25. Round the corner from the YMCA, the *Rajah Cafe* does cheap rotis and dahl curry.

While you're in the north try a Jaffna mango too. They're reputed to be the finest in Sri Lanka and I'm in definite agreement!

Getting There

There are four train services daily and an additional service on Fridays from Colombo via Anuradhapura to Jaffna. The trip takes 7½ to 11 hours depending on the train. From Anuradhapura takes 3½ to 4½ hours. Fares from Colombo are Rs 198 in 1st, Rs 126.80 in 2nd, Rs 51.50 in 3rd.

The three times weekly Inter-City Express operates Colombo-Anuradhapura -Jaffna and takes just 6½ hours. The fare on this new one-class, limited stop train service is Rs 51 from Colombo Fort, Rs 48 from Anuradhapura.

There are also buses operating to Jaffna including direct services from Colombo and Trincomalee.

Getting Around

An extensive network of bus routes fan out from Jaffna. Taxis and auto-rickshaws operate around the city.

AROUND THE PENINSULA

The peninsula country looks quite unlike other parts of Sri Lanka – the intensive agriculture is all a result of irrigation and for the southern coconut palms Jaffna substitutes the stark looking palmyrah. Fear not toddy addicts, there is a palmyrah toddy too – it's said to be best on the island of Delft.

The peninsula is famous for its tidal wells – it rests on a limestone platform and deep wells of water rise and fall, though seemingly out of harmony with the tides. The deepest of these wells, at Neerveli, is fresh for the first 15 or so metres, but salt for the balance of its 45 metre depth. At Keerimalai on the north coast of the peninsula there is a fresh water spring right by the beach. Manalkadu, at the eastern end of the peninsula, is a unique mini-desert with shifting sand dunes and occasional sand storms. Further east still there's the relatively inaccessible Hundikkulam wildlife sanctuary which is noted for its rich birdlife.

Jaffna has a number of good beaches although it's a long, long way from being the sort of beach resort centre you find on the east and west coasts in the south. Popular beaches include Kalmunai Point near Jaffna and Palm Beach on the north coast, but tranquil Casuarina on the island of Karaitivu is best known although the water here is very shallow and you have to walk a fair distance out from the shore.

There are numerous kovils dotted around the peninsula. The Kandaswamy Kovil at Maviddapuram, 15 km north of Jaffna near Keerimalai, has a car festival rivalling that of its namesake temple in Jaffna. Dutch kirks can be seen at Achchubeli and Vadukkodia, two Dutch toll-gates at Point Pedro, and the ruins of Portuguese churches at Myliddy and Chankanai. Erected in 1641 the Chankanai

church is still in reasonably good repair.

The dagobas at Kantarodai are reached via Chunnakam, directly north of Jaffna about half way to Kankesanturai. There are nearly 100 of these curious miniature dagobas crammed into one tiny area of not much over a hectare – the largest is only about four metres in diameter. They were first discovered in 1916 but comprehensive excavations only commenced in 1966. You can find out more about these dagobas, thought to be over two thousand years old, in the Jaffna Archaeological Museum.

ISLANDS

The islands off the peninsula are virtually as well known as Jaffna itself, particularly the island of Delft. Three of the major islands – Kayts, Karaitivu and Punkudutivu – are joined to the mainland by causeways over the shallow waters around the peninsula.

Close to the town of Kayts, at the northern tip of the island of Kayts, stands the island fort of Hammenhiel which is accessible by boat from Kayts. Ask for the fort caretaker in Kayts. The name means 'heel-of-the-ham' and relates to the Dutch view that Sri Lanka was shaped rather like a ham. There are other Dutch forts at Velanai on Kayts, on the island of Delft and at Elephant Pass on the mainland. The Delft and Velanai forts were built over earlier Portuguese ones.

Most of the ferry services run from Kayts, including the very short hop across to Karaitivu which is joined to the mainland by a causeway but not, as maps seem to indicate, to Kayts. You can do a round trip by catching one of the frequent buses to Kayts, taking the hourly ferry across to Karaitivu and then another bus back to Jaffna.

Delft

Delft, named after the Dutch town of that name, is about 15 km out and reached by boat services from Siriputu. The island is noted for the locally bred Delft ponies (of

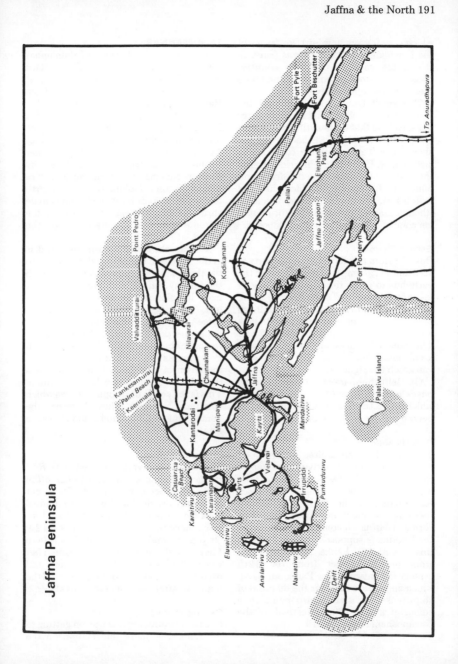

Jaffna Peninsula

which very few are now left), for traces of the Portuguese and Dutch eras (such as the Dutch garrison captain's country-house with a stone pigeon-cote) and for its bleak, windswept beauty.

The small Dutch fort is behind the hospital, only a short walk from the ferry dock. Behind that is a beautiful beach with many exquisite shells washed up on the shore. The Tamil Catholic cemetery is also nearby. If you take a bus ride around the island you'll notice the hundreds and hundred of stone walls which, like the Dutch fort, are made of huge, beautiful (though grayed) chunks of the brain and fan coral of which the island is composed.

Getting There

Bus 776 from the Jaffna depot departs at 7.20 and 11.20 am – you need to be on the early bus to make the trip in one day. It takes 50 minutes and costs Rs 7.50 to the boat dock. You can then take the 9 am boat across and have enough time to look around before the last boat back at 2 pm. The boat trip takes an hour but there aren't many boats each day. Make sure you catch the right one.

On Delft there are only two round-trip buses a day – if you take the first one, which meets the boat, you can then get an overall picture of the island.

Other Islands

The usually uninhabited islands of Kachchativu and Palativu host major Roman Catholic festivals during the months of February or March each year. At Nagadipa on the island of Nainativu there is the most important Buddhist shrine in Jaffna – it commemorates a visit the Buddha is supposed to have made to this region of Sri Lanka. Nainativu has a stone-inscribed edict from the 12th century Polonnaruwa king Parakramabahu, which announces rules for the disposal of shipwrecks. The island is also the site for a colourful annual Hindu festival at the Nagaposhani Ammal Kovil.

TALAIMANNAR

The island of Mannar (Talaimannar literally means 'Mannar Head') is a place many visitors pass through but few linger, for this is where the India ferry from Rameswaram arrives. Mannar is probably the driest and most barren area in Sri Lanka and the landscape is chiefly notable for the many baobab trees – a native of Africa and Madagascar; the Mannar baobabs were probably introduced by Arab traders many centuries ago. They're a most peculiar looking tree with a girth that often exceeds their height. The jungle shrine of Madhu (see 'Festivals' in the introduction) can also be found on the island.

Mannar, the major town on the island, is at the landward end of the island – close to the three-km long causeway across which the railway runs. It's uninteresting apart from its picturesque Portuguese/Dutch fort. The town of Talaimannar is about three km before the pier – the ferry departure point for India. A little further west an abandoned lighthouse at South Point marks the start of Adam's Bridge, the chain of reefs, sandbanks and islets that almost connects Sri Lanka to India. This is the series of stepping stones which Hanuman used to follow Rawana, the demon king of Lanka, in his bid to rescue Sita.

Places to Stay

There is a (generally booked out) *Rest House* in Talaimannar but you can often find private accommodation for Rs 15 per bed or Rs 30 a double. Just a few minutes' walk from the pier *Demsey Rest* is a low-price place to stay, rooms start at Rs 20. Or you can make a 40 minute bus ride to Mannar and stay at the small *Jacobian Inn* where doubles cost Rs 40. There will usually be somebody touting it around the platform after train or ferry arrivals.

Getting There

See the introductory section on getting to Sri Lanka for more information on the

Talaimannar-Rameswaram ferry service. There are two daily train services Columbo – Anuradhapura – Talaimannar but on Monday, Wednesday and Friday the overnight service to and from Talaimannar is timed to connect with ferry arrivals and departures. Fares from Colombo are Rs 168.50 in 1st class, Rs 107.90 in 2nd, Rs 43.90 in 3rd.

Wildlife Parks

It's perhaps a little astonishing that Sri Lanka – small and densely populated as it is – manages to set aside 10% of its total area for wildlife sanctuaries. Some of these are designated as Strict Natural Reserves where no visitors are allowed – they're for the animals only. Others are Nature Reserves – populated, but animal and bird life is protected. Or simply Jungle Corridors – seasonal migrating paths such as those that elephants might follow as their usual water sources dry up. For the overseas visitor the most interesting are the National Parks where you can see animals in their natural habitat.

Sri Lanka has a wide variety of wildlife but the two that attract most attention are the elephants and the leopards, both of which a park visitor stands a very good chance of seeing. Less exotic animals you may well come across include the mongoose, wild buffalo, mouse deer, sloth bear, loris, sambhur, jackal, monkey and wild boar. The latter animal is one that hunters are still welcome to take a shot at since the Sri Lankans reckon that there are far too many of them! Reptile life includes a wide variety of goannas, lizards, snakes (including some very fair size pythons) and crocodiles – so watch where you swim. Bird life is even more abundant with hornbills, flycatchers, bee-eaters, minivets, orioles, woodpeckers, flamingoes, pelicans, fishing eagles, a varied assortment of storks, spoonbills, coots and many others.

There are a number of national parks, each with specialities for certain animals or birds, but the best known and most visited are Wilpattu and Ruhuna, better known as Yala. Entry into these parks is strictly regulated – visitors are only allowed in vehicles, a park warden must accompany them, and except at certain designated spots you are not allowed to leave your vehicle. There are jungle bungalows where you can stay for more extended study of the wildlife – they can be booked through the Department of Wildlife Conservation (tel 714146), Anagarika Dharmapala Mawatha, Dehiwala in the premises of the Colombo Zoo.

Due to the forests being dangerously dry at that time, Wilpattu is closed to visitors during September while Yala is closed in August, September and for the first half of October.

WILPATTU

Covering 1085 square km, the Wilpattu National Park is on the north-west coast, directly west of Anuradhapura, which is the usual jumping off point for park visits. From Anuradhapura it is only about 30 km to the park turnoff (at milestone 27) and from there it is another seven km to the park entrance.

The park gets its name from the many *villus*, small seasonal lakes, which dot the generally dry landscape. Between the lakes the park is generally grassy plains, sand dunes and forestland – particularly in the eastern part of the park where there are also a number of ancient Sinhalese ruins. Approximately 270 km of jeep track loops confusingly through the park, it would be easy to get lost.

Wilpattu is best known for its leopards, you have the best chance in Sri Lanka of seeing leopards here. Other animals you may see are spotted deer, wild boar, wild buffalo and the mongoose. In the *villus* you have a good chance of spotting crocodiles and large goannas will often scuttle out of your path. Wilpattu has much bird life with certain of the lakes absolutely alive with birds during the November, December and January nesting time. There are a number of bungalows in the park.

The information below on my visit to

the park is now incorrect in one important detail – you cannot bring outside vehicles into the park any longer. If you wish to visit the park you must either hire a jeep from the park authorities or go on one of their minibus tours. In either case there is a Rs 50 admission charge to the park. Seats in the minibus cost Rs 150 and there are departures at 6.30 am and 2.30 to 3 pm. Jeeps with driver cost Rs 125 per person but with a minimum charge of Rs 500. If you really want to see wildlife you're likely to have much more luck in a jeep.

A Visit to Wilpattu

Two or three other people at our guest house had been to the park and seen leopards so we were easily persuaded to join a group and hire a Land-Rover. Between six of us it cost Rs 650, including the driver and admission to the park, Sandwiches packed the night before, we got up at 4 am, an ungodly early hour in easy-going Sri Lanka. With a little persuasion and a push-start our vehicle got moving and we trundled off, all a little bleary-eyed. Early morning or around sunset are the best times to visit the park since so many of the animals are nocturnal and sleep during the heat of the day. It can also get very hot for bumping around in an open jeep later in the day.

By the time we'd got to the park, signed in and collected our guide it was closer to 6 am. We'd already seen a mongoose before we arrived in the park and our second rushed across the road as soon as we entered. With the canvas roof rolled back we all stood in the back, scanning the trackside for signs of movement and shivering since it was still rather cold at this time of morning. We soon came across storks, pelicans, goannas, many deer and some wild buffalo but naturally it was a leopard we all wanted. We paused at one waterhole and were rewarded with the sight of a crocodile yawning widely, inviting some foolish bird to hop inside.

Several times we met other jeeps but each time the answer was the same – no leopards. When the king of the Sri Lankan beasts did deign to show his spotted face it was totally unexpected. Suddenly the Land-Rover stopped and there he was, lapping water from a stream only a short distance from the track. We'd all been busy watching the lake on the other side. Hardly daring to breathe (but cameras clicking)

we watched him finish his leisurely pre-breakfast drink and then, with scarcely a disdainful glance in our direction, stroll back into the jungle. Perhaps looking for a deer or something to really get his teeth into.

We drove on to a jungle bungalow and stopped for our sandwiches and tea but afterwards it was simply more of the same, no more leopards. By 10 am it was getting uncomfortably hot so we were glad to drop our guide off, roll the roof back into place and head back to Anuradhapura in time for lunch.

Places to Stay

Outside the park there's the *Hotel Wilpattu* (tel 0145-201) at Kala Oya. There are 35 rooms with bed and breakfast prices of Rs 180 for singles, Rs 250 for doubles. The food isn't very good. Or at Pahalamaragahawewa (wow!) there's the *Preshamel Safari Hotel* (contact phone 32469) with similar prices and 12 rooms.

Inside the park there are seven jungle bungalows with a cook provided although you must bring your own bedding and food. If you want to see birds the *Nature & Wildlife Conservation Society Bungalow* is a great place to stay. You can even watch the birds from the porch! The bungalow costs Rs 170 per night for up to three people, Rs 50 extra for each additional person. It will hold 10 people in all. You can book the bungalow through the Wildlife Society (tel 25248), Marine Drive, Fort, Colombo – opposite the lighthouse. The bungalow only costs Rs 20 a night for Sri Lankans.

Getting There

From Colombo take an Anuradhapura bus and get off at the park turn-off. If you can't get a ride from here you have a seven km walk ahead of you. From Anuradhapura there is a bus to the park twice daily. A taxi from Anuradhapura will cost about Rs 330 to 350 and the driver will wait while you visit the park.

YALA

The 1249 square km of the Ruhuna National Park lies on the south-eastern corner of the island – it's generally known as Yala. You can approach Yala either from the south coast or the hill country, turn off to Tissamaharama which is the usual jumping off point for the park. Yala is a mixture of scrub, plains, brackish lagoons and rocky outcrops. Part of the park is a Strict Natural Reserve and the easternmost section, Kumana, is particularly good for bird life. Visits to Kumana are usually made from Pottuvil on the east coast rather than from Tissamaharama.

Yala has much the same variety of wildlife as Wilpattu but it is particularly known for its elephant population. As at Wilpattu the best time for seeing the animals is October through December.

Outside jeeps are no longer allowed into the park; you can take a jeep from Tissamaharama the last 25 km to the park gate (minimum cost Rs 250 for the round trip) and from there you must pay a Rs 50 admission charge plus Rs 90 per person for the government safari bus plus Rs 10 to take photos. The view is, unfortunately, not as good as from a jeep and you can't get the driver to stop whenever you want him to. The three-hour morning tour starts from about 6 am, group tours get in first. A jeep costs Rs 125 per person with a minimum charge of Rs 500. One writer reported that block one is the best area in Yala.

Places to Stay

Outside the park there is accommodation at Kataragama, Tissamaharama and Wirawila. These places are covered in the West Coast section.

Within the park there are six bungalows and two more over in the Kumana region, known as Yala East. As at Wilpattu the nightly cost is Rs 200 per person for non-Sri Lankans (Rs 20 for Sri Lankans) and you must provide bedding and food but the bungalow warden cooks.

GAL OYA

The Gal Oya park covers about 540 square km, a little inland from the east coast. It has a huge tank, the Senanayake Samudra, and March to July is the best time to see wildlife here. Elephants are the main attraction, as in Yala.

You visit Gal Oya by taking a small motor boat around the lake, watching the animals on the shore or the birds. It's possible to drift right in close to herds of elephants. The park entrance fee is Rs 50 per person and the boat, which will hold five to eight people, costs Rs 400. The boat ride last 2½ to three hours – take the morning excursion (around 6.30 am) if you want to see birds, the afternoon trip (around 2.30 pm) for elephants.

Places to Stay Accommodation is available at the 22 room *Inginiyagala Safari Inn* (tel 063-2499) where rooms cost around Rs 300/350 or Rs 500/750 including all meals.

OTHER PARKS

The great majority of visitors head for either Wilpattu or Yala but there are a number of others. The Lahugala Sanctuary is a very small park also renowned for its seasonal elephant population. Situated near Pottuvil on the east coast it is covered in the East Coast section.

There are many smaller bird sanctuaries including the Chundikkulam Sanctuary (near Jaffna), Wirawila (near Hambantota and Tissamaharama), Kumana, Bundala, Udawattakele (in Kandy), Peak Wilderness, Giants Tank, Kokilai Lagoon and Pallemalala.

If you visit the Ministry of Forests in Colombo you may be able to get permission to visit the Sinharaja rainforest just south of Pelmadulla near Ratnapura. It's 'one of the few pieces of primary rainforest left outside of South America'. What about Cape Tribulation in northern Queensland, huh?

For more about Sri Lanka's flora and fauna, see pages 25 to 27.

Maldives

The Maldives are a long string of tropical islands to the south-west of India and Sri Lanka. They're normally reached through Sri Lanka and have acquired something of a 'lost paradise' image over the past few years – with good reason, they're beautiful, virtually unspoilt and as far away from everything as you could possibly ask. People coming to the Maldives are mainly bound for the various resort islands in the archipelago although there are also dhoni trips which go around a number of islands.

Although the islands are so beautiful and the diving can be terrific the Maldives are essentially a place for watersport enthusiasts or for lying under a palm tree and doing nothing. To visit the Maldives you need to either be wealthy enough to afford the expensive resorts or hardy and enterprising enough to find your way around the islands on fishing boats.

HISTORY

The Maldives have almost always been an independent nation, although for the period from 1887 until independence in 1965 they were a British protectorate. For a short period from 1558 to 1575 the Portuguese conquered Male. There was a major British airbase at Gan, the furthest south of the islands, but it is now deserted. The Maldivians were always traders and their islands were strategically placed on the old Indian Ocean trading routes.

FACTS

Population The population of the Maldives is about 160,000, making it the smallest country in south Asia. Male, the capital and only town in the islands, has a population of 45,000. Only 200 of the 2000 odd islands are inhabited.

Economy Male is the only town in the country and the only place with any sort of 'industry', apart from fishing. The economy of the country was totally based on fishing until tourism began to develop from the early '70s. There are now more than 20 resorts in operation with more being planned. Male is fairly affluent, despite the last president fleeing with half the national account.

Geography The Maldives stretch for 764 km from just north of the equator but the archipelago is only 128 km wide at its widest. The total land area is only 298 square km. Male, which is at the centre of the archipelago, is 670 km from Colombo in Sri Lanka. Officially there are 1196 islands but if you add tiny spits and bars the figure is probably over 2000. The islands are almost uniform in their appearance – tiny spots in the ocean, ringed by a white sandy beach, a coral reef and crystal clear water. You can divide the islands into four groups – Male with its town, the resort islands (most resorts occupy an entire island), the fishing islands where the 'rural' population of the Maldives lives, and the many uninhabited islands. Most of the resorts are in Male Atoll, close to the island of Male.

Religion The Maldives may originally have been Buddhists but in 1163 the ruler became Moslem and the population is now entirely Islamic. It's a low key, easy going brand of the religion, however.

INFORMATION

The Maldives Tourist Board is part of the Department of Information in Male. The various resorts are owned by government organisations – principally Crescent Tourist Agency on Marine Drive or Universal at 15 Chandani Rd. The tourist information counter at the airport has a list of all guest houses on the fishing islands.

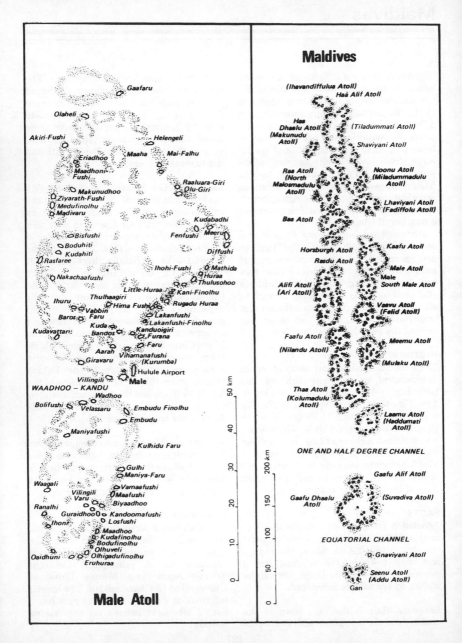

Maldives

(Ihavandiffulua Atoll)
Haa Alif Atoll

Haa
Dhaalu Atoll
(Makunudu
Atoll)

(Tiladummati Atoll)

Shaviyani Atoll

Raa Atoll
(North
Malosmadulu
Atoll)

Noonu Atoll
(Miladummadulu
Atoll)

Lhaviyani Atoll
(Fadiffolu Atoll)

Baa Atoll

Horsburgh Atoll

Kaafu Atoll

Rasdu Atoll

Male Atoll

Alifi Atoll
(Ari Atoll)

Male
South Male Atoll

Vaavu Atoll
(Felid Atoll)

Faafu Atoll

Meemu Atoll

(Nilandu Atoll)

(Mulaku Atoll)

Thaa Atoll
(Kolumadulu
Atoll)

Laamu Atoll
(Haddumati
Atoll)

ONE AND HALF DEGREE CHANNEL

Gaafu Alif Atoll

Gaafu Dhaalu
Atoll

(Suvadiva Atoll)

EQUATORIAL CHANNEL

Gnaviyani Atoll

Seenu Atoll
(Addu Atoll)

Gan

Male Atoll

Gaafaru

Olaheli

Akiri-Fushi

Helengeli

Eriadhoo
Maaha
Mai-Falhu

Maadhoni
Fushi

Raaluara-Giri
Olu-Giri

Makunudhoo

Ziyarath-Fushi

Medufinolhu

Madivaru

Kudabadhi

Fenfushi
Meeru

Bisfushi

Boduhiti

Kudahiti

Diffushi

Rasfaree

Mathida

Nakachaafushi

Ihohi-Fushi
Huraa
Thulusohoo

Little-Huraa
Kani-Finolhu

Thulhaagiri
Hima Fushi
Rugadu Huraa

Ihuru

Vabbin
Faru
Lakanfushi

Baros

Lakanfushi-Finolhu

Kuda
Bandos
Kanduoigiri

Kudavattaru
Furana

Faru

Aarah
Vihamanafushi
(Kurumba)

Giravaru

Hulule Airport

Villingili
Male

WAADHOO – KANDU

Wadhoo

Bolifushi
Velassaru
Embudu Finolhu

Embudu

Maniyafushi

Kulhidu Faru

Gulhi
Maniya-Faru

Waagali
Vamaafushi

Vilingili
Maafushi

Varu
Biyaadhoo

Ranalhi
Guraidhoo
Kandoomafushi

Ihoni
Losfushi

Maadhoo
Kudafinolhu
Bodufinolhu
Olhuveli

Oaidhuni
Olhigadufinolhu
Eruhuraa

50 km
40
30
20
10
0

200 km
150
100
50
0

Every island has an office which is in contact with Male daily. Cable & Wireless have set up such a good communications network in the Maldives that it is possible to get a line to Europe from the Male post office in one minute! This also means that the government always knows where you are.

TIMES & HOURS

Maldives time is five hours ahead of GMT, a half hour time change form Sri Lanka. Post offices are open from Saturday to Thursday from 7.30 am to 1.30 pm and from 3 to 5 pm. Banks are open Sunday to Thursday from 9 am to 1 pm. Government offices normally operate Saturday to Thursday from 7.30 am to 1.30 pm. Friday is the usual weekly holiday.

VISAS

No visas are required but a Rs 150 tax is charged for stays beyond one month.

MONEY

The Maldivian rupee is divided into 100 larees. The exchange rate is approximately Rs 9 to the US dollar. Although rupees are, of course, the everyday currency US dollars are usually required for airline ticket purchases and can be spent in tourist shops and for other such purposes. At the resort islands only US dollars are accepted. Every visitor has to pay a daily tax of US$3, which makes the Maldives fairly expensive, particularly since the exchange rate is rather poor.

CLIMATE

The tropical climate of the Maldives is almost always tempered by cooling sea breezes. No place on the Maldives is more than a couple of metres above sea level. November to March is the main season in the Maldives, from May to October the south-east monsoon usually brings some rain each day and this is the only time of year to consider avoiding. Otherwise it's sunny and dry most of the year.

ACCOMMODATION

Few visitors stay long in Male, it's only a jumping off point for the other islands. Indeed the Male airport is on nearby Hulule Island and most resorts pick their guests up straight from the airport. A number of the resorts in the Male atoll are close enough to Male to commute into the capital. Accommodation in the resorts usually costs from around US$50 a night. for a double with full board. There are, however, a number of cheaper guest houses in Male. Most resort visitors will have booked their accommodation as a package from Europe. You can, however, book through travel agents in Colombo and quite possibly pick up a good deal in this way.

You are not supposed to sleep on the beaches of uninhabited islands but can on inhabited ones that do not have guest houses. The best bet is probably to speak to any traveller you meet in Male and try to get an idea of an island you will like. Once you get there it is far cheaper to lie on the beach or snorkel than to island hop. Don't count on being able to find a guest house (or food, markets, toilets, etc) on just any island. Guest houses will probably start from around US$8 including food.

FOOD

Although some of the southern islands grow a little food most food, including vegetables, is imported. The obvious exception is fish and other seafoods. Some fruit – principally coconuts, bananas, mangoes, breadfruit, limes and papayas are also grown, but it's not surprising that things are expensive. No alcohol is allowed into the Maldives.

GETTING THERE

There are occasional ships from Colombo in Sri Lanka, the trip takes a couple of days, but apart from that the usual route to the Maldives is by air. Check with C V Soerensen (tel 93256, 98732) at 169 Stafford Place in Colombo 10 about their weekly shipping service to Male. In Male the agent is Imad's Agency (tel 2964), MA Javahiriya, 39/2 Chandani Magu.

Indian Airlines flies to Male from Trivandrum or you can fly from Colombo with Air Lanka or Maldives International Airlines. There are two flights a day from Colombo almost every day of the week and the fare is Rs 1557. At present Maldives Airlines is simply an Indian Airlines flight operated in their name but there is talk of actually establishing an airline. Airport tax on departure is US$6.

If you're young and not in a resort group your baggage is likely to be thoroughly searched on arrival. Furthermore, reported one visitor, 'if you've not got a cholera vaccination certificate when coming from Sri Lanka you get vaccinated on arrival and then have to spend five days in Male, before you can visit the islands. Strangely this doesn't seem to apply if you're staying at a $100-a-day resort!'

GETTING AROUND

Ferries operate approximately hourly between Hulule airport and Male, the fare is Rs 0.50. Male is the only place in the Maldives with cars and all taxis operate from a stand outside the Government Hospital. The town is small enough to walk around or you can hire bicycles.

Before you can visit the islands you must get a permit from the Atolls Administration Office in Male. The permit is free but limited to three islands. At the moment the government is having an Islamic-purity campaign and trying to limit contact between islanders and visitors. Island guest houses are being shut and regulations about carrying tourists on fishing boats are being tightened up. The resort islands have their own boats, of course, but individuals can hire dhonis, the local dhow-like fishing boats, by the day or for longer periods.

Ask around the fish market for a boat going to the island you want to get to. It costs US$5 per person to travel to any island – there are no ferries as such, all

inter-island travel is done on fishing boats, always at US$5 per trip. Since boats are infrequent and irregular, once you get to an island you're stuck – the 'boat is not working' or 'weather is too bad' syndrome will probably apply. This can be a problem if you don't like the island. Leave your island at least a day early and spend your last night in Male, so you can be certain you will catch your flight.

THINGS TO BUY

Hopefully the government is clamping down on the large scale export of turtle shell products – before the turtles are hunted to extinction. Apart from tourist souvenirs the main things to buy are seashells, woven grass mats and *felis* – local made sarongs.

LANGUAGE

The national language is Dhivehi, which is related to Sinhala. You can pick up a locally produced phrase book called *In Maldives* while you are in Male. English is widely spoken.

MALE

Male is the capital city and also the name of the island. Although most visitors merely pause here before heading out to the other islands you can happily spend some time looking at the market, the fishing boats, dhonis being built or repaired, the museum and the various mosques. The waterfront Marine Drive is the location for the GPO, the resort island offices and the bank. Chandani Magu and Orchid Magu are the main shopping streets.

Places to Stay

More expensive hotels in Male include the 18 room *Alia Hotel*, the smaller *Sosunge* and *Blue Haven*. There are many guest houses in Male such as the *Malam International Guest House* at 8 Majeed Magu, not far from where the airport ferry drops you. It's a pleasant place to stay

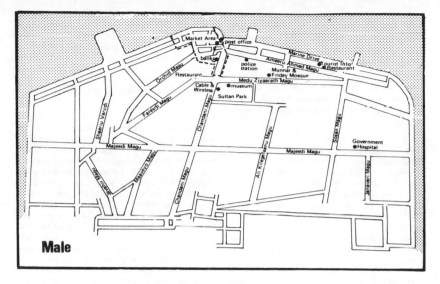

Male

with singles/doubles for US$5/10. Meals add another US$4 per person. There are usually a few room touts at the airport seeking solo travellers. If you go with one you do at least get a free ferry ride but their commission gets added to the bill.

Places to Eat

Rather expensive food is available at the *Alia Hotel* or at *Food City* on Chandani Magu. There are two cheap cafes on Orchid Magu, the *Moon* is the better of them. They serve up very sweet black tea and a table full of cakes and savouries. You pay for what you eat. At night before 8 pm it is just possible to get some rice and fish in these places.

For local food try the *Neon Hotel* on Chandani Magu, the *Crest Hotel* on January Magu or *Majeedee Ufaa* on Majeedee Magu. Cold drinks can be found at *Icege* on Orchid Magu, *Icecone* on Chandani Magu or *Beach Crescent* on Marine Drive.

RESORT ISLANDS

The Male Atoll extends for a little over 100 km from the southern end of South Male to the northern end of the main Male Atoll. Male itself and nearby Hulule, where the airport is located, are at the southern end of the main Male Atoll. Most of the resort islands are in the Male Atoll, many of them 10 km or less out of Male. The local word for island is fushi, thus Furana island might be referred to as Furanafushi.

Some of the island resorts include: Alimat (56 km from Male), Bandos (8), Baros (16), Boduhithi, Embodu, Farukolhu (7), Furana (10), Helengeli, Ihuru (19), Kanifinolhu (27), Kuramathi (64), Kuredu (131), Kurumba (4), Little Huraa (16), Loi Meerufen (43), Medufinolhu, Nakachcha, Nolhivaranfaru (210), Ranalhi (43), Vaadho (or Wadu) (8), Vabbinfaru (15), Velassaru (11) and Villingili (3). Farukolhu is the site of the Male Club Mediterranee.

At most of the resorts, nightly costs with meals run from around US$50 for a double. Resorts range from smaller places with just half a dozen rooms to resorts like Bandos or Villingili with over 100 rooms. Dhoni trips around the Maldives – from

Australia they are operated by Australian Himalayan Expeditions and Peregrine Expeditions – usually camp on fishing village islands or uninhabited islands. Solo travellers could, no doubt, do the same. Many of the uninhabited islands have wells so drinking water is available. A few island and boat trip reports from visitors:

Gulhi Island is very small with a nice beach. On Maafushi there is a German guest house costing US$8 each for half board. It is run by a German and his Maldivian wife and it's really a home from home although the beach here is not one of the best. There are masks, snorkels and even a dinghy which you can use.

Rannali is highly recommended. It's a small, oval island with a self-contained resort (capacity about 150 people), about 2½ hours by slow boat, south of Male. The reef here is the best I've ever seen, both in terms of coral and fish. Forget your swimsuit, people don't use such things there. Accommodation, about US$40 with meals, consists of pleasant huts ringing the island. They're comfortable, clean and each has beach frontage and shade trees. Rooms have a ceiling fan and bathrooms with saltwater (ugh!) showers. The restaurant is excellent, if you like seafood, with a different fresh fish each night. The island has a great open-air bar, cold beer and European ice cream. Plus good music, some entertainment and sports facilities including, of course, a diving shop.

There are several small dhonis for rent at very low rates which you can take out with or without a boatman. There are also powerboats which will take you to the neighbouring islands, of which there are many – some inhabited.

Dhonis trips are not for the soft. There's little fresh water for washing and the diet can be monotonous. You generally sleep on board or on a beach – there are no mosquitoes. The boats carry very little safety equipment and the water can get very rough, fortunately they're good sailors but in a mishap your chances would be slim. You rarely wear more than a swimsuit (at the most) so bring more than one.

Some of the islands we went to included Halaveli – an idyllic though very small island in a perfect atoll. Ukulhas you could walk right around in 20 minutes. Ten minutes was long enough to do a circuit of Rasdhu, very near Kuramathi, a German resort island. On Alifu Atoll there was actually a small town on Toddu, which took half an hour to walk right around. Giraavanu was a very small resort island.

Some islands have better food than others. The German resort islands generally bring their food straight from Germany via the charter airliner Condor. On other islands the food may be much more limited in quantity and quality. There are German, French, Australian (Furana Island) and Maldivian run resort islands.

Glossary

Adam's Bridge – chain of sandbars and islands that almost connects Sri Lanka to India.

Ambalamas – wayside shelters for pilgrims.

Amudes – loin cloths worn by gem miners, very similar to the G-strings worn by tourists at Hikkaduwa!

Arrack – distilled toddy, often very potent indeed.

Avalokitesvera – one of the Buddha's most importance disciples.

Ayurvedic – traditional naturopathic medical attention using herbal medicines.

Baas – skilled workman.

Banian – long, loose sleeved, over-shirt.

Banyan tree – a type of Bo-tree.

Baobab – strange water-holding, African, dry-land trees which were introduced into the northern regions of the island by Arab traders.

Beedis – small hand-rolled cigars.

Bel Kalla – a 'Bell Fragment', name given to a newly discovered archaeological find, after H C P Bell the first British Government Archaeologist.

Betel – nut of the betel tree chewed as a mild intoxicant.

Bhikku – Buddhist Monk.

Bhodhisattva – follower of the Buddha.

Bo-tree – *Ficus religiosa* – large spreading tree under which the Buddha was sitting when he attained enlightenment.

Bund – built up bank or dyke around a tank.

Burgher – Eurasians, generally descended from Portuguese or Dutch-Sinhalese inter-marriage.

Chena – primitive slash-and-burn agriculture, also the fields created in this way. Leonard Woolf's *The Village in the Jungle* describes the life of turn-of-the-century chena farmers.

Chola – a powerful, ancient south Indian kingdom which invaded Ceylon on several occasions.

Choli – short jacket worn with a sari.

Coir – matting or rope made from coconut fibres.

Copra – dried coconut kernel, used to make cooking oil.

Crore – 10 million, of anything but most often rupees.

CTB – Ceylon Transport Board, responsible for Sri Lanka's all encompassing bus system; much improved since the introduction of private competition.

Culavamsa – the 'Genealogy of the Lesser Dynasty' continues the history of the Mahavamsa right up to 1758, just 40 years before the last King of Kandy, Sri Wickrema Rajasinha, surrendered to the British.

Curd – yoghurt, usually buffalo-curd and always delicious.

Dagoba – Sinhala word for Buddhist religious monument composed of a solid hemisphere containing relics of the Buddha. Known as a pagoda, stupa or chedi in other countries.

Devala – temple or shrine, can be Buddhist or Hindu.

D-form – currency exchange form on which you used to have to record all foreign currency transactions.

Dhal – a thick soup made of split lentils.

Dharma – Buddhist teachings (Sanskrit word, in Pali it is Dhamma).

Dhobi – laundryman.

Dhoni – the dhow-like sailing boats used between the islands in the Maldives.

Dravidian – southern Indian race which includes Tamils.

Ganga – river

Gedige – ancient Sinhalese architectural style, extremely thick walls and a corbelled roof.

Gopuram – towering entrance tower to a Hindu temple, a style of Dravidian architecture found principally in south India.

Groote Kerk – the old Dutch churches in Jaffna and Galle.

Guardstone – carved ornamental stones that flank doorways or entrances to temples.

Hopper – popular Sri Lankan snack meal – either string hoppers or egg hoppers.

Howdah – seating structure on an elephant's back.

Illama – gem bearing strata in gem fields.

Jaggery – hard, brown, sugar-like sweetener made from kitul palm sap.

Jataka – stories from the Buddha's previous lives.

Juggernauts – huge, extravagantly decorated temple 'cars' which are dragged through the streets during Hindu festivals.

Kachchan – a hot, dry wind.
Kachcheri – government secretariat or residency.
Karava – fisherfolk of Indian descent.
Kavadi – decorated framework carried in festivals as a form of penance by Hindu devotees.
Kharma – law of cause and effect (Sanskrit word, in Pali it is Khamma).
Kitul – one of the Sri Lankan palm trees, used to make jaggery and treacle.
Kolam – masked dance drama.
Kotte – the most important southern Sinhalese capital after the fall of Polonnaruwa – today it is Colombo.
Kovil – Hindu temple.
Kul – spicy chowder dish, popular in Jaffna.

Lakh – 100,000, a standard large unit in Sri Lanka and India.
Laksala – government run arts and handicrafts shop.
Lamprai – rice and curry wrapped up and cooked in a banana leaf.
Loris – small, nocturnal, tree-climbing animal.

Maha – the north-east monsoon season.
Mahavamsa – 'Genealogy of the Great Dynasty', a recorded Sri Lankan history running from the arrival of Vijaya in 543 BC through the meeting of King Devanampaya Tissa with Mahinda and on to the great kings of Anuradhapura.
Mahawell Ganga – Sri Lanka's biggest river, starts in the hill country near Adam's Peak, flows through Kandy and eventually reaches the sea near Trincomalee. The only river which flows north from the hill country.
Mahayana – large vehicle Buddhism.
Mahinda – son of the Indian Buddhist-Emperor Ashoka, credited with introducing Buddhism to Sri Lanka.
Mahout – elephant rider/master.
Maitreya – future Buddha.
Mawatha – Avenue.
Moonstone – semi-precious stone or a carved stone 'doorstep' at temple entrances.
Mouse deer – very small variety of Sri Lankan deer.
Mudra – hand and body position of a Buddha image.

Naga – cobra, usually used religiously.
Nibbana – pali word for nirvana.
Nirvana – the ultimate aim of Buddhist existence, a state where one leaves the cycle of existence and does not have to suffer further rebirths.
Nuwara – city.

Ola – palm leaf used in traditional books.
Oya – stream or small river.

Paddy – unhusked rice.
Padma – lotus flower.
Pagoda – see dagoba.
Pali – the original language in which the Buddhist scriptures were recorded, scholars still look to the original Pali texts for the true interpretation.
Palmyrah – tall palm trees found in the dry northern region.
Paranibbana – the transition stage to nibbana, as in the reclining Buddha images where the Buddha is in the state of entering nirvana.
Perahera – procession, usually with dancers, drummers and even elephants.
Pettah – bazaar area of Colombo.
Pittu – steamed mixture of rice, flour and coconut.
Plantains – bananas, come in many varieties in Sri Lanka.
Pola – special food market on certain day of the week.
Pooja – religious service.
Potgul – library.
Poya – full moon holiday.

Rawana – the 'demon king of Lanka' who abducts Rama's beautiful wife Sita in the Hindu epic the *Ramayana*.
Relic Chamber – chamber in a dagoba housing a relic of the Buddha but also representing the Buddhist concept of the cosmos.
Ruhuna – ancient southern centre of Sinhalese power which stood even when Anuradhapura and Polonnaruwa fell to Indian invaders, it was located near Tissamaharama.

Sadhu Sadhu – 'blessed, blessed', the words pilgrims cry out as they climb Adam's Peak.
Sambhur – species of deer.
Samudra – large tank or inland sea.
Sangamitta – Mahinda's sister, she brought the sapling from which the sacred Bo-tree at Anuradhapura has grown.
Sangha – the brotherhood of the Buddhist monks.

Sanskrit – ancient Indian language, the oldest known language of the Indo-European family.
Sari – traditional female garment in Sri Lanka and India.
School pen – ballpoint pen.
Singing fish – mysterious 'fish' which sing from the lagoon in Batticaloa.
Sinhala – language of the Sinhalese people.
Sinhalese – majority population of Sri Lanka, principally Sinhala speaking Buddhists.
SLFP – Sri Lanka Freedom Party.
Sloth bear – large, shaggy, honey-eating Sri Lankan bear.

Tamil – people of Indian descent who compromise the largest minority population in Sri Lanka.
Tank – artificial water storage lake, many of the tanks in Sri Lanka are both very large and very ancient.
Tantric Buddhism – Hindu influenced Buddhism with strong sexual and occult overtones, Tibetan Buddhism.
Taylor, James – not the rock singer, this one set up the first tea plantation in Ceylon.
Thambili – king coconut, makes a very refreshing drink.
Theravada – small vehicle Buddhism, as practised in Sri Lanka.

Tiffin – lunch, a colonial English expression.
Tiffin boys – they pick up the city workers' tiffins from their homes and transport them into the city.
Toddy – mildly alcoholic drink tapped from the palm tree.
Toddy tapper – the people who perform acrobatic feats in order to tap toddy from the tops of palm trees.
Tripitaka – the 'three baskets', one of the classical Buddhist scriptures.

UNP – United National Party, first Sri Lankan political party to hold power after independence.

Vanni – the northern plains, the tank country.
Vatadage – ancient Sinhalese architectural style; 'circular relic house' with a small dagoba flanked by Buddha images and encircled by rows of columns.
Veddah – the original people of Sri Lanka prior to the arrival of the Sinhalese, still struggling on in isolated pockets.
Villus – small seasonal lake-lets found in the Wilpattu park.

Wewa – irrigation tanks, artificial lakes.

Yala – the south-west monsoon season.

LONELY PLANET NEWSLETTER

We collect an enormous amount of information here at Lonely Planet. Apart from our research we also get a steady stream of letters from people out on the road – some of them are just one line on a postcard, others go on for pages. Plus we always have an ear to the ground for the latest on cheap airfares, new visa regulations, borders opening and closing. A lot of this information goes into our new editions or 'update supplements' in reprints. But we like to make faster use of this information so we are now producing a quarterly newsletter packed full of the latest news from out on the trail.

The newsletter covers all the countries we cover and usually ranges from 10 to 20 pages in length. It appears in February, May, August and November of each year. If you'd like an airmailed copy of the most recent newsletter just send us A$5 (to our Australian address) or US$5 (to our US address) for a year's subscription. For a single copy please send A$2 or US$2.

Index

Lonely Planet travel guides
Africa on a Shoestring
Australia – a travel survival kit
Alaska – a travel survival kit
Bali & Lombok – a travel survival kit
Burma – a travel survival kit
Bushwalking in Papua New Guinea
Canada – a travel survival kit
China – a travel survival kit
Hong Kong, Macau & Canton
India – a travel survival kit
Japan – a travel survival kit
Kashmir, Ladakh & Zanskar
Kathmandu & the Kingdom of Nepal
Korea & Taiwan – a travel survival kit
Malaysia, Singapore & Brunei – a travel survival kit
Mexico – a travel survial kit
New Zealand – a travel survival kit
Pakistan – a travel survival kit kit
Papua New Guinea – a travel survival kit
The Philippines – a travel survival kit
South America on a Shoestring
South-East Asia on a Shoestring
Sri Lanka – a travel survival kit
Thailand – a travel survival kit
Tramping in New Zealand
Trekking in the Himalayas
Turkey – a travel survival kit
USA West
West Asia on a Shoestring

Lonely Planet phrasebooks
Indonesia Prasebook
Nepal Phrasebook
Thailand Phrasebook

Lonely Planet travel guides are available around the world. If you can't find them, ask your bookshop to order them from one of the distributors listed below. For countries not listed or if you would like a free copy of our latest booklist write to Lonely Planet in Australia.

Australia
Lonely Planet Publications, PO Box 88, South Yarra, Victoria 3141.
Canada
Milestone Publications, Box 2248, Sidney British Columbia, V8L 3S8.
Denmark
Scanvik Books aps, Store Kongensgade 59 A, DK-1264 Copenhagen K.
Hong Kong
The Book Society, GPO Box 7804.
India & Nepal
UBS Distributors, 5 Ansari Rd, New Delhi.
Israel
Geographical Tours Ltd, 8 Tverya St, Tel Aviv 63144.
Japan
Intercontinental Marketing Corp, IPO Box 5056, Tokyo 100-31.
Malaysia
MPH Distributors, 13 Jalan 13/6, Petaling Jaya, Selangor.
Netherlands
Nilsson & Lamm bv, Postbus 195, Pampuslaan 212, 1380 AD Weesp.
New Zealand
Roulston Greene Publishing Associates Ltd, Box 33850, Takapuna, Auckland 9.
Papua New Guinea
Gordon & Gotch (PNG), PO Box 3395, Port Moresby.
Singapore
MPH Distributors, 116-DJTC Factory Building, Lorong 3, Geylang Square, Singapore, 1438.
Sweden
Esselte Kartcentrum AB, Vasagatan 16, S-111 20 Stockholm.
Thailand
Chalermnit, 1-2 Erawan Arcade, Bangkok.
UK
Roger Lascelles, 47 York Rd, Brentford, Middlesex, TW8 0QP.
USA
Lonely Planet Publications, PO Box 2001A, Berkeley, CA 94702.
West Germany
Buchvertrieb Gerda Schettler, Postfach 64, D3415 Hattorf a H.